George B. Mertzios

Graph Classes based on Interval Structures

George B. Mertzios

Graph Classes based on Interval Structures

Combinatorial Optimization and Recognition of Graph Classes with Applications to Related Models

Südwestdeutscher Verlag für Hochschulschriften

Impressum/Imprint (nur für Deutschland/ only for Germany)
Bibliografische Information der Deutschen Nationalbibliothek: Die Deutsche Nationalbibliothek verzeichnet diese Publikation in der Deutschen Nationalbibliografie; detaillierte bibliografische Daten sind im Internet über http://dnb.d-nb.de abrufbar.

Alle in diesem Buch genannten Marken und Produktnamen unterliegen warenzeichen-, marken- oder patentrechtlichem Schutz bzw. sind Warenzeichen oder eingetragene Warenzeichen der jeweiligen Inhaber. Die Wiedergabe von Marken, Produktnamen, Gebrauchsnamen, Handelsnamen, Warenbezeichnungen u.s.w. in diesem Werk berechtigt auch ohne besondere Kennzeichnung nicht zu der Annahme, dass solche Namen im Sinne der Warenzeichen- und Markenschutzgesetzgebung als frei zu betrachten wären und daher von jedermann benutzt werden dürften.

Verlag: Südwestdeutscher Verlag für Hochschulschriften Aktiengesellschaft & Co. KG
Dudweiler Landstr. 99, 66123 Saarbrücken, Deutschland
Telefon +49 681 37 20 271-1, Telefax +49 681 37 20 271-0
Email: info@svh-verlag.de
Zugl.: Aachen, RWTH Aachen University, Dissertation, 2009

Herstellung in Deutschland:
Schaltungsdienst Lange o.H.G., Berlin
Books on Demand GmbH, Norderstedt
Reha GmbH, Saarbrücken
Amazon Distribution GmbH, Leipzig
ISBN: 978-3-8381-1195-7

Imprint (only for USA, GB)
Bibliographic information published by the Deutsche Nationalbibliothek: The Deutsche Nationalbibliothek lists this publication in the Deutsche Nationalbibliografie; detailed bibliographic data are available in the Internet at http://dnb.d-nb.de.

Any brand names and product names mentioned in this book are subject to trademark, brand or patent protection and are trademarks or registered trademarks of their respective holders. The use of brand names, product names, common names, trade names, product descriptions etc. even without a particular marking in this works is in no way to be construed to mean that such names may be regarded as unrestricted in respect of trademark and brand protection legislation and could thus be used by anyone.

Publisher: Südwestdeutscher Verlag für Hochschulschriften Aktiengesellschaft & Co. KG
Dudweiler Landstr. 99, 66123 Saarbrücken, Germany
Phone +49 681 37 20 271-1, Fax +49 681 37 20 271-0
Email: info@svh-verlag.de

Printed in the U.S.A.
Printed in the U.K. by (see last page)
ISBN: 978-3-8381-1195-7

Copyright © 2010 by the author and Südwestdeutscher Verlag für Hochschulschriften Aktiengesellschaft & Co. KG and licensors
All rights reserved. Saarbrücken 2010

Abstract

This thesis mainly deals with the structure of some classes of perfect graphs that have been widely investigated, due to both their interesting structure and their numerous applications. By exploiting the structure of these graph classes, we provide solutions to some open problems on them (in both the affirmative and negative), along with some new representation models that enable the design of new efficient algorithms.

In particular, we first investigate the classes of interval and proper interval graphs, and especially, path problems on them. These classes of graphs have been extensively studied and they find many applications in several fields and disciplines such as genetics, molecular biology, scheduling, VLSI design, archaeology, and psychology, among others. Although the Hamiltonian path problem is well known to be linearly solvable on interval graphs, the complexity status of the longest path problem, which is the most natural optimization version of the Hamiltonian path problem, was an open question. We present the first polynomial algorithm for this problem with running time $O(n^4)$. Furthermore, we introduce a matrix representation for both interval and proper interval graphs, called the Normal Interval Representation (NIR) and the Stair Normal Interval Representation (SNIR) matrix, respectively. The whole information of both NIR and SNIR matrices for a graph with n vertices can be captured in $O(n)$ space. We illustrate the use of this succinct matrix representation (SNIR) for proper interval graphs to solve in optimal $O(n)$ time the k-fixed-endpoint path cover problem, which is another optimization variant of the Hamiltonian path problem.

Next, we investigate the classes of tolerance and bounded tolerance graphs, which generalize in a natural way both interval and permutation graphs. This class of graphs has attracted many research efforts since its introduction by Golumbic and Monma in 1982, as it finds many important applications in bioinformatics, constrained-based temporal reasoning, resource allocation, and scheduling, among others. We present the first non-trivial intersection model for tolerance graphs, given by three-dimensional parallelepipeds. Apart of being important on its own, this new intersection model enables the design of efficient algorithms on tolerance graphs. Namely, given a tolerance graph G with n vertices, we present optimal $O(n \log n)$ time algorithms for the minimum coloring and the maximum clique problems, as well as an improved $O(n^2)$ time algorithm for the maximum weighted independent set problem on G.

In spite of the extensive study of these classes, the recognition of both tolerance and bounded tolerance graphs have been the most fundamental open problems since their introduction. Therefore, all existing efficient algorithms assumed that the input graph is given along with a tolerance or a bounded tolerance representation, respectively. We prove that both recognition problems are NP-complete, thereby settling a long standing open question. These hardness results are surprising, since it was expected that the recognition of these graph classes is polynomial.

Finally, we investigate a scheduling model, which is closely related to the concept of interval and tolerance graphs. Namely, we deal with the scheduling of weighted jobs with release times and with equal processing time each on a single machine. In our model, the scheduling of the jobs is preemptive, i.e. the processing of a job can be interrupted by another one. Our goal is to find a schedule of the given jobs with the minimum weighted sum of completion times. The complexity status of this problem has been stated as an open question. We present for this problem the first polynomial algorithm for the case where the number of different weights of the jobs is constant.

Acknowledgements

First of all, I wish to express my gratitude to Professor Dr. Berthold Vöcking for giving me the opportunity and trusting me to study this interesting topic in his Chair of Algorithms and Complexity under his supervision, as well as to my advisor Privat Dozent Dr. Walter Unger for his care and interest on my work, for stimulating discussions, and for his valuable advises on a number of issues during the thesis.

I also wish to express my sincere thanks and appreciation to Professor Stavros Nikolopoulos for his invitation at the Department of Computer Science, University of Ioannina, Greece, as well as for our productive collaboration and our several stimulating discussions.

I wish to express my gratitude and appreciation to Professor Shmuel Zaks for his invitation at the Department of Computer Science, Technion, Israel, as well as for his valuable interest and his insight during our stimulating discussions. It was always a pleasure for me to work with him.

Marcel Ochel and Michaël Thomazo deserve many thanks for the proofreading of this thesis. Moreover, I wish to thank the Empirikion Foundation in Athens, Greece, for its support.

Finally, I wish to thank my family and friends, who supported me in difficult moments, each of them in his/her own way.

Contents

Abstract   iii

Acknowledgements   v

List of Figures   ix

List of algorithms   xi

1 Introduction   1
    1.1 Basic definitions and notation 1
    1.2 Interval and proper interval graphs 7
    1.3 Tolerance and bounded tolerance graphs 9
    1.4 Preemptive scheduling 10

2 The longest path problem on interval graphs   13
    2.1 Structural properties of interval graphs 14
       2.1.1 Normal paths 16
    2.2 Interval graphs and the longest path problem 18
       2.2.1 The stable-connection interval graph H 19
       2.2.2 Computing a longest path of H 22
       2.2.3 Computing a longest path of G 23
    2.3 Correctness and complexity 24
       2.3.1 Correctness of Algorithm 2.1 24
       2.3.2 Correctness of Algorithm 2.3 34
       2.3.3 Total complexity 36

3 A matrix representation of interval and proper interval graphs   39
    3.1 The NIR and the SNIR matrices 40
       3.1.1 Interval graphs and the NIR matrix 40
       3.1.2 Proper interval graphs and the SNIR matrix 45
    3.2 The kPC problem on proper interval graphs 49
       3.2.1 Singular points in a proper interval graph 51
       3.2.2 The 2HP problem 53

		3.2.2.1	Necessary and sufficient conditions	53

            3.2.2.1   Necessary and sufficient conditions 53
            3.2.2.2   The decision of 2HP in $O(n)$ time 57
      3.2.3 The kPC problem 57
            3.2.3.1   The algorithm 57
            3.2.3.2   Correctness and complexity of Algorithm 3.5 60

4 A new intersection model for tolerance graphs   **65**
  4.1 A new intersection model 66
  4.2 Coloring and Clique Algorithms in $O(n \log n)$ 70
      4.2.1 A canonical representation 70
      4.2.2 Minimum coloring 75
      4.2.3 Maximum clique 76
      4.2.4 Optimality of the running time 77
  4.3 Weighted Independent Set Algorithm in $O(n^2)$ 77

5 The recognition of tolerance and bounded tolerance graphs   **83**
  5.1 Trapezoid graphs and representations 85
      5.1.1 Acyclic permutation and trapezoid representations 85
      5.1.2 Structural properties of trapezoid graphs 88
      5.1.3 A splitting algorithm 93
  5.2 The recognition of bounded tolerance graphs 99
      5.2.1 The permutation graph P_ϕ 99
      5.2.2 The trapezoid graphs G_ϕ and H_ϕ 102
  5.3 The recognition of tolerance graphs 107

6 Preemptive scheduling of equal-length jobs   **111**
  6.1 Properties of an optimal schedule 113
  6.2 The dynamic programming algorithm 115
      6.2.1 Definitions and boundary conditions 115
      6.2.2 The recursive computation 118
      6.2.3 The algorithm 125

7 Concluding remarks   **129**

Publications   **133**

References   **135**

List of Figures

2.1 The right-end vertex ordering and a normal path of an interval graph . . 16
2.2 The stable-connection graph H of an interval graph G 19
2.3 A subgraph $H(i,j)$ of the stable-connection graph H 21

3.1 The NIR and the SNIR matrices 44
3.2 The computation of the values $s(w)$ and $e(w)$ 52
3.3 A singular point w of $G_{i,j}$ 52
3.4 The construction of a Hamiltonian path with endpoints u, v 56
3.5 The case $e_1 \leq t_1$ 61
3.6 The case, where there is no singular point of G among $\{1, \ldots, t_1\}$ 62
3.7 The case, where there are singular points of G among $\{1, \ldots, t_1 - 1\}$ and t_1 is a regular point of G 63

4.1 The parallelograms that correspond to bounded and to unbounded vertices 67
4.2 The intersection model for tolerance graphs 68
4.3 The cases where the currently processed point p_i is (a) dominated by a point $p_j \in A_i$ and (b) an extreme point of the set A_i 75
4.4 An example of the vertex sets $L_i(j)$, R_j, and $S(v_i, v_j)$ 79

5.1 (a) A permutation graph P, (b) a permutation representation R of P, (c) the transitive orientation Φ_R of P, and (d) the corresponding simple directed graph F_R 87
5.2 A trapezoid representation R of a trapezoid graph G 89
5.3 The movement of the left line of the trapezoid T_u in the construction of a standard trapezoid representation with respect to u 96
5.4 The six lines of the permutation graph P_ϕ, which correspond to a clause of the boolean formula ϕ 100
5.5 The permutation representation R_P of the permutation graph P_ϕ 101
5.6 An acyclic permutation representation R_0 of P_ϕ and the corresponding transitive orientation Φ_{R_0} of P_ϕ 103
5.7 The construction of the trapezoid graph H_ϕ from the trapezoid graph G_ϕ 104
5.8 The relative positions of the lines a_i, b_i, c_i, d_i, e_i, and f_i for three truth assignments of the clause α_i 106

6.1 The impossible case $C_i > C_k$, where job J_i is partially executed in $[r_k, C_k)$ 113
6.2 The impossible case $r_\ell^j \leq s_i$, where $j \leq i$ and $C_\ell^j > s_i$ 119
6.3 The case $s_{t_{\max}} = y$ 122

List of Algorithms

2.1	Computation of a longest binormal path of H	22
2.2	Computation of all binormal paths of $H(i,j)$	23
2.3	Computation of a longest path of an interval graph G	24
3.1	Computation of the values $s(w)$ and $e(w)$ for all vertices w	51
3.2	Construction of a Hamiltonian path P in G with u,v as endpoints	55
3.3	Computation of $C(G,T)$ for a proper interval graph G	58
3.4	Computation of $C(G,T)$, if G is connected and $|T| \leq 1$	59
3.5	Computation of $C(G,T)$, where G is connected, $|T| \geq 2$, $t_1 \notin S(G)$	60
4.1	Construction of a canonical representation of a tolerance graph G	74
4.2	Minimum coloring of a tolerance graph G	75
4.3	Maximum weight independent set of a tolerance graph G	80
5.1	Split-U	94
6.1	Computation of the value of an optimal schedule with n jobs	126

Chapter 1

Introduction

A set of graphs defined by a common structure is called a structured family of graphs. Elaboration of inherent properties of certain structured graph families has motivated a search for new algorithms on them. In this thesis we investigate properties, algorithms, and representations of some important graph classes that are based on relations of intervals, as well as of a scheduling model, which relates to the investigated graph classes.

1.1 Basic definitions and notation

An *undirected* graph $G = (V, E)$ consists of a finite set V of *vertices* and a set E of *edges*, which are subsets of V with two distinct elements each [45]. For clarity reasons, we may use the notation $V(G)$ and $E(G)$ to denote the sets of vertices and of edges of the graph G, respectively. An edge between two vertices u and v in an undirected graph is denoted by uv or by vu, and in this case u is said to be *adjacent* to v, or equivalently, u *sees* v. The set $N(v) = \{u \in V \mid uv \in E\}$ is called the *neighborhood* of the vertex v in G, sometimes denoted by $N_G(v)$ for clarity reasons. The set $N[v] = N(v) \cup \{v\}$ is called the *closed neighborhood* of the vertex v of G. A *directed* graph $G = (V, E)$ (or *digraph*) consists of a finite set V of vertices and a set E of *arcs*, which are *ordered* subsets of V with two distinct elements each. An arc from u to v in a directed graph is denoted by $\langle uv \rangle$. All undirected and directed graphs considered in this thesis are *simple*, i.e. with no self loops and no multiple edges or arcs, respectively. In the following of the thesis, any investigated graph is undirected, unless it is stated otherwise.

A *path* P of a graph $G = (V, E)$ is a sequence $(v_1, v_2, \ldots, v_k)$ of vertices, such that $v_i v_{i+1} \in E$ for every i, $1 \leq i \leq k-1$. Similarly, a *cycle* C of G is a sequence $(v_1, v_2, \ldots, v_k, v_1)$ of vertices, such that $v_k v_1 \in E$ and $v_i v_{i+1} \in E$, for every i, $1 \leq i \leq k-1$. We denote by $V(P)$ and $V(C)$ the set of vertices of a path P and a cycle C, respectively. A path P (resp. a cycle C) is called *simple* if all vertices of $V(P)$ (resp. of $V(C)$) are distinct. All paths and cycles considered in this thesis are simple. Thus, for simplicity, we will refer in the sequel to a simple path and to a simple cycle just by *path* and *cycle*. The *length* of a path P, denoted by $|P|$, is defined as the number of vertices of P, i.e. $|P| = |V(P)|$. Similarly, the *length* of a cycle C, denoted by $|C|$, is defined as the number of vertices of C, i.e. $|C| = |V(C)|$. A path P (resp. a cycle C) is called *Hamiltonian* if every vertex of G appears in P (resp. in C) exactly once, i.e. if $|P| = |V|$ (resp. if $|C| = |V|$). The *Hamiltonian path problem* and the *Hamiltonian cycle problem* are to decide whether a given graph G has a Hamiltonian path or a Hamiltonian cycle, respectively. Clearly, if a graph G has a Hamiltonian cycle C, we can construct a Hamiltonian path of G by removing an arbitrary edge of C. In the following of the thesis, a graph that has at least one Hamiltonian path will be called a *Hamiltonian graph*.

The most natural optimization version of the Hamiltonian path problem is the *longest path* problem. That is, given a graph G, to compute a path P of G with the greatest possible length. Another optimization version of the Hamiltonian path problem is the *path cover* problem. That is, given a graph G, to cover all vertices of G with the smallest number of simple paths. Clearly, the Hamiltonian path problem is a special case of the longest path and the path cover problems. Namely, a graph $G = (V, E)$ is Hamiltonian if and only if the longest path of G has $|V|$ vertices, or equivalently, if the minimum path cover of G has value one.

For a graph G, $\overline{G}$ denotes the *complement* of G, i.e. $\overline{G} = (V, \overline{E})$, where $uv \in \overline{E}$ if and only if $uv \notin E$. Given a subset of vertices $S \subseteq V$, the graph $G[S]$ denotes the graph *induced* by the vertices in S, i.e. $G[S] = (S, E')$, where for any two vertices $u, v \in S$, $uv \in E'$ if and only if $uv \in E$. Furthermore, we use $E[S]$ to denote $E(G[S])$. A subset $S \subseteq V$ is an *independent set* in G if the graph $G[S]$ has no edges. For a subset $K \subseteq V$, the induced subgraph $G[K]$ is a *complete subgraph* of G, or a *clique*, if each two of its vertices are adjacent (equivalently, K is an independent set in $\overline{G}$). For simplicity reasons, if $G[K]$ is a clique, we will often refer also to the set K itself as a clique. The maximum cardinality of an independent set in G is denoted by $\alpha(G)$ and is termed the *independence number* of G. Similarly, the maximum cardinality of a clique in G is denoted by $\omega(G)$ and is termed the *clique number* of G. A *proper coloring* of G is an assignment of different colors to adjacent vertices, which results in a partition of V into independent sets. The minimum number of colors for which there exists a proper coloring in G is denoted by $\chi(G)$ and is termed the *chromatic number* of G. A partition of V into $\chi(G)$ independent sets, the *color classes*, is called a *minimum coloring* of G. In any graph G, clearly $\chi(G) \geq \omega(G)$.

An important and well studied class of graphs is that of perfect graphs. A graph G is called *perfect* if $\chi(H) = \omega(H)$ for every induced subgraph H of G [57, 100]. A *hole* in a graph is a chordless cycle, i.e. an induced cycle, of length at least five, while an *antihole* is the complement of a hole. A hole or antihole is *even* or *odd*, depending on its length, i.e. on the number of vertices it contains. It can be easily seen by definition that odd holes are not perfect. An important result on perfect graphs is the *perfect graph theorem* [89], which states that a graph is perfect if and only if its complement is also perfect. Thus, it follows easily by the definition of perfect graphs and by the perfect graph theorem that odd antiholes are also not perfect.

Berge conjectured in 1963 that a graph G is perfect if and only if G does not contain any odd holes or odd antiholes; this conjecture has been known as the *strong perfect graph conjecture*. The graphs that do not contain any odd holes or odd antiholes are known as *Berge* graphs. Recently, this conjecture has been answered in the affirmative [33], and thus, it became the *strong perfect graph theorem*. That is, a graph is Berge if and only if it is perfect.

The *recognition* problem for a class $\mathcal{G}$ of graphs is, given a graph G, to decide whether $G \in \mathcal{G}$ or not. This is a central problem for every class of graphs. The recognition of perfect graphs is known to be polynomial, by an $O(n^9)$ time algorithm given in [32], where n is the number of vertices in the input graph. The proof of this algorithm is independent of the proof of the strong perfect graph theorem in [33].

Perfect graphs include many important families of graphs, and serve to unify results relating colorings and cliques in those families. For instance, in all perfect graphs, the minimum coloring, maximum clique, and maximum independent set problems can all be solved in polynomial time [63]. However, these algorithms are not very efficient and therefore, it makes sense to devise specific fast algorithms for these problems on subclasses of perfect graphs that are of particular interest.

A graph $G = (V, E)$ is the *intersection graph* of a family $F = \{S_1, \ldots, S_n\}$ of distinct nonempty subsets of a set S if there exists a bijection $\mu : V \to F$ such that for any two distinct vertices $u, v \in V$, $uv \in E$ if and only if $\mu(u) \cap \mu(v) \neq \emptyset$. In that case, we say that F is an *intersection model* of G. It is easy to see that each graph has a trivial intersection model based on adjacency relations [92]. Some intersection models provide a natural and intuitive understanding of the structure of a class of graphs, and turn out to be very helpful to find efficient algorithms to solve optimization problems [92]. Therefore, it is of great importance to establish non-trivial intersection models for families of graphs.

In the following we review some well known classes of perfect graphs; for an overview see [21, 57]. A graph is called *chordal*, or *triangulated*, if it has no induced cycle of length strictly greater than three. That is, every cycle of length at least four possesses a *chord*, i.e. an edge joining two non-consecutive vertices of the cycle. There are several known characterizations of chordal graphs. One of them uses the notion of a perfect elimination ordering, which is defined as follows. A vertex v of a graph $G = (V, E)$ is called *simplicial* if $N[v]$ induces a clique in G. An ordering $\pi = (v_1, v_2, \ldots, v_n)$ of the vertices of V, where $|V| = n$, is called a *perfect elimination ordering* if each vertex v_i, $1 \leq i \leq n$, is a simplicial vertex in the induced subgraph $G[\{v_i, v_{i+1}, \ldots, v_n\}]$ of G. Then, a graph G is chordal if and only if G has a perfect elimination ordering [50]. This characterization of chordal graphs leads to a linear time recognition algorithm [86, 102].

Another graph class that is characterized using vertex orderings is that of perfectly orderable graphs. Let $G = (V, E)$ be a graph with n vertices. A vertex ordering $\pi = (v_1, v_2, \ldots, v_n)$ of the vertices of V is called *perfect* if G contains no induced path $P = (v_i, v_j, v_k, v_\ell)$ with $i < j$ and $\ell < k$. A graph is called *perfectly orderable* if it admits a perfect ordering. Furthermore, chordal graphs are a subclass of perfectly orderable graphs.

Another characterization of chordal graphs as intersection graphs, is that chordal graphs are exactly the intersection graphs of a family of subtrees of a tree [25, 55, 116]. Let T be a tree and $\mathcal{T} = \{T_i\}_{i=1}^n$ be a collection of subtrees of a tree. We may think of the host tree T either as a *continuous* model of a tree embedded in the plane, thus generalizing the real line from the one-dimensional case, or as a *discrete* model of a tree, i.e. a connected graph of vertices and edges having no cycles, thus generalizing the notion of an induced path from the one-dimensional case.

Moreover, the usual definition of the intersection graph $G = (V, E)$ of a collection $\mathcal{T} = \{T_i\}_{i=1}^{n}$ of a tree T can be interpreted in two ways. One the one hand, we may interpret intersection to mean sharing at least one vertex of the host tree T in the discrete case, or a point in the continuous case; in this case, G is called the *vertex intersection* graph. On the other hand, we may interpret intersection to mean sharing at least one edge of the host tree T in the discrete case, or a measurable segment in the continuous case; in this case, G is called the *edge intersection* graph. These two definitions lead in general to different classes of graphs [62]. Chordal graphs are the *vertex* intersection graphs of a family of subtrees of a tree [62]. Two other well known classes that can be characterized similarly are the classes of vertex and edge intersection graphs of *paths* in a tree, also known as *VPT* and *EPT* graphs, respectively. The classes of VPT and EPT graphs are not equal; moreover, none of them is included in the other. For more details, see [62].

A graph is called *interval* if it is the intersection graph of a set of closed intervals on the real line. It follows now by the definition of interval graphs and by the characterization of chordal graphs as intersection graphs, that interval graphs are a subclass of chordal graphs. In particular, interval graphs are a strict subclass of chordal graphs [21]. An intersection model of an interval graph is often called an *interval representation* of it. If an interval graph G has an interval representation, in which no interval properly includes another, then G is called a *proper interval* graph. Proper interval graphs form a strict subclass of interval graphs, since they are exactly interval graphs without containing any induced claw $K_{1,3}$ [19, 21]. Furthermore, if an interval graph G has an interval representation, in which all intervals have equal length, then G is called a *unit interval* graph. The subclasses of proper and unit interval graphs are equal [19, 101], Another well known subclass of interval graphs is that of threshold graphs. A graph $G = (V, E)$ is called *threshold* if there exists a real number s (the threshold) and a real weight w_v for every vertex $v \in V$, such that uv is an edge if and only if $w_u + w_v \geq s$.

A graph G is called *trapezoid*, if it is the intersection graph of trapezoids between two parallel lines L_1 and L_2 [57]. Similarly, a graph G is called *parallelogram* (resp. *permutation*), if it is the intersection graph of parallelograms (resp. line segments) between two parallel lines L_1 and L_2 [57]. Such a representation with trapezoids (resp. parallelograms, line segments) is called a *trapezoid* (resp. *parallelogram, permutation*) *representation* of G. Permutation graphs are a strict subclass of parallelogram graphs [21], while parallelograms graphs are a strict subclass of trapezoid graphs [103]. Interval graphs can be viewed as the intersection graphs of rectangles between two parallel lines L_1 and L_2, and thus, interval graphs are a subclass of parallelogram graphs. In particular, interval graphs are a strict subclass of parallelogram graphs, since for instance the induced cycle with four vertices is a parallelogram graph but not an interval graph (since it is also not a chordal graph, by the definition of chordal graphs).

Two classes of perfect graphs that share a similar structure with interval graphs, are the those of *convex* and *biconvex* graphs. Recall first that a graph $G = (V, E)$ is called *bipartite* if its vertex set V can be partitioned into two sets V_1 and V_2, such that every edge of E connects a vertex of V_1 to a vertex of V_2; i.e. V_1 and V_2 are independent sets. In this case, G is often writen as $G = (V_1, V_2, E)$. Equivalently, a bipartite graph is a graph that does not contain any odd-length cycles [21]. An ordering π of the vertices of V_1 in a bipartite graph $G = (V_1, V_2, E)$ has the *adjacency property* if for every vertex $v \in V_2$, $N(v)$ consists of vertices that are consecutive (an interval) in the ordering π of V_1. A graph G is *convex* if it is a bipartite graph $G = (V_1, V_2, E)$, such that there is an ordering of V_1 (or of V_2) that fulfills the adjacency property. Furthermore, a graph G is *biconvex* if it is a bipartite graph $G = (V_1, V_2, E)$, such that there is an ordering of V_1 *and* an ordering of V_2 that both fulfill the adjacency property.

The classes of chordal, VPT, EPT, interval, proper interval, threshold, trapezoid, parallelogram, permutation, bipartite, convex, and biconvex graphs are *hereditary*. That is, if G is a graph that belongs to one of these classes, then every induced subgraph of G belongs also to the same class.

A graph is called *comparability* if it admits a *transitive orientation* [21]. Such an orientation consists of an assignment of a direction to each edge of the graph such that the resulting directed graph satisfies a transitive law: if the directed arcs $\langle xy \rangle$ and $\langle yz \rangle$ exist, then the arc $\langle xz \rangle$ exists as well. In other words, a comparability graph connects pairs of elements that are related to each other in a partial order. These graphs are also known as *transitively orientable* graphs, *partially orderable* graphs, and *containment* graphs [21]. A *cocomparability* graph is a graph whose complement is a comparability graph. Interval, trapezoid, parallelogram, and permutation graphs are all cocomparability graphs [57]. In particular, the class of permutation graphs coincides with the intersection of comparability and cocomparability graphs [57, 98].

A graph $G = (V, E)$ on n vertices is called *tolerance* if there is a set $I = \{I_i \mid i = 1, \ldots, n\}$ of closed intervals on the real line and a set $T = \{t_i > 0 \mid i = 1, \ldots, n\}$ of positive real numbers, called *tolerances*, such that for any two vertices $v_i, v_j \in V$, $v_i v_j \in E$ if and only if $|I_i \cap I_j| \geq \min\{t_i, t_j\}$, where $|I|$ denotes the length of the interval I. In other words, tolerance graphs model interval relations in such a way that intervals can tolerate a certain degree of overlap without being in conflict. The pair $\langle I, t \rangle$ is called a *tolerance representation* of G. If G has a tolerance representation $\langle I, t \rangle$, such that $t_i \leq |I_i|$ for every $i = 1, 2, \ldots, n$, then G is called a *bounded tolerance* graph and $\langle I, t \rangle$ a *bounded tolerance representation* of G. A graph is bounded tolerance if and only if it is a parallelogram graph [18, 83], and thus, also a cocomparability graph. On the contrary, tolerance graphs are not cocomparability graphs [57, 62].

Similarly to the case of interval graphs, if $\langle I, t \rangle$ is a tolerance representation of G such that no interval is properly included in another (resp. all intervals have equal length), then G is called a *proper* (resp. *unit*) tolerance graph and $\langle I, t \rangle$ a *proper* (resp. *unit*) tolerance representation of G. Although the subclasses of unit and proper interval graphs are equal [19, 101], the corresponding tolerance subclasses are different [18].

1.2 Interval and proper interval graphs

Interval and proper interval graphs arise naturally in biological applications, such as the physical mapping of DNA and the genome reconstruction [28, 56, 57, 107, 117]. Furthermore, they find applications in genetics, molecular biology, scheduling, VLSI circuit design, information storage retrieval, as well as in archaeology, psychology, and social sciences [57]. Except due to their applicability to several practical problems, interval graphs have been extensively studied also due to their interesting structure. Namely, many NP-hard problems admit efficient algorithms, such as maximum clique [64], minimum coloring [96], maximum independent set [64, 69], Hamiltonian cycle [76], Hamiltonian path, path cover [3, 29], domination problems [99], domatic partition [29], and bandwidth [108] among others. These algorithms exploit several structural properties of interval graphs. However, some interesting problems remain NP-hard, when the input is restricted to be an interval graph, such as optimal linear arrangement [34], sum coloring [91,110], hypo-coloring [51], harmonious coloring [4], and pair-complete coloring [17].

In Chapters 2 and 3, we investigate two different path problems on interval and proper interval graphs, as well as we introduce two matrix representations of them. First, we investigate in Chapter 2 the complexity status of the longest path problem on the class of interval graphs. Even if a graph is not Hamiltonian, it makes sense in several applications to search for a longest path, or equivalently, to find a maximum induced subgraph of the graph that is Hamiltonian. However, computing a longest path seems to be more difficult than deciding whether or not a graph admits a Hamiltonian path. Indeed, it has been proved that even if a graph is Hamiltonian, the problem of computing a path of length $n - n^{\varepsilon}$ for any $\varepsilon < 1$ is NP-hard, where n is the number of vertices of the input graph [74]. Moreover, there is no polynomial-time constant-factor approximation algorithm for the longest path problem unless P=NP [74]. In contrast to the Hamiltonian path problem, there are only few known polynomial algorithms for the longest path problem, and these restrict to trees and some other small graph classes. In particular, the complexity status of the longest path problem on interval graphs was as an open question [113,114], although the Hamiltonian path problem on an interval graph $G = (V, E)$ is well known to be solved by a greedy approach in linear time $O(|V|+|E|)$ [3]. We resolve this problem by presenting in Chapter 2 the first polynomial algorithm for the longest path problem on interval graphs with running time $O(n^4)$, which is based on a dynamic programming approach [P1].

Next, we present in Chapter 3 a new matrix representation of both interval and proper interval graphs, called the *Normal Interval Representation (NIR)* and the *Stair Normal Interval Representation (SNIR)* matrix, respectively [P2]. Given a (proper) interval graph G, the (S)NIR matrix of G is a special form of its adjacency matrix, according to a specific ordering of the vertices. Although an adjacency matrix of a graph with n vertices needs $O(n^2)$ space in worst case, the whole information of the (S)NIR matrix can be captured in $O(n)$ space. Apart of being important on its own, we use this succinct representation (SNIR) for proper interval graphs to solve efficiently another optimization variant of the Hamiltonian path problem, namely the k-fixed-endpoint path cover problem [P5]. The *k-fixed-endpoint path cover* problem is, given a graph G and k arbitrary vertices of G, to cover all vertices of G with the smallest possible number of simple paths, such that the given k vertices are only allowed to be endpoints of these paths. In particular, exploiting the SNIR structure, we provide in Chapter 3 an optimal $O(n)$ time algorithm for this problem on proper interval graphs [P5], assuming that the endpoints of the intervals are sorted.

1.3 Tolerance and bounded tolerance graphs

Tolerance graphs were introduced by Golumbic and Monma in 1982 [59], in order to generalize some of the well known applications of interval graphs. The main motivation was in the context of resource allocation and scheduling problems, in which resources, such as rooms and vehicles, can tolerate sharing among users [62]. If we replace in the definition of tolerance graphs the operator *min* by the operator *max*, we obtain the class of *max-tolerance* graphs. Both tolerance and max-tolerance graphs find in a natural way applications in biology and bioinformatics, as in the comparison of DNA sequences from different organisms or individuals [75], by making use of a software tool like BLAST [2, 75]. Tolerance graphs find numerous other applications in constrained-based temporal reasoning, data transmission through networks to efficiently scheduling aircraft and crews, as well as contributing to genetic analysis and studies of the brain [61, 62]. This class of graphs has attracted many research efforts [18, 26, 46, 60–62, 66, 77, 95], as it generalizes in a natural way both interval graphs (when all tolerances are equal) and permutation graphs (when $t_i = |I_i|$ for every $i = 1, 2, \ldots, n$) [59]. For a detailed survey on tolerance graphs we refer to [62].

As already mentioned in Section 1.1, the existence of a suitable non-trivial intersection model for some graph class may be very helpful, in order to design efficient algorithms for difficult optimization problems [92]. The class of bounded tolerance graphs is well known to be equal to that of parallelogram graphs [18, 83]. However, no non-trivial intersection model for tolerance graphs was known until now. Therefore, all algorithms have been based on a given tolerance representation $\langle I, t \rangle$ of the input graph G, which however is no intersection model (two intervals may intersect in $\langle I, t \rangle$, but the corresponding vertices may be not adjacent). We present in Chapter 4 the first non-trivial intersection model for tolerance graphs, given by three-dimensional parallelepipeds [P3], which extends the widely known intersection model of parallelograms in the plane that characterizes bounded tolerance graphs. This new intersection model enables the design of efficient algorithms on tolerance graphs. Namely, we illustrate its usefulness by presenting in Chapter 4 optimal $O(n \log n)$ time algorithms for the minimum coloring and the maximum clique problems, as well as an improved $O(n^2)$ time algorithm for the maximum weighted independent set problem on a tolerance graph G with n vertices [P3].

In spite of the extensive study of these classes, the recognition of both tolerance and bounded tolerance graphs have been the most fundamental open problems since their introduction [62]. Therefore, all existing algorithms assumed that the input graph is given along with a tolerance or a bounded tolerance representation, respectively. Since very few subclasses of perfect graphs are known to be NP-hard to recognize (for instance, perfectly orderable graphs [93] or EPT graphs [58]), it was believed that the recognition of tolerance graphs was polynomial. Furthermore, as bounded tolerance graphs –which are equivalent to parallelogram graphs– are a natural subclass of trapezoid graphs and share a very similar structure with them, and since the recognition of trapezoid graphs is well known to be polynomial [90, 107], it was plausible that that their recognition was also polynomial.

Surprisingly, we prove in Chapter 5 that both recognition problems of tolerance and of bounded tolerance graphs are NP-complete, providing a reduction from the monotone Not-All-Equal-3-SAT problem [P4]. For the proof of our reduction, we extend the notion of an acyclic orientation of permutation and trapezoid graphs. Our main tool is a new algorithm that transforms a given trapezoid graph into a permutation graph by splitting some specific vertices, while preserving this new acyclic orientation property. One of the main advantages of this algorithm is that the constructed permutation graph does not depend on any particular trapezoid representation of the input graph G.

1.4 Preemptive scheduling

As already mentioned in Sections 1.2 and 1.3, both interval and tolerance graphs find natural applications in scheduling and resource allocation. In Chapter 6 we investigate a preemptive scheduling model, in which several jobs $J_1, J_2, \ldots, J_n$ have to be scheduled on a single machine. Here, *preemption* means job splitting, i.e. the execution of a job J_i may be interrupted for the execution of another job J_j. In our model, every job J_i has a release time r_i, i.e. a time point, after which J_i is available for execution on the machine, and a positive weight w_i. A schedule of the given jobs is called *feasible* if the execution of every job J_i starts not earlier than its release time r_i. Furthermore, all

Chapter 1. *Introduction* 11

jobs have equal processing time. In a particular feasible schedule, the time at which a job J_i is completed is called its *completion time* C_i. Our goal is to find a feasible preemptive schedule of the given n jobs, such that the weighted sum of the completion times $\sum_{i=1}^{n} w_i C_i$ is minimized.

The complexity status of this problem has been stated as an open question [11,12,14,23]. On the contrary, the complexity status of most of the closely related problems is already known [82,87]. We provide for this problem the first polynomial algorithm for the case where there is a constant number k of different weight values [P6]. The running time of this algorithm, which is based on a dynamic programming approach, is $O((\frac{n}{k}+1)^k n^8)$, where n is the number of the jobs to be scheduled and k is the number of different weights. These results provide evidence that the problem under consideration could admit a polynomial solution even in the case of arbitrarily many different weights.

Chapter 2

The longest path problem on interval graphs

Since the Hamiltonian path problem is a special case of the longest path problem, it is clear that the longest path problem is NP-hard on every class of graphs, on which the Hamiltonian path problem is NP-complete. The Hamiltonian path problem is known to be NP-complete in general graphs [53, 54], and remains NP-complete even when restricted to some small classes of graphs such as bipartite graphs [81], split graphs [57], chordal bipartite graphs, split strongly chordal graphs [94], circle graphs [39], planar graphs [54], and grid graphs [72]. However, it makes sense to investigate the tractability of the longest path problem on the classes of graphs for which the Hamiltonian path problem admits polynomial time solutions. Such classes include interval graphs [3], circular-arc graphs [40], convex bipartite graphs [94], and cocomparability graphs [41]. Note that the problem of finding a longest path on proper interval graphs is easy, since all connected proper interval graphs have a Hamiltonian path which can be computed in linear time [15]. On the contrary, not all interval graphs are Hamiltonian; in the case where an interval graph has a Hamiltonian path, it can be computed in linear time [3,29]. However, in the case where an interval graph is not Hamiltonian, there was no known algorithm for computing a longest path on it.

As already mentioned in Section 1.2, computing a longest path seems to be more difficult than deciding whether or not a graph admits a Hamiltonian path. In contrast to the Hamiltonian path problem, there are few known polynomial algorithms for the longest path problem, and these restrict to trees and some small graph classes. Specifically, a linear time algorithm for finding a longest path in a tree was proposed by Dijkstra around 1960, a formal proof of which can be found in [24]. Later, through a generalization of Dijkstra's algorithm for trees, a linear time algorithm $O(n + m)$ on weighted trees and block graphs, as well as an $O(n^2)$ time algorithm for cacti have been presented for the longest path problem [114], where n and m denote the number of vertices and edges of the input graph, respectively.

More recently, polynomial algorithms have been proposed that solve the longest path problem on bipartite permutation graphs in $O(n)$ time and space [115], and on ptolemaic graphs in $O(n^5)$ time and $O(n^2)$ space [111]. Furthermore, a subclass of interval graphs, namely interval biconvex graphs, has been introduced in [113], which is a superclass of proper interval and threshold graphs. In the same paper, an $O(n^3(m + n \log n))$ time algorithm has been presented for the longest path problem on this class. As a corollary, it has been shown that a longest path of a threshold graph can be computed in $O(n+m)$ time. The complexity status of the longest path problem on interval graphs has been left open [113, 114].

In this chapter, we present the first polynomial algorithm for the longest path problem on interval graphs [P1]. This algorithm computes a longest path problem on a given interval graph G with n vertices in $O(n^4)$ time and space, using a dynamic programming approach. This result, not only answers the open question on interval graphs, but also improves the known time complexity of this problem on interval biconvex graphs, a subclass of interval graphs.

The rest of this chapter is organized as follows. In Section 2.1, we review some structural properties of interval graphs and introduce the notion of a *normal path*, which is central for our algorithm. In Section 2.2, we present our algorithm for computing a longest path problem on an interval graph, which includes three phases. In Section 2.3 we prove the correctness and compute the time and space complexity of this algorithm.

2.1 Structural properties of interval graphs

One of the most common ways to represent an interval graph G is to sort the intervals of the intersection model of G according to their right endpoints [3]. This vertex numbering has been proposed in [99] as follows.

Lemma 2.1 ([99]). *The vertices of any interval graph G can be numbered with integers $1, 2, \ldots, |V(G)|$ such that if $i < j < k$ and $ik \in E(G)$, then $jk \in E(G)$.*

An equivalent vertex numbering has been presented in [96]. This numbering can be obtained in $O(|V(G)| + |E(G)|)$ time [96, 99]. An ordering of the vertices according to this numbering has been proved quite useful in solving efficiently some graph theoretic problems on interval graphs [3, 96, 99]. Throughout this chapter, such an ordering is called a *right-end ordering* of G. Let u and v be two vertices of G; if π is a right-end ordering of G, denote $u <_\pi v$ if u appears before v in π. In particular, if $\pi = (u_1, u_2, \ldots, u_{|V(G)|})$ is a right-end ordering of G, then $u_i <_\pi u_j$ if and only if $i < j$.

We call *right endpoint* of a path $P = (v_1, v_2, \ldots, v_k)$ the last vertex v_k of P. Moreover, let $P = (v_1, v_2, \ldots, v_{i-1}, v_i, v_{i+1}, \ldots, v_j, v_{j+1}, v_{j+2}, \ldots, v_k)$ and $P_0 = (v_i, v_{i+1}, \ldots, v_j)$ be two paths of a graph. Sometimes, we shall denote for simplicity reasons the path P by $P = (v_1, v_2, \ldots, v_{i-1}, P_0, v_{j+1}, v_{j+2}, \ldots, v_k)$. The following lemma appears to be useful in obtaining some important results in the sequel.

Lemma 2.2. *Let G be an interval graph, and let π be a right-end ordering of G. Let $P = (v_1, v_2, \ldots, v_k)$ be a path of G, and let $v_\ell \notin V(P)$ be a vertex of G such that $v_1 <_\pi v_\ell <_\pi v_k$ and $v_\ell v_k \notin E(G)$. Then, there exist two consecutive vertices v_{i-1} and v_i in P, $2 \leq i \leq k$, such that $v_{i-1} v_\ell \in E(G)$ and $v_\ell <_\pi v_i$.*

Proof. Consider the intersection model F of G, from which we obtain the right-end ordering π of G. Let I_i denote the interval which corresponds to the vertex v_i in F, and let $l(I_i)$ and $r(I_i)$ denote the left and the right endpoint of the interval I_i, respectively. Without loss of generality, we may assume that all values $l(I_i)$ and $r(I_i)$ are distinct. Since $P = (v_1, v_2, \ldots, v_k)$ is a path from v_1 to v_k, it is clear from the intersection model F of G that at least one vertex of P sees v_ℓ. Recall that $v_k v_\ell \notin E(G)$; let v_{i-1}, $2 \leq i \leq k$, be the last vertex of P such that $v_{i-1} v_\ell \in E(G)$, i.e. $v_j v_\ell \notin E(G)$ for every index j, $i \leq j \leq k$. Thus, since $v_\ell <_\pi v_k$, it follows that $r(I_\ell) < l(I_j) < r(I_j)$ for every index j, $i \leq j \leq k$, and thus, $v_\ell <_\pi v_j$. Therefore, in particular, $v_\ell <_\pi v_i$. This completes the proof. □

2.1.1 Normal paths

Our algorithm for constructing a longest path of an interval graph G uses a specific type of paths, namely normal paths. We next define the notion of a normal path of an interval graph G.

Definition 2.1. *Let G be an interval graph, and let π be a right-end ordering of G. The path $P = (v_1, v_2, \ldots, v_k)$ of G is called* normal*, if v_1 is the leftmost vertex of $V(P)$ in π, and for every i, $2 \leq i \leq k$, the vertex v_i is the leftmost vertex of $N(v_{i-1}) \cap \{v_i, v_{i+1}, \ldots, v_k\}$ in π.*

In Figure 2.1 an interval representation of an interval graph G with six vertices $u_1, u_2, u_3, u_4, u_5, u_6$ is presented. The right-end ordering of these vertices is $\pi = (u_1, u_2, u_3, u_4, u_5, u_6)$ (the intervals are sorted increasingly according to their right endpoints). In this example, the path $P = (v_1, v_2, v_3, v_4, v_5, v_6) = (u_1, u_2, u_4, u_3, u_6, u_5)$, which is indicated by the directed arrows in the figure, is a normal path of G.

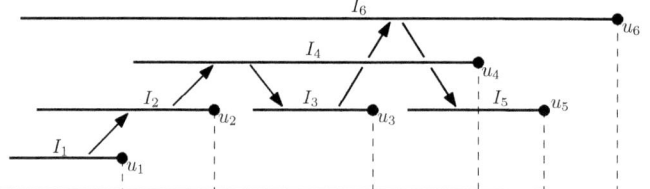

FIGURE 2.1: The right-end ordering $\pi = (u_1, u_2, u_3, u_4, u_5, u_6)$ of the vertices of an interval graph G, and the normal path $P = (v_1, v_2, v_3, v_4, v_5, v_6) = (u_1, u_2, u_4, u_3, u_6, u_5)$ of G.

The notion of a normal path of an interval graph G is an extension of the notion of a typical path of G; the path $P = (v_1, v_2, \ldots, v_k)$ of an interval graph G is called a *typical* path, if v_1 is the leftmost vertex of $V(P)$ in π. The notion of a typical path has been introduced in [3], in order to solve the path cover problem on interval graphs, where the following result has been proved.

Lemma 2.3 ([3]). *Let P be a path of an interval graph G. Then, there exists a typical path P' in G such that $V(P') = V(P)$.*

The following lemma extends Lemma 2.3, and is the basis of our algorithm for solving the longest path problem on interval graphs.

Lemma 2.4. *Let P be a path of an interval graph G. Then, there exists a normal path P' of G, such that $V(P') = V(P)$.*

Proof. Let G be an interval graph, let π be a right-end ordering of G, and let $P = (v_1, v_2, \ldots, v_k)$ be a path of G. If $k = 1$, the lemma clearly holds. Suppose that $k \geq 2$. We will prove that for every index i, $2 \leq i \leq k$, there exists a path $P_i = (v'_1, v'_2, \ldots, v'_k)$, such that $V(P_i) = V(P)$, v'_1 is the leftmost vertex of $V(P_i)$ in π, and for every index j, $2 \leq j \leq i$, the vertex v'_j is the leftmost vertex of $N(v'_{j-1}) \cap \{v'_j, v'_{j+1}, \ldots, v'_k\}$ in π. The proof will be done by induction on i.

Due to Lemma 2.3, we may assume that $P = (v_1, v_2, \ldots, v_k)$ is typical, i.e. that v_1 is the leftmost vertex of $V(P)$ in π. Let $i = 2$. Assume that $v_j \in V(P)$, $j > 2$, is the leftmost vertex of $N(v_1) \cap \{v_2, v_3, \ldots, v_k\}$ in π. Then, since $G[V(P)]$ is an interval graph, and since $v_1 <_\pi v_j <_\pi v_2$ and $v_1v_2, v_1v_j \in E(G)$, it follows that $N[v_j] \cap \{v_1, v_2, \ldots, v_k\} \subseteq N[v_2] \cap \{v_1, v_2, \ldots, v_k\}$. Thus, there exists a path

$$P_2 = (v'_1, v'_2, \ldots, v'_k) = (v_1, v_j, v_{j-1}, \ldots, v_3, v_2, v_{j+1}, v_{j+2} \ldots, v_k)$$

of G, such that $V(P_2) = V(P)$, v'_1 is the leftmost vertex of $V(P_2)$ in π, and v'_2 is the leftmost vertex of $N(v'_1) \cap \{v'_2, v'_3, \ldots, v'_k\}$ in π. This proves the induction basis.

Consider now an arbitrary index i, $2 \leq i \leq k-1$, and let $P_i = (v'_1, v'_2, \ldots, v'_k)$ be a path of G, such that $V(P_i) = V(P)$, v'_1 is the leftmost vertex of $V(P_i)$ in π, and for every index j, $2 \leq j \leq i$, the vertex v'_j is the leftmost vertex of $N(v'_{j-1}) \cap \{v'_j, v'_{j+1}, \ldots, v'_k\}$ in π. In particular, it follows that the subpath $(v'_1, v'_2, \ldots, v'_i)$ of P_i is normal. We will now prove that for any vertex $v'_\ell \in \{v'_{i+1}, v'_{i+2}, \ldots, v'_k\}$, where $v'_\ell <_\pi v'_i$, it holds $v'_\ell v'_i \in E(G)$. Indeed, suppose otherwise that $v'_\ell v'_i \notin E(G)$, for such a vertex v'_ℓ. Then, since $v'_1 <_\pi v'_\ell <_\pi v'_i$, it follows by Lemma 2.2 that there are two consecutive vertices v'_{j-1} and v'_j in P_i, $2 \leq j \leq i$, such that $v'_{j-1}v'_\ell \in E(G)$ and $v'_\ell <_\pi v'_j$. Thus, v'_j is not the leftmost vertex of $N(v'_{j-1}) \cap \{v'_j, v'_{j+1}, \ldots, v'_\ell, \ldots, v'_k\}$ in π, which is a contradiction. Therefore, for any vertex $v'_\ell \in \{v'_{i+1}, v'_{i+2}, \ldots, v'_k\}$, where $v'_\ell <_\pi v'_i$, it holds $v'_\ell v'_i \in E(G)$.

Assume that $v'_j \in V(P_i)$, $j > i+1$, is the leftmost vertex of $N(v'_i) \cap \{v'_{i+1}, v'_{i+2}, \ldots, v'_k\}$ in π. Consider first the case where $v'_i <_\pi v'_j$. Then, for every vertex $v'_\ell \in \{v'_{i+1}, v'_{i+2}, \ldots, v'_k\}$ it holds $v'_i <_\pi v'_\ell$. Indeed, suppose otherwise that $v'_\ell <_\pi v'_i <_\pi v'_j$ for such a vertex v'_ℓ. Then, as we have proved above, $v'_\ell v'_i \in E(G)$, which is a contradiction, since v'_j is the leftmost vertex of $N(v'_i) \cap \{v'_{i+1}, v'_{i+2}, \ldots, v'_k\}$ in π and $v'_\ell <_\pi v'_j$.

Thus, $v'_i <_\pi v'_\ell$ for every vertex $v'_\ell \in \{v'_{i+1}, v'_{i+2}, \ldots, v'_k\}$. Therefore, since $G[V(P_i)]$ is an interval graph, and since $v'_i <_\pi v'_j <_\pi v'_{i+1}$ and $v'_i v'_{i+1}, v'_i v'_j \in E(G)$, it follows that $N[v'_j] \cap \{v'_i, v'_{i+1}, \ldots, v'_k\} \subseteq N[v'_{i+1}] \cap \{v'_i, v'_{i+1}, \ldots, v'_k\}$. Then, there exists the path

$$P_{i+1} = (v''_1, v''_2, \ldots, v''_i, v''_{i+1}, \ldots, v''_k) = (v'_1, v'_2, \ldots, v'_i, v'_j, v'_{j-1}, \ldots, v'_{i+2}, v'_{i+1}, v'_{j+1}, \ldots, v'_k)$$

of G, such that $V(P_{i+1}) = V(P_i)$, v''_1 is the leftmost vertex of $V(P_{i+1})$ in π, and for every index j, $2 \leq j \leq i+1$, the vertex v''_j is the leftmost vertex of $N(v''_{j-1}) \cap \{v''_j, v''_{j+1}, \ldots, v''_k\}$ in π.

Consider now the case where $v'_j <_\pi v'_i$. Then, v'_j is the leftmost vertex of $\{v'_{i+1}, v'_{i+2}, \ldots, v'_k\}$ in π. Indeed, suppose otherwise that $v'_\ell <_\pi v'_j <_\pi v'_i$ for a vertex $v'_\ell \in \{v'_{i+1}, v'_{i+2}, \ldots, v'_k\}$. Then, as we have proved above, $v'_\ell v'_i \in E(G)$, which is a contradiction, since v'_j is the leftmost vertex of $N(v'_i) \cap \{v'_{i+1}, v'_{i+2}, \ldots, v'_k\}$ in π and $v'_\ell <_\pi v'_j$. Thus, there exists by Lemma 2.3 a typical path P_0, such that $V(P_0) = \{v'_{i+1}, v'_{i+2}, \ldots, v'_k\}$. Since P_0 is typical and v'_j is the leftmost vertex of $V(P_0)$ in π, it follows that v'_j is the first vertex of P_0. Then, since $v'_i v'_j \in E(G)$, there exists the path

$$P_{i+1} = (v''_1, v''_2, \ldots, v''_i, v''_{i+1}, \ldots, v''_k) = (v'_1, v'_2, \ldots, v'_i, P_0)$$

of G, such that $V(P_{i+1}) = V(P_i)$, v''_1 is the leftmost vertex of $V(P_{i+1})$ in π, and for every index j, $2 \leq j \leq i+1$, the vertex v''_j is the leftmost vertex of $N(v''_{j-1}) \cap \{v''_j, v''_{j+1}, \ldots, v''_k\}$ in π. This proves the induction step.

Thus, the path $P' = P_k$ is a normal path of G, such that $V(P') = V(P)$. □

2.2 Interval graphs and the longest path problem

In this section we present our algorithm (Algorithm 2.3) for solving the longest path problem on interval graphs; it consists of three phases and works as follows:

- Phase 1: construct an auxiliary interval graph H from the input interval graph G;
- Phase 2: compute a longest path P of H using Algorithm 2.1;
- Phase 3: compute a longest path $\widehat{P}$ on G from the path P;

The proposed algorithm computes a longest path P of the graph H using dynamic programming techniques, and then it computes a longest path $\widehat{P}$ of G from the path P.

We next describe in detail the three phases of our algorithm and prove properties of the constructed graph H which will be used for proving the correctness of the algorithm.

2.2.1 The stable-connection interval graph H

In this section we present Phase 1 of Algorithm 2.3: given an interval graph G and a right-end ordering π of G, we construct the auxiliary interval graph H and a right-end ordering σ of H.

▶ **Construction of H and σ:** Let G be an interval graph and let $\pi = (v_1, v_2, \ldots, v_{|V(G)|})$ be a right-end ordering of G. Initially, set $V(H) = V(G)$, $E(H) = E(G)$, $\sigma = \pi$, and $A = \emptyset$. Traverse the vertices of π from left to right and do the following: for every vertex v_i add two vertices $a_{i,1}$ and $a_{i,2}$ to $V(H)$ and make both these vertices to be adjacent to every vertex in $N_G[v_i] \cap \{v_i, v_{i+1}, \ldots, v_{|V(G)|}\}$; add $a_{i,1}$ and $a_{i,2}$ to A. Update σ such that $a_{1,1} <_\sigma a_{1,2} <_\sigma v_1$, and $v_{i-1} <_\sigma a_{i,1} <_\sigma a_{i,2} <_\sigma v_i$ for every i, $2 \leq i \leq |V(G)|$.

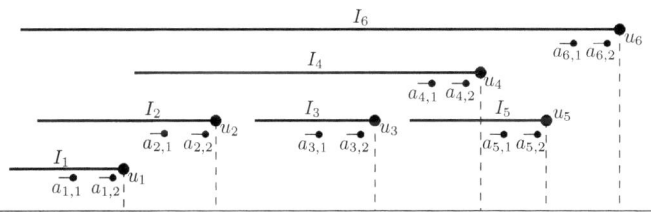

FIGURE 2.2: The stable-connection graph H of the graph G of Figure 2.1.

We call the constructed graph H the *stable-connection graph* of the graph G. It is easy to see by the construction of H that G is an induced subgraph of H. The stable-connection graph H of the graph G of Figure 2.1 is illustrated in Figure 2.2. Hereafter, we will denote by n the number $|V(H)|$ of vertices of the graph H and by $\sigma = (u_1, u_2, \ldots, u_n)$ the constructed ordering of H. By construction, the vertex set of the graph H consists of the vertices of the set $C = V(G)$ and the vertices of the set A. We will refer to C as the set of the *connector vertices* c of the graph H and to A as the set of *stable vertices* a of the graph H; we denote these sets by $C(H)$ and $A(H)$, respectively. Note that $|A(H)| = 2|V(G)|$.

By the construction of the stable-connection graph H, all neighbors of a stable vertex $a \in A(H)$ are connector vertices $c \in C(H)$, such that $a <_\sigma c$. Moreover, observe that all neighbors of a stable vertex form a clique in G, and thus, also in H. For every connector vertex $u_i \in C(H)$, we denote by $u_{f(u_i)}$ and $u_{h(u_i)}$ the leftmost and rightmost neighbor of u_i in σ that appears before u_i in σ, respectively, i.e. $u_{f(u_i)} <_\sigma u_{h(u_i)} <_\sigma u_i$. Note that $u_{f(u_i)}$ and $u_{h(u_i)}$ are distinct stable vertices, for every connector vertex u_i.

Lemma 2.5. *Let G be an interval graph. The stable-connection graph H of G is an interval graph, and the vertex ordering σ is a right-end ordering of H.*

Proof. Consider the intersection model F of G, from which we obtain the right-end ordering $\pi = (v_1, v_2, \ldots, v_{|V(G)|})$ of G. Let I_i denote the interval which corresponds to the vertex v_i in F, and let $l(I_i)$ and $r(I_i)$ denote the left and the right endpoint of the interval I_i, respectively. Without loss of generality, we may assume that all values $l(I_i)$ and $r(I_i)$ are distinct. Let ε be the smallest distance between two interval endpoints in F.

For every interval I_i which corresponds to a vertex $v_i \in C$, we replace its right endpoint $r(I_i)$ by $r(I_i) + \frac{\varepsilon}{2}$, and we add two non-intersecting intervals $I_{i,1} = [r(I_i), r(I_i) + \frac{\varepsilon}{8}]$ and $I_{i,2} = [r(I_i) + \frac{\varepsilon}{4}, r(I_i) + \frac{3\varepsilon}{8}]$ (one for each vertex $a_{i,1}$ and $a_{i,2}$ of A, respectively). The two new intervals do not intersect with any interval I_k, such that $r(I_k) < r(I_i)$. Additionally, the two new intervals intersect with the interval I_i, and with every interval I_ℓ, such that $r(I_\ell) > r(I_i)$ and I_ℓ intersects with I_i. After processing all intervals I_i, $1 \leq i \leq |V(G)|$, of the intersection model F of G, we obtain an intersection model of H. Thus, H is an interval graph, and the ordering which results from numbering the intervals after sorting them according to their right endpoints is identical to the vertex ordering σ of H, and thus, σ is a right-end ordering of H. □

Definition 2.2. *Let H be the stable-connection graph of an interval graph G, and let $\sigma = (u_1, u_2, \ldots, u_n)$ be the right-end ordering of H. For every pair of indices i, j, $1 \leq i \leq j \leq n$, we define the graph $H(i, j)$ to be the subgraph $H[S]$ of H, induced by the set $S = \{u_i, u_{i+1}, \ldots, u_j\} \setminus \{u_k \in C(H) \mid u_{f(u_k)} <_\sigma u_i\}$.*

The stable-connection H of Figure 2.2 is illustrated in Figure 2.3, where its 18 vertices (both stable and connector vertices) are numbered according to the right-end ordering σ of H. The subgraph $H(2, 12)$ for $i = 2$ and $j = 12$ is illustrated in Figure 2.3, where the vertices $V(H(2,12)) = \{u_2, u_4, u_5, u_7, u_8, u_9, u_{10}, u_{11}, u_{12}\}$ are drawn bold for better visibility.

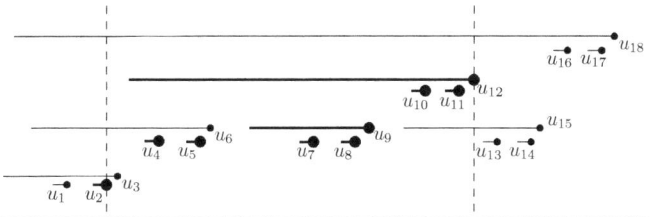

FIGURE 2.3: The subgraph $H(2,12)$ of the stable-connection H of Figure 2.2, for $i = 2$ and $j = 12$.

The following properties hold for every induced subgraph $H(i,j)$, $1 \leq i \leq j \leq n$, and they are used for proving the correctness of Algorithm 2.1. In particular, the next two observations follow easily by the construction of H and σ.

Observation 2.1. *Let u_k be a connector vertex of $H(i,j)$, i.e. $u_k \in C(H(i,j))$. Then, for every vertex $u_\ell \in V(H(i,j))$, such that $u_k <_\sigma u_\ell$ and $u_k u_\ell \in E(H(i,j))$, u_ℓ is also a connector vertex of $H(i,j)$.*

Observation 2.2. *No two stable vertices of $H(i,j)$ are adjacent.*

Lemma 2.6. *Let $P = (v_1, v_2, \ldots, v_k)$ be a normal path of $H(i,j)$. Then:*

(a) For any two stable vertices v_r and v_ℓ in P, v_r appears before v_ℓ in P if and only if $v_r <_\sigma v_\ell$.

(b) For any two connector vertices v_r and v_ℓ in P, if v_ℓ appears before v_r in P and $v_r <_\sigma v_\ell$, then v_r does not see the previous vertex $v_{\ell-1}$ of v_ℓ in P.

Proof. The proof will be done by contradiction.

(a) Let v_r and v_ℓ be any two stable vertices of $H(i,j)$ that belong to the normal path $P = (v_1, v_2, \ldots, v_k)$, such that v_r appears before v_ℓ in P, and assume that $v_\ell <_\sigma v_r$. Then, clearly $v_\ell \neq v_1$, since v_r appears before v_ℓ in P. Since P is a normal path of $H(i,j)$, v_1 is the leftmost vertex of $V(P)$ in σ. Thus, $v_1 <_\sigma v_\ell <_\sigma v_r$, and since no two stable vertices of $H(i,j)$ are adjacent due to Observation 2.2, it follows that $v_r v_\ell \notin E(H(i,j))$. Thus, by Lemma 2.2 there exist two consecutive vertices u and u' in P that appear between v_1 and v_r in P, such that $uv_\ell \in E(H(i,j))$ and $v_\ell <_\sigma u'$. Thus, since P is a normal path, v_ℓ should be the next vertex of u in P instead of u', which is a contradiction. Therefore, $v_r <_\sigma v_\ell$.

(b) Let v_r and v_ℓ be any two connector vertices of $H(i,j)$ that belong to the normal path $P = (v_1, v_2, \ldots, v_k)$, such that v_ℓ appears before v_r in P and $v_r <_\sigma v_\ell$. Since P is a normal path of $H(i,j)$, v_1 is the leftmost vertex of $V(P)$ in σ. Since $v_r <_\sigma v_\ell$, it follows that $v_\ell \neq v_1$, and thus, there exists a vertex $v_{\ell-1}$ which appears before v_ℓ in P. Assume that $v_r v_{\ell-1} \in E(H(i,j))$. Since $v_r <_\sigma v_\ell$, and since P is a normal path, v_r should be the next vertex of $v_{\ell-1}$ in P instead of v_ℓ, which is a contradiction. Therefore, $v_r v_{\ell-1} \notin E(H(i,j))$. □

2.2.2 Computing a longest path of H

In this section we present Phase 2 of Algorithm 2.3. Let G be an interval graph and let H be the stable-connection graph of G constructed in Phase 1. We next provide Algorithm 2.1, which computes a longest path of the graph H. Let us first give some definitions and notations necessary for the description of the algorithm.

Definition 2.3. *Let H be a stable-connection graph, and let P be a path of $H(i,j)$, $1 \leq i \leq j \leq n$. The path P is called* binormal *if P is a normal path of $H(i,j)$, both endpoints of P are stable vertices, and no two connector vertices are consecutive in P.*

Algorithm 2.1 Computation of a longest binormal path of H

Input: A stable-connection graph H and the right-end ordering $\sigma = (u_1, u_2, \ldots, u_n)$ of H
Output: A longest binormal path of H

1: **for** $j = 1$ to n **do**
2:   **for** $i = j$ downto 1 **do**
3:     **if** $i = j$ and $u_i \in A(H)$ **then**
4:       $\ell(u_i; i, i) \leftarrow 1$; $P(u_i; i, i) \leftarrow (u_i)$
5:     **if** $i \neq j$ **then**
6:       **for** every stable vertex $u_k \in A(H)$, $i \leq k \leq j-1$ **do**
7:         $\ell(u_k; i, j) \leftarrow \ell(u_k; i, j-1)$; $P(u_k; i, j) \leftarrow P(u_k; i, j-1)$ {initialization}
8:       **if** u_j is a stable vertex of $H(i,j)$, i.e. $u_j \in A(H)$ **then**
9:         $\ell(u_j; i, j) \leftarrow 1$; $P(u_j; i, j) \leftarrow (u_j)$
10:      **if** u_j is a connector vertex of $H(i,j)$, i.e. $u_j \in C(H)$ and $i \leq f(u_j)$ **then**
11:         Execute Procedure 2.2 on $H(i,j)$
12: Compute $\ell = \max\{\ell(u_k; 1, n) \mid u_k \in A(H)\}$ and the corresponding path $P = P(u_k; 1, n)$
13: **return** ℓ and P

Procedure 2.2 Computation of all binormal paths of $H(i,j)$

Input: A subgraph $H(i,j)$ of H, where $i \neq j$, $u_j \in C(H)$, and $i \leq f(u_j)$
Output: The paths $P(u_k;i,j)$ for every $u_k \in A(H(f(u_j)+1,j-1))$

1: **for** $y = f(u_j) + 1$ to $j - 1$ **do**
2:    **for** $x = f(u_j)$ to $y - 1$ **do** $\{u_x \text{ and } u_y \text{ are adjacent to } u_j\}$
3:       **if** $u_x, u_y \in A(H)$ **then**
4:          $w_1 \leftarrow \ell(u_x;i,j-1);\ P_1' \leftarrow P(u_x;i,j-1)$
5:          $w_2 \leftarrow \ell(u_y;x+1,j-1);\ P_2' \leftarrow P(u_y;x+1,j-1)$
6:          **if** $w_1 + w_2 + 1 > \ell(u_y;i,j)$ **then**
7:             $\ell(u_y;i,j) \leftarrow w_1 + w_2 + 1;\ P(u_y;i,j) \leftarrow (P_1', u_j, P_2')$
8: **return** the value $\ell(u_k;i,j)$ and the path $P(u_k;i,j)$, $\forall u_k \in A(H(f(u_j)+1,j-1))$

Notation 2.1. *Let H be a stable-connection graph, and let $\sigma = (u_1, u_2, \ldots, u_n)$ be the right-end ordering of H. For every stable vertex $u_k \in A(H(i,j))$, we denote by $P(u_k;i,j)$ a longest binormal path of $H(i,j)$ with u_k as its right endpoint, and by $\ell(u_k;i,j)$ the length of $P(u_k;i,j)$.*

Since any binormal path is a normal path, Lemma 2.6 holds also for binormal paths. Moreover, since $P(u_k;i,j)$ is a binormal path, it follows that its right endpoint u_k is also the rightmost stable vertex of P in σ, due to Lemma 2.6(a).

Algorithm 2.1 computes (calling Procedure 2.2 as a subroutine) for every induced subgraph $H(i,j)$ and for every stable vertex $u_k \in A(H(i,j))$, the length $\ell(u_k;i,j)$ and the corresponding path $P(u_k;i,j)$. Since $H(1,n) = H$, it follows that the maximum among the values $\ell(u_k;1,n)$, where $u_k \in A(H)$, is the length of a longest binormal path $P(u_k;1,n)$ of H. In Section 2.3.2 we prove that the length of a longest path of H equals to the length of a longest binormal path of H. Thus, the binormal path $P(u_k;1,n)$ computed by Algorithm 2.1 is also a longest path of H.

2.2.3 Computing a longest path of G

During Phase 3 of Algorithm 2.3, we compute a path $\widehat{P}$ from the longest binormal path P of H, computed by Algorithm 2.1, by simply deleting all the stable vertices of P. In Section 2.3.2 we prove that the resulting path $\widehat{P}$ is a longest path of the interval graph G. Note that Steps 1, 2, and 3 of Algorithm 2.3 correspond to the presented Phases 1, 2, and 3, respectively.

Algorithm 2.3 Computation of a longest path of an interval graph G

Input: An interval graph G and a right-end ordering π of G
Output: A longest path $\widehat{P}$ of G

1: Construct the stable-connection graph H of G and the right-end ordering σ of H; let $V(H) = C \cup A$, where $C = V(G)$ and A are the sets of the connector and stable vertices of H, respectively
2: Compute a longest binormal path P of H, using Algorithm 2.1; let $P = (v_1, v_2, \ldots, v_{2k}, v_{2k+1})$, where $v_{2i} \in C$, $1 \leq i \leq k$, and $v_{2i+1} \in A$, $0 \leq i \leq k$
3: Compute the longest path $\widehat{P} = (v_2, v_4, \ldots, v_{2k})$ of G, by deleting all stable vertices $\{v_1, v_3, \ldots, v_{2k+1}\}$ from the longest binormal path P of H

2.3 Correctness and complexity

In this section we prove the correctness of our algorithm and compute its complexity. More specifically, in Section 2.3.1 we show that Algorithm 2.1 computes a longest binormal path P of the graph H (this path is also a longest path of H, cf. Lemma 2.13), while in Section 2.3.2 we show that the length of a longest binormal path P of H is equal to $2k + 1$, where k is the length of a longest path of G. Finally, we show that the path $\widehat{P}$ computed by Algorithm 2.3 (at at Step 3) is indeed a longest path of G.

2.3.1 Correctness of Algorithm 2.1

We next prove that Algorithm 2.1 correctly computes a longest binormal path of the stable-connection graph H. The following three lemmas appear useful in the proof of the algorithm's correctness.

Lemma 2.7. *Let H be a stable-connection graph, and let $\sigma = (u_1, u_2, \ldots, u_n)$ be the right-end ordering of H. Let P be a longest binormal path of $H(i,j)$ with u_y as its right endpoint, let u_k be the rightmost connector vertex of $H(i,j)$ in σ, and let $u_{f(u_k)+1} \leq_\sigma u_y \leq_\sigma u_{h(u_k)}$. Then, there exists a longest binormal path P' of $H(i,j)$ with u_y as its right endpoint, which contains the connector vertex u_k.*

Proof. Let P be a longest binormal path of $H(i,j)$ with u_y as its right endpoint, which does not contain the connector vertex u_k. Assume first that $P = (u_y)$. Since u_k is a connector vertex of $H(i,j)$ and $u_{f(u_k)}$ is a stable vertex of $H(i,j)$, we have that $u_i \leq_\sigma u_{f(u_k)} <_\sigma u_y <_\sigma u_k$. Thus, there exists the binormal path $P_1 = (u_{f(u_k)}, u_k, u_y)$, where $|P_1| > |P|$. However, this is a contradiction to the assumption that P is a longest binormal path of $H(i,j)$.

Therefore, assume now that $P = (u_p, \ldots, u_q, u_\ell, u_y)$. By assumption, P is a longest binormal path of $H(i,j)$ with u_y as its right endpoint that does not contain the connector vertex u_k. Since the connector vertex u_ℓ sees the stable vertex u_y and, also, since u_k is the rightmost connector vertex of $H(i,j)$ in σ, it follows by Observation 2.1 that $u_{f(u_k)} <_\sigma u_y <_\sigma u_\ell <_\sigma u_k$. Thus, u_k sees the connector vertex u_ℓ. Consider first the case where u_k does not see the stable vertex u_q, i.e. $u_q <_\sigma u_{f(u_k)} <_\sigma u_y <_\sigma u_\ell <_\sigma u_k$. Then, it is easy to see that the connector vertex u_ℓ sees $u_{f(u_k)}$, where $u_{f(u_k)}$ is always a stable vertex, and also, from Lemma 2.6(a) it follows that the vertex $u_{f(u_k)}$ does not belong to the path P. Therefore, there exists a binormal path $P_2 = (u_p, \ldots, u_q, u_\ell, u_{f(u_k)}, u_k, u_y)$ in $H(i,j)$, such that $|P_2| > |P|$. This is a contradiction to our assumption that P is a longest binormal path.

Consider now the case where u_k sees the stable vertex u_q. Then, there exists a path $P' = (u_p, \ldots, u_q, u_k, u_y)$ of $H(i,j)$ with u_y as its right endpoint that contains the connector vertex u_k, such that $|P| = |P'|$; since P is a binormal path, it is easy to see that P' is also a binormal path. Thus, the path P' is a longest binormal path of $H(i,j)$ with u_y as its right endpoint, which contains the connector vertex u_k. □

Lemma 2.8. *Let H be a stable-connection graph, and let σ be the right-end ordering of H. Let $P = (P_1, v_\ell, P_2)$ be a binormal path of $H(i,j)$, and let v_ℓ be a connector vertex of $H(i,j)$. Then, P_1 and P_2 are binormal paths of $H(i,j)$.*

Proof. Let $P = (v_1, v_2, \ldots, v_{\ell-1}, v_\ell, v_{\ell+1}, \ldots, v_k)$ be a binormal path of $H(i,j)$. Then, from Definition 2.1, v_1 is the leftmost vertex of $V(P)$ in σ, and for every index r, $2 \leq r \leq k$, the vertex v_r is the leftmost vertex of $N(v_{r-1}) \cap \{v_r, v_{r+1}, \ldots, v_k\}$ in σ. It is easy to see that $P_1 = (v_1, v_2, \ldots, v_{\ell-1})$ is a normal path of $H(i,j)$. Indeed, since $V(P_1) \subset V(P)$, v_1 is also the leftmost vertex of $V(P_1)$ in σ, and additionally, v_r is the leftmost vertex of $N(v_{r-1}) \cap \{v_r, v_{r+1}, \ldots, v_{\ell-1}\}$ in σ, for every index r, $2 \leq r \leq \ell - 1$. Furthermore, since P is binormal and v_ℓ is a connector vertex, it follows that $v_{\ell-1}$ is a stable vertex, and thus, P_1 is a binormal path of $H(i,j)$ as well.

Consider now the path $P_2 = (v_{\ell+1}, v_{\ell+2}, \ldots, v_k)$ of $H(i,j)$. Since P is a binormal path and v_ℓ is a connector vertex, it follows that $v_{\ell+1}$ is a stable vertex, and thus, $v_{\ell+1} <_\sigma v_\ell$ due to Observation 2.1. We first prove that $v_{\ell+1}$ is the leftmost vertex of $V(P_2)$ in σ.

Since P is a binormal path, we obtain from Lemma 2.6(a) that $v_{\ell+1}$ is the leftmost stable vertex of $V(P_2)$ in σ. Moreover, consider a connector vertex v_t of P_2. Then, its previous vertex v_{t-1} in P_2 is a stable vertex and, thus, $v_{t-1} <_\sigma v_t$ due to Observation 2.1. Since $v_{\ell+1}$ is the leftmost stable vertex of $V(P_2)$ in σ, we have that $v_{\ell+1} \leq_\sigma v_{t-1}$, and thus, $v_{\ell+1} <_\sigma v_t$. Therefore, $v_{\ell+1}$ is the leftmost vertex of $V(P_2)$ in σ. Additionally, since P is a binormal path, it is straightforward that for every index r, $\ell + 2 \leq r \leq k$, the vertex v_r is the leftmost vertex of $N(v_{r-1}) \cap \{v_r, v_{r+1}, \ldots, v_k\}$ in σ. Thus, P_2 is a normal path. Finally, since P is binormal and $v_{\ell+1}$ is a stable vertex, P_2 is a binormal path as well. $\square$

Lemma 2.9. *Let H be a stable-connection graph, and let $\sigma = (u_1, u_2, \ldots, u_n)$ be the right-end ordering of H. Let P_1 be a binormal path of $H(i, j-1)$ with u_x as its right endpoint, and let P_2 be a binormal path of $H(x+1, j-1)$ with u_y as its right endpoint, such that $V(P_1) \cap V(P_2) = \emptyset$. Suppose that u_j is a connector vertex of H and that $u_i \leq_\sigma u_{f(u_j)} \leq_\sigma u_x$. Then, $P = (P_1, u_j, P_2)$ is a binormal path of $H(i,j)$ with u_y as its right endpoint.*

Proof. Let P_1 be a binormal path of $H(i, j-1)$ with u_x as its right endpoint, and let P_2 be a binormal path of $H(x+1, j-1)$ with u_y as its right endpoint, such that $V(P_1) \cap V(P_2) = \emptyset$. Let u_z be the first vertex of P_2. Since u_j is a connector vertex of H such that $u_i \leq_\sigma u_{f(u_j)} \leq_\sigma u_x$, it follows that u_j sees the right endpoint u_x of P_1. Additionally, since $u_z \in V(H(x+1, j-1))$, we have $u_{f(u_j)} \leq_\sigma u_x <_\sigma u_{x+1} \leq_\sigma u_z <_\sigma u_j$, and thus u_j sees u_z. Therefore, since $V(P_1) \cap V(P_2) = \emptyset$, it follows that $P = (P_1, u_j, P_2)$ is a path of H. Additionally, since $H(i, j-1)$ and $H(x+1, j-1)$ are induced subgraphs of $H(i,j)$, it follows that P is a path of $H(i,j)$. In the rest of this proof $P_1 = (v_1, v_2, \ldots, v_{p-1})$, $P_2 = (v_{p+1}, v_{p+2}, \ldots, v_\ell)$, $u_x = v_{p-1}$, $u_y = v_\ell$, and $u_j = v_p$.

We first show that $P = (v_1, v_2, \ldots, v_p, \ldots, v_\ell)$ is a normal path. Since v_1 is the leftmost vertex of $V(P_1)$ in σ, it follows that $v_1 \leq_\sigma u_x$. Furthermore, since for every vertex $v_k \in V(P_2)$ it holds $u_x <_\sigma u_{x+1} \leq_\sigma v_k$, it follows that v_1 is the leftmost vertex of $V(P)$ in σ. We next show that for every k, $2 \leq k \leq \ell$, the vertex v_k is the leftmost vertex of $N(v_{k-1}) \cap \{v_k, v_{k+1}, \ldots, v_\ell\}$ in σ.

Consider first the case where $2 \leq k \leq p-1$, i.e. $v_k \in V(P_1)$. Since P_1 is a normal path, v_k is the leftmost vertex of $N(v_{k-1}) \cap \{v_k, v_{k+1}, \ldots, v_{p-1}\}$ in σ. Assume that v_{k-1} is a stable vertex. Then, Lemma 2.6(a) implies that $v_{k-1} <_\sigma v_{p-1} = u_x$ and, due to

Observation 2.2, it follows that $N(v_{k-1}) \cap \{v_k, v_{k+1}, \ldots, v_\ell\}$ is a set of connector vertices. Since every connector vertex $v_r \in V(P_2)$ is a vertex of $H(x+1, j-1)$, it follows that $v_{k-1} <_\sigma u_{x+1} \leq_\sigma u_{f(v_r)}$, and thus, $v_r \notin N(v_{k-1})$. Additionally, since $v_p = u_j$ is the rightmost vertex of $H(i,j)$ in σ, it follows that $v_k <_\sigma v_p$. Therefore, since v_k is the leftmost vertex of $N(v_{k-1}) \cap \{v_k, v_{k+1}, \ldots, v_{p-1}\}$ in σ, it follows that v_k is the leftmost vertex of $N(v_{k-1}) \cap \{v_k, v_{k+1}, \ldots, v_\ell\}$ in σ. Assume now that v_{k-1} is a connector vertex. Since P_1 is a binormal path, v_k is a stable vertex, such that $v_k \leq_\sigma u_x$ and v_k is the leftmost vertex of $N(v_{k-1}) \cap \{v_k, v_{k+1}, \ldots, v_{p-1}\}$ in σ. Since for every r, $p+1 \leq r \leq \ell$, the vertex $v_r \in V(H(x+1, j-1))$, it follows that $v_k \leq_\sigma u_x <_\sigma v_r$. Additionally, $v_k <_\sigma u_{x+1} <_\sigma v_p$. Therefore, v_k is the leftmost vertex of $N(v_{k-1}) \cap \{v_k, v_{k+1}, \ldots, v_\ell\}$ in σ.

Consider now the case where $k = p$. Since P_1 is a normal path and $v_{p-1} = u_x$ is a stable vertex, $N(v_{p-1}) \cap \{v_p, v_{p+1}, \ldots, v_\ell\}$ is a set of connector vertices, due to Observation 2.2. Additionally, since every connector vertex $v_r \in V(P_2)$ is a vertex of $H(x+1, j-1)$, it follows that $v_{p-1} <_\sigma u_{x+1} \leq_\sigma u_{f(v_r)}$, and thus, $v_r \notin N(v_{p-1})$. Therefore, $N(v_{p-1}) \cap \{v_p, v_{p+1}, \ldots, v_\ell\} = \{v_p\}$, and thus, v_p is the leftmost vertex of $N(v_{p-1}) \cap \{v_p, v_{p+1}, \ldots, v_\ell\}$ in σ. Now, in the case where $k = p+1$, we have that v_{p+1} is the leftmost vertex of $V(P_2) = \{v_{p+1}, v_{p+2}, \ldots, v_\ell\}$ in σ, since P_2 is a normal path. Therefore, it easily follows that v_{p+1} is the leftmost vertex of $N(v_p) \cap \{v_{p+1}, v_{p+2}, \ldots, v_\ell\}$ in σ. Finally, in the case where $p+2 \leq k \leq \ell$, since P_2 is a normal path it directly follows that v_k is the leftmost vertex of $N(v_{k-1}) \cap \{v_k, v_{k+1}, \ldots, v_\ell\}$ in σ.

Concluding, we have shown that P is a normal path of $H(i,j)$. Additionally, since P_1 and P_2 are binormal paths of $H(i,j)$, the path P has stable vertices as endpoints and no two connector vertices are consecutive in P. Therefore, P is a binormal path of $H(i,j)$ with u_y as its right endpoint. □

Now, we are ready to prove the correctness of Algorithm 2.1.

Lemma 2.10. *Let H be a stable-connection graph, and let σ be the right-end ordering of H. For every induced subgraph $H(i,j)$ of H, $1 \leq i \leq j \leq n$, and for every stable vertex $u_y \in A(H(i,j))$, Algorithm 2.1 computes the length $\ell(u_y; i, j)$ of a longest binormal path of $H(i,j)$, which has u_y as its right endpoint, and also the corresponding path $P(u_y; i, j)$.*

Proof. Let P be a longest binormal path of the stable-connection graph $H(i,j)$, which has a vertex $u_y \in A(H(i,j))$ as its right endpoint. Consider first the case where

$C(H(i,j)) = \emptyset$; the graph $H(i,j)$ is consisted of a set of stable vertices $A(H(i,j))$, which is an independent set, due to Observation 2.2. Therefore, in this case Algorithm 2.1 sets $\ell(u_y; i, j) = 1$ for every vertex $u_y \in A(H(i,j))$, which is indeed the length of the longest binormal path $P(u_y; i, j) = (u_y)$ of $H(i,j)$ which has u_y as its right endpoint. Therefore, the lemma holds for every induced subgraph $H(i,j)$, for which $C(H(i,j)) = \emptyset$.

We examine next the case where $C(H(i,j)) \neq \emptyset$. Let $C(H) = \{c_1, c_2, \ldots, c_k, \ldots, c_t\}$ be the set of connector vertices of H, where $c_1 <_\sigma c_2 <_\sigma \ldots <_\sigma c_k <_\sigma \ldots <_\sigma c_t$. Let $\sigma = (u_1, u_2, \ldots, u_n)$ be the vertex ordering of H constructed in Phase 1. Recall that, by the construction of H, $n = 3t$, and $A(H) = V(H) \setminus C(H)$ is the set of stable vertices of H.

Let $H(i,j)$ be an induced subgraph of H, and let c_k be the rightmost connector vertex of $H(i,j)$ in σ. The proof of the lemma is done by induction on the index k of the rightmost connector vertex c_k of $H(i,j)$. More specifically, given a connector vertex c_k of H, we prove that the lemma holds for every induced subgraph $H(i,j)$ of H, which has c_k as its rightmost connector vertex in σ. To this end, in both the induction basis and the induction step, we distinguish three cases on the position of the stable vertex u_y in the ordering σ: $u_i \leq_\sigma u_y \leq_\sigma u_{f(c_k)}$, $u_{h(c_k)} <_\sigma u_y \leq_\sigma u_j$, and $u_{f(c_k)+1} \leq_\sigma u_y \leq_\sigma u_{h(c_k)}$. In each of these three cases, we examine first the length of a longest binormal path of $H(i,j)$ with u_y as its right endpoint, and then we compare this value to the length of the path computed by Algorithm 2.1. Moreover, we prove that the path computed by Algorithm 2.1 is a binormal path with u_y as its right endpoint.

We first show that the lemma holds for $k = 1$. In the case where $u_i \leq_\sigma u_y \leq_\sigma u_{f(c_1)}$ or $u_{h(c_1)} <_\sigma u_y \leq_\sigma u_j$, it is easy to see that the length $\ell(u_y; i, j)$ of a longest binormal path P of $H(i,j)$ with u_y as its right endpoint is equal to 1. Indeed, in these cases, if $u_y \neq u_{f(c_1)}$, then u_y does not see the unique connector vertex c_1 of $H(i,j)$, and thus, the longest binormal path with u_y as its right endpoint is consisted of the vertex u_y. Now, in the case where $u_y = u_{f(c_1)}$, the connector vertex c_1 sees u_y, however, c_1 does not belong to any binormal path with u_y as its right endpoint, since u_y is the leftmost neighbor of c_1 in σ. Therefore, in the case where $u_i \leq_\sigma u_y \leq_\sigma u_{f(c_1)}$ or $u_{h(c_1)} <_\sigma u_y \leq_\sigma u_j$, Algorithm 2.1 computes the length of the longest binormal path $P(u_y; i, j) = (u_y)$ of $H(i,j)$ with u_y as its right endpoint. In the case where $u_{f(c_1)+1} \leq_\sigma u_y \leq_\sigma u_{h(c_1)}$, Algorithm 2.1 computes (in the call of Procedure 2.2) for every stable vertex u_x of $H(i,j)$, such that $u_{f(c_1)} \leq_\sigma u_x \leq_\sigma u_{y-1}$, the value $\ell(u_x; i, j-1) + \ell(u_y; x+1, j-1) + 1 = 1 + 1 + 1 = 3$ and sets

$\ell(u_y; i, j) = 3$. It is easy to see that the path $P(u_y; i, j) = (u_x, c_1, u_y)$, computed by Algorithm 2.1 in this case, is indeed a longest binormal path of $H(i, j)$ with u_y as its right endpoint.

Let now c_k be a connector vertex of H, such that $2 \leq k \leq t$. Assume that the lemma holds for every induced subgraph $H(i, j)$ of H, which has c_ℓ as its rightmost connector vertex in σ, where $1 \leq \ell \leq k-1$. That is, we assume that for every such graph $H(i, j)$, the value $\ell(u_y; i, j)$ computed by Algorithm 2.1 is the length of a longest binormal path $P(u_y; i, j)$ of $H(i, j)$ with u_y as its right endpoint. We will show that the lemma holds for every induced subgraph $H(i, j)$ of H, which has c_k as its rightmost connector vertex in σ.

Case 1: $u_i \leq_\sigma u_y \leq_\sigma u_{f(c_k)}$. In this case, it holds $\ell(u_y; i, j) = \ell(u_y; i, h(c_k))$ (note that $u_{h(c_k)}$ is the previous vertex of c_k in σ). Indeed, on the one hand, using similar arguments as in the induction basis, it easily follows that the connector vertex c_k does not belong to any binormal path of $H(i, j)$ with u_y as its right endpoint. On the other hand, since c_k is the rightmost connector vertex of $H(i, j)$, it follows that every vertex u_ℓ of $H(i, j)$, where $c_k <_\sigma u_\ell \leq_\sigma u_j$, is a stable vertex, and thus, u_ℓ does not see u_y, due to Observation 2.2. Therefore, we obtain that $\ell(u_y; i, j) = \ell(u_y; i, h(c_k))$.

Next, we show that this is the result computed by Algorithm 2.1 in this case. Note first that, since $h(c_k) < j$, Algorithm 2.1 has already computed the value $\ell(u_y; i, h(c_k))$ at a previous iteration, where j was equal to $h(c_k)$. Additionally, this computed value $\ell(u_y; i, h(c_k))$ equals indeed to the length of a longest binormal path $P(u_y; i, h(c_k))$ of $H(i, h(c_k))$ with u_y as its right endpoint. Namely, consider first the case where $H(i, h(c_k))$ is a graph for which $C(H(i, h(c_k))) = \emptyset$, i.e. $H(i, h(c_k))$ has only stable vertices. Then, as we have shown in the first paragraph of the proof, the computed value $\ell(u_y; i, h(c_k)) = 1$ equals the length of a longest binormal path of $H(i, h(c_k))$ with u_y as its right endpoint. Consider now the case where $H(i, h(c_k))$ is a graph for which $C(H(i, h(c_k))) \neq \emptyset$, i.e. $H(i, h(c_k))$ has at least one connector vertex, and let c_ℓ be its rightmost connector vertex in σ. Then, $c_\ell <_\sigma c_k$, since $u_{h(c_k)} <_\sigma c_k$. Therefore, by the induction hypothesis, the computed value $\ell(u_y; i, h(c_k))$ by Algorithm 2.1 equals indeed the length of a longest binormal path of $H(i, h(c_k))$ with u_y as its right endpoint.

We now show that in Case 1 Algorithm 2.1 computes $\ell(u_y; i, j) = \ell(u_y; i, h(c_k))$. Consider first the case where u_j is a connector vertex of $H(i, j)$, i.e. $u_j = c_k$. Then, Algorithm 2.1

computes $\ell(u_y; i, j) = \ell(u_y; i, j-1)$, which equals to $\ell(u_y; i, h(c_k))$, since in this case $j - 1 = h(c_k)$. Consider now the case where u_j is a stable vertex; then $j - 1 > h(c_k)$. If $j - 1 = h(c_k) + 1$, then Algorithm 2.1 computes $\ell(u_y; i, j) = \ell(u_y; i, j-1)$, which is equal to $\ell(u_y; i, h(c_k) + 1)$; moreover, since $u_{h(c_k)+1} = c_k$ is a connector vertex, it follows that $\ell(u_y; i, h(c_k) + 1) = \ell(u_y; i, h(c_k))$, and thus, $\ell(u_y; i, j) = \ell(u_y; i, h(c_k))$. Similarly, if $j - 1 > h(c_k) + 1$, then Algorithm 2.1 computes $\ell(u_y; i, j) = \ell(u_y; i, j-1)$, which is again equal to $\ell(u_y; i, h(c_k))$. Therefore, in Case 1, where $u_i \leq_\sigma u_y \leq_\sigma u_{f(c_k)}$, Algorithm 2.1 computes $\ell(u_y; i, h(c_k))$ as the length of a longest binormal path of $H(i, j)$ with u_y as its right endpoint and, also, computes $P(u_y; i, j) = P(u_y; i, h(c_k))$. Then, by the induction hypothesis, this path is also binormal. Thus, in Case 1 the lemma holds.

Case 2: $u_{h(c_k)} <_\sigma u_y \leq_\sigma u_j$. Since c_k is the rightmost connector vertex of $H(i, j)$, and since u_y is a stable vertex, it follows that u_y does not see any vertex of $H(i, j)$. Thus, the longest binormal path of $H(i, j)$ with u_y as its right endpoint is consisted of the vertex u_y, i.e. $\ell(u_y; i, j) = 1$. One can easily see that in this case Algorithm 2.1 computes the length $\ell(u_y; i, j) = 1$, and the path $P(u_y; i, j) = (u_y)$, which is clearly a binormal path. Thus, in Case 2 the lemma holds.

Case 3: $u_{f(c_k)+1} \leq_\sigma u_y \leq_\sigma u_{h(c_k)}$. In this case, the connector vertex c_k sees u_y. Let $P = (u_{x'}, \ldots, u_x, c_k, u_{y'}, \ldots, u_y)$ be a longest binormal path of $H(i, j)$ with u_y as its right endpoint, which contains the connector vertex c_k; due to Lemma 2.7, such a path always exists. Let u_x be the previous vertex of c_k in the path P; thus, $u_{f(c_k)} \leq_\sigma u_x <_\sigma u_y$. Since P is a binormal path, the vertices $u_{x'}$, u_x, $u_{y'}$, and u_y are all stable vertices. Also, since c_k sees u_y, which is the rightmost stable vertex of P in σ, all stable vertices of P belong to the graph $H(i, h(c_k))$. Additionally, since c_k is the rightmost connector vertex of $H(i, j)$ in σ, all connector vertices of P belong to the graph $H(i, h(c_k) + 1)$. Therefore, all vertices of P belong to the graph $H(i, h(c_k) + 1)$. Thus, the path P is a longest binormal path of $H(i, h(c_k) + 1)$ with u_y as its right endpoint, which contains the connector vertex c_k. Therefore, for every graph $H(i, j)$, for which c_k is its rightmost connector vertex in σ and $h(c_k) + 1 \leq j$, we have that $\ell(u_y; i, j) = \ell(u_y; i, h(c_k) + 1)$. Thus, we will examine only the case where $h(c_k) + 1 = j$, that is, c_k is the rightmost vertex u_j of $H(i, j)$ in σ.

Next, we examine the length $\ell(u_y; i, j)$ of a longest binormal path of $H(i, j)$ with u_y as its right endpoint, in the case where $h(c_k) + 1 = j$. Consider removing the connector vertex c_k from the path P. Then, we obtain the paths $P_1 = (u_{x'}, \ldots, u_x)$ and

$P_2 = (u_{y'}, \ldots, u_y)$. Since P is a binormal path of $H(i,j)$, we obtain from Lemma 2.8 that P_1 and P_2 are binormal paths of $H(i,j)$. Since, as we have shown, all vertices of P belong to $H(i, h(c_k) + 1)$, and since $c_k = u_j$ is the rightmost vertex of $H(i,j)$ in σ, it follows that all vertices of P_1 and P_2 belong to the graph $H(i, h(c_k)) = H(i, j-1)$. Since P is a binormal path, it follows from Lemma 2.6(a) that for every stable vertex $u_{\ell_1} \in V(P_1)$, we have $u_i \leq_\sigma u_{x'} \leq_\sigma u_{\ell_1} \leq_\sigma u_x$. Additionally, for every stable vertex $u_{\ell_2} \in V(P_2)$, we have $u_x <_\sigma u_{\ell_2} \leq_\sigma u_y \leq_\sigma u_{j-1}$, where $u_{j-1} = u_{h(c_k)}$ is the rightmost vertex of $H(i, j-1)$ in σ, since $u_j = c_k$. Therefore, for every stable vertex $u_{\ell_1} \in V(P_1)$ it holds $u_{\ell_1} \in A(H(i,x))$, and for every stable vertex $u_{\ell_2} \in V(P_2)$ it holds $u_{\ell_2} \in A(H(x+1, j-1))$.

Similarly, since P_1 is a binormal path, u_x is the rightmost stable vertex of $V(P_1)$ in σ, due to Lemma 2.6(a). Moreover, since P_1 is binormal, every connector vertex $c_{\ell_1} \in V(P_1)$ sees at least one stable vertex (in particular, it sees at least two stable vertices) of P_1, and thus, $u_i \leq_\sigma u_{f(c_{\ell_1})} \leq_\sigma u_x$. Therefore, for every connector vertex $c_{\ell_1} \in V(P_1)$, we have that $c_{\ell_1} \in C(H(i, j-1)) \setminus \{c_\ell \in C(H(i, j-1)) \mid u_x <_\sigma u_{f(c_\ell)}\} = C(H(i, j-1)) \setminus C(H(x+1, j-1))$.

Additionally, from Lemma 2.6(b) we have that every connector vertex $c_{\ell_2} \in V(P_2)$ does not see the vertex u_x, i.e. $u_x <_\sigma u_{f(c_{\ell_2})} <_\sigma c_{\ell_2} \leq_\sigma u_{j-1}$; thus, $c_{\ell_2} \in C(H(x+1, j-1))$. Summarizing, let H_1 and H_2 be the induced subgraphs of $H(i, j-1)$, with vertex sets $V(H_1) = A(H(i,x)) \cup C(H(i, j-1)) \setminus C(H(x+1, j-1))$ and $V(H_2) = A(H(x+1, j-1)) \cup C(H(x+1, j-1))$, respectively. Note that the graphs H_1 and H_2 are defined with respect to a stable vertex u_x, where $u_{f(c_k)} \leq_\sigma u_x <_\sigma u_{j-1}$, and that $H_2 = H(x+1, j-1)$. Now, it is easy to see that $V(H_1) \cap V(H_2) = \emptyset$. Moreover, note that $V(P_1) \cap V(P_2) = \emptyset$, since P_1 and P_2 belong to H_1 and H_2, respectively.

Since $P = (P_1, c_k, P_2)$ is a longest binormal path of $H(i,j)$ with u_y as its right endpoint, and since the paths P_1 and P_2 belong to two disjoint induced subgraphs of $H(i,j)$, it follows that P_1 is a longest binormal path of H_1 with u_x as its right endpoint, and that P_2 is a longest binormal path of H_2 with u_y as its right endpoint. Thus, since $H_2 = H(x+1, j-1)$, we obtain that $|P_2| = \ell(u_y; x+1, j-1)$. We will now show that $|P_1| = \ell(u_x; i, j-1)$. To this end, consider a longest binormal path P_0 of $H(i, j-1)$ with u_x as its right endpoint. Due to Lemma 2.6(a), u_x is the rightmost stable vertex of P_0 in σ, and thus, all stable vertices of P_0 belong to $A(H_1) = A(H(i,x))$. Furthermore, since P_0 is binormal, every connector vertex c_ℓ of P_0 sees at least one stable vertex (in particular, it sees at least two stable vertices) of P_0, and thus, $u_{f(c_\ell)} \leq_\sigma u_x$, i.e. $c_\ell \in C(H_1) = C(H(i,j-1)) \setminus C(H(x+1,j-1))$. It follows that $V(P_0) \subseteq V(H_1)$, and thus, $|P_0| \leq |P_1|$. On the other hand, $|P_1| \leq |P_0|$, since H_1 is an induced subgraph of $H(i,j-1)$. Thus, $|P_1| = |P_0| = \ell(u_x; i, j-1)$. Therefore, for the length $|P| = \ell(u_y; i, j)$ of a longest binormal path P of $H(i,j)$ with u_y as its right endpoint, it follows that $\ell(u_y; i, j) = \ell(u_x; i, j-1) + \ell(u_y; x+1, j-1) + 1$.

Hereafter, we examine the results computed by Algorithm 2.1 in Case 3. Let P' be the path of the graph $H(i,j)$ with u_y as its right endpoint computed by Algorithm 2.1, in the case where $u_{f(c_k)+1} \leq_\sigma u_y \leq_\sigma u_{h(c_k)}$. Consider first the case where u_j is a connector vertex of $H(i,j)$, i.e. $u_j = c_k$. It is easy to see that the path P' constructed by Algorithm 2.1 (in the call of Procedure 2.2) contains the connector vertex c_k. Algorithm 2.1 computes the length of the path $P' = (P'_1, c_k, P'_2)$, for two paths P'_1 and P'_2 as follows. The path $P'_1 = P(u_x; i, j-1)$ is a path of $H(i, j-1)$ with u_x as its right endpoint, where u_x is a neighbor of c_k, such that $u_{f(c_k)} \leq_\sigma u_x <_\sigma u_y$. The path $P'_2 = P(u_y; x+1, j-1)$ is a path of $H(x+1, j-1)$ with u_y as its right endpoint, where $u_{f(c_k)+1} \leq_\sigma u_y \leq_\sigma u_{h(c_k)}$. Actually, in this case, Algorithm 2.1 computes (in the call of Procedure 2.2) the value $w_1 + w_2 + 1 = |P'_1| + |P'_2| + 1$, for every stable vertex u_x, where $u_{f(c_k)} \leq_\sigma u_x <_\sigma u_y$, and sets $|P'|$ to be equal to the maximum among these values. Additionally, Algorithm 2.1 computes the corresponding path $P' = (P'_1, c_k, P'_2)$.

Note that the path $P'_1 = P(u_x; i, j-1)$ (resp. $P'_2 = P(u_y; x+1, j-1)$) has been already computed by Algorithm 2.1 at a previous iteration, where j was smaller by one. Additionally, the computed path $P(u_x; i, j-1)$ (resp. $P(u_y; x+1, j-1)$) is indeed a longest binormal path of $H(i, j-1)$ (resp. of $H(x+1, j-1)$) with u_x (resp. with u_y) as its right endpoint. Namely, consider first the case where $H(i, j-1)$ (resp. $H(x+1, j-1)$) is a graph for which $C(H(i,j-1)) = \emptyset$ (resp. $C(H(x+1,j-1)) = \emptyset$), i.e. $H(i, j-1)$ (resp. $H(x+1, j-1)$) has only stable vertices. Then, as we have shown in the first paragraph of the proof, the computed path $P(u_x; i, j-1)$ (resp. $P(u_y; x+1, j-1)$) is a longest binormal path of $H(i, j-1)$ (resp. of $H(x+1, j-1)$) with u_x (resp. with u_y) as its right endpoint. Consider now the case where $H(i, j-1)$ (resp. $H(x+1, j-1)$) is a graph for which $C(H(i,j-1)) \neq \emptyset$ (resp. $C(H(x+1,j-1)) \neq \emptyset$), i.e. $H(i, j-1)$ (resp. $H(x+1, j-1)$) has at least one connector vertex, and let c_ℓ be its rightmost connector vertex in σ. Then, $c_\ell <_\sigma c_k$, since $u_{j-1} <_\sigma u_j = c_k$. Therefore, by the induction hypothesis, the computed path $P(u_x; i, j-1)$ (resp. $P(u_y; x+1, j-1)$) by Algorithm 2.1 is indeed a longest binormal path of $H(i, j-1)$ (resp. of $H(x+1, j-1)$) with u_x (resp. with u_y) as its right endpoint.

Since by the induction hypothesis, P_1' and P_2' are binormal paths of $H(i, j-1)$ with u_x and u_y as their right endpoints, respectively, it follows similarly to the above that P_1' and P_2' belong to the graphs H_1 and H_2, respectively. Recall that the graphs H_1 and H_2 are defined with respect to a stable vertex u_x, where $u_{f(c_k)} \leq_\sigma u_x <_\sigma u_{j-1}$. Since, as we have shown, $V(H_1) \cap V(H_2) = \emptyset$, it follows that $V(P_1') \cap V(P_2') = \emptyset$. Therefore, we obtain from Lemma 2.9 that the computed path $P' = (P_1', u_j, P_2')$ is a binormal path as well. Moreover, since Algorithm 2.1 computes (in the call of Procedure 2.2) for every stable vertex u_x, where $u_{f(c_k)} \leq_\sigma u_x <_\sigma u_y$, the value $\ell(u_x; i, j-1) + \ell(u_y; x+1, j-1) + 1$, and sets $|P'|$ to be equal to the maximum among these values, the computed path P' is a longest binormal path of $H(i, j)$ with u_y as its right endpoint.

Consider now the case where u_j is a stable vertex of $H(i, j)$. Let c_k be the rightmost connector vertex of $H(i, j)$ in σ; then $h(c_k) + 1 < j$. Assume first that $h(c_k) + 1 = j - 1$. Since u_j is a stable vertex and also the rightmost vertex of $H(i, j)$, u_j does not see any vertex of $H(i, h(c_k) + 1)$. In this case, Algorithm 2.1 correctly computes the path $P' = P(u_y; i, j-1) = P(u_y; i, h(c_k) + 1)$, with length $|P'| = \ell(u_y; i, h(c_k) + 1)$. Similarly, in the case where $h(c_k) + 1 < j - 1$, Algorithm 2.1 computes the path $P' = P(u_y; i, j-1) = P(u_y; i, h(c_k) + 1)$, with length $|P'| = \ell(u_y; i, j-1) = \ell(u_y; i, h(c_k) + 1)$. Algorithm 2.1 has already computed the value $\ell(u_y; i, h(c_k) + 1)$ at a previous iteration, where j was equal to $h(c_k) + 1$ (i.e. $u_j = c_k$), and also the computed path $P' = P(u_y; i, h(c_k) + 1)$ is binormal.

Concluding, in both cases where u_j is a connector or a stable vertex of $H(i, j)$, the path P' of $H(i, j)$ with u_y as its right endpoint computed by Algorithm 2.1 is a longest binormal path $P(u_y; i, j)$ of $H(i, j)$ with u_y as its right endpoint, and $|P'| = \ell(u_y; i, j)$. Thus, the lemma holds in Case 3 as well. □

Due to Lemma 2.10, and since the output of Algorithm 2.1 is the maximum among the lengths $\ell(u_y; 1, n)$, $u_y \in A(H(1, n))$, along with the corresponding path, it follows that Algorithm 2.1 computes a longest binormal path of $H(1, n)$ with right endpoint a vertex $u_y \in A(H(1, n))$. Thus, since $H(1, n) = H$, we obtain the following result.

Lemma 2.11. *Let G be an interval graph. Algorithm 2.1 computes a longest binormal path of the stable-connection graph H of the graph G.*

2.3.2 Correctness of Algorithm 2.3

In this section we show that Algorithm 2.3 correctly computes a longest path of an interval graph G. The correctness proof is based on the following property: for any longest path P of G there exists a longest binormal path P' of H, such that $|P'| = 2|P|+1$ and vice versa (cf. Lemma 2.12). Therefore, we obtain that the length of a longest binormal path P of H computed by Algorithm 2.1, is equal to $2k + 1$, where k is the length of a longest path $\widehat{P}$ of G. Next, we show that the length of a longest binormal path of H equals to the length of a longest path of H. Finally, we show that the path $\widehat{P}$ computed at Step 3 of Algorithm 2.3 is indeed a longest path of the input interval graph G.

Lemma 2.12. *Let H be the stable-connection graph of an interval graph G. Then, for any longest path P of G there exists a longest binormal path P' of H, such that $|P'| = 2|P| + 1$ and vice versa.*

Proof. Let σ be the right-end ordering of H, constructed in Phase 1.

($\Rightarrow$) Let $P = (v_1, v_2, \ldots, v_k)$ be a longest path of G, i.e. $|P| = k$. We will show that there exists a binormal path P' of H such that $|P'| = 2k + 1$. Since G is an induced subgraph of H, the path P of G is a path of H as well. We construct a path $\widehat{P}$ of H from P, by adding to P the appropriate stable vertices, using the following procedure. Initially, set $\widehat{P} = P$ and for every subpath (v_i, v_{i+1}) of the path $\widehat{P}$, $1 \leq i \leq k - 1$, do the following: consider first the case where $v_i <_\sigma v_{i+1}$; then, by the construction of H, v_{i+1} is adjacent to both stable vertices $a_{i,1}$ and $a_{i,2}$ associated with the connector vertex v_i. If $a_{i,1}$ has not already been added to $\widehat{P}$, then replace the subpath (v_i, v_{i+1}) by the path $(v_i, a_{i,1}, v_{i+1})$; otherwise, replace the subpath (v_i, v_{i+1}) by the path $(v_i, a_{i,2}, v_{i+1})$. Similarly, in the case where $v_{i+1} <_\sigma v_i$, replace the subpath (v_i, v_{i+1}) by the path $(v_i, a_{i+1,1}, v_{i+1})$ or $(v_i, a_{i+1,2}, v_{i+1})$, respectively. Finally, consider the endpoint v_1 (resp. v_k) of $\widehat{P}$. If $a_{1,1}$ (resp. $a_{k,1}$) has not already been added to $\widehat{P}$, then add $a_{1,1}$ (resp. $a_{k,1}$) as the first (resp. last) vertex of $\widehat{P}$; otherwise, add $a_{1,2}$ (resp. $a_{k,2}$) as the first (resp. last) vertex of $\widehat{P}$.

By the construction of $\widehat{P}$ it is easy to see that for every connector vertex v of P we add two stable vertices as neighbors of v in $\widehat{P}$, and since in H there are exactly two stable vertices associated with every connector vertex v, it follows that every stable vertex of H appears at most once in $\widehat{P}$. Furthermore, since we add in total $k+1$ stable vertices to P, where $|P| = k$, it follows that $|\widehat{P}| = 2k+1$. Denote now by P' a normal path of H such that $V(P') = V(\widehat{P})$. Such a path exists, due to Lemma 2.4. Due to the above construction, the path $\widehat{P}$ is consisted of $k+1$ stable vertices and k connector vertices. Thus, since no two stable vertices are adjacent in H due to Observation 2.2, and since P' is a normal path of H, it follows that P' is a binormal path of H. Thus, for any longest path P of G there exists a binormal path P' of H, such that $|P'| = 2|P| + 1$.

($\Leftarrow$) Consider now a longest binormal path $P' = (v_1, v_2, \ldots, v_\ell)$ of H. Since P' is binormal, it follows that $\ell = 2k+1$, and that P' has k connector vertices and $k+1$ stable vertices, for some $k \geq 1$. We construct a path P by deleting all stable vertices from the path P' of H. By the construction of H, all neighbors of a stable vertex a are connector vertices and form a clique in G; thus, for every subpath (v, a, v') of P', v is adjacent to v' in G. It follows that P is a path of G. Since we removed all the $k+1$ stable vertices of P', it follows that $|P| = k$, i.e. $|P'| = 2|P| + 1$.

Summarizing, we have constructed a binormal path P' of H from a longest path P of G such that $|P'| = 2|P| + 1$, and a path P of G from a longest binormal path P' of H such that $|P'| = 2|P| + 1$. This completes the proof. $\square$

In the next lemma, we show that the length of a longest path of H is equal to the length of a longest binormal path of H.

Lemma 2.13. *For any longest path P and any longest binormal path P' of H, it holds $|P'| = |P|$.*

Proof. Let P be a longest path of H and P' be a longest binormal path of H, i.e. a binormal path of H with maximum length. Then, clearly $|P'| \leq |P|$. Suppose that P has k connector and ℓ stable vertices. Since no two stable vertices of H are adjacent due to Observation 2.2, it holds clearly that $\ell \leq k+1$. Similarly to the second part of the proof of Lemma 2.12, we can obtain a path $\widehat{P}$ of H with k vertices, by removing all ℓ stable vertices from P. Then, similarly to the first part of the proof of Lemma 2.12, there exists a binormal path P'' of H, where $|P''| = 2k + 1 \geq k + \ell = |P| \geq |P'|$. However,

$|P''| \leq |P'|$, since P' be a longest binormal path of H. Therefore, $|P'| = |P|$. This completes the proof. □

We can now state our main theorem of this chapter.

Theorem 2.1. *Algorithm 2.3 computes a longest path of an interval graph G.*

Proof. Let P be the longest binormal path of H computed in Step 2 of Algorithm 2.3, using Algorithm 2.1. Then, Algorithm 2.3 computes in Step 3 the path $\widehat{P}$ by deleting all stable vertices from P. By the construction of H, all neighbors of a stable vertex a are connector vertices and form a clique in G; thus, for every subpath (v, a, v') of P, v is adjacent to v' in G. It follows that $\widehat{P}$ is a path of G. Moreover, since P is binormal, it has k connector vertices and $k+1$ stable vertices, i.e. $|P| = 2k+1$, where $k \geq 1$. Thus, since we have removed all $k+1$ stable vertices of P, it follows that $|\widehat{P}| = k$, and thus, $\widehat{P}$ is a longest path of G due to Lemma 2.12. □

2.3.3 Total complexity

The following theorem states the total complexity of Algorithm 2.3 for computing a longest path of a given interval graph.

Theorem 2.2. *A longest path of an interval graph $G = (V, E)$, where $|V| = n$ and $|E| = m$, can be computed in $O(n^4)$ time and space, while the computation of the length of a longest path needs $O(n^3)$ space.*

Proof. First, we can obtain the right-end ordering π of G, which results from numbering the intervals after sorting them on their right endpoints, in $O(n+m)$ time [96, 99]. Step 1 of Algorithm 2.3, which constructs the stable-connection graph H of the graph G, needs $O(n^2)$ time. Indeed, for every of the n vertices of G, we can add the corresponding two stable vertices to $V(H)$ in $O(1)$ time and we can compute the neighborhoods of these two vertices in $O(n)$ time. Then, $|V(H)| = 3n$. Step 2 of Algorithm 2.3 includes the execution of Algorithm 2.1. Procedure 2.2 needs $O(n^2)$ time, due to the $O(n^2)$ pairs of the neighbors u_x and u_y of the connector vertex u_j in the graph $H(i,j)$. Furthermore, Procedure 2.2 is executed at most once for each subgraph $H(i,j)$ of H, $1 \leq i \leq j \leq |V(H)|$, i.e. it is executed $O(n^2)$ times. Thus, Algorithm 2.1 needs $O(n^4)$ time. Step 3 of Algorithm 2.3 can be executed in $O(n)$ time, since we simply traverse the vertices of the path P, constructed by Algorithm 2.1, and delete every stable vertex. Therefore, the total time complexity of Algorithm 2.1 is $O(n^4)$.

Regarding the space complexity, in order to compute the length of a longest path, we need to store one value for every induced subgraph $H(i,j)$ and for every stable vertex u_y of $H(i,j)$. Thus, since there are in total $O(n^2)$ such subgraphs $H(i,j)$, $1 \leq i \leq j \leq |V(H)|$, and since each one has at most $O(n)$ stable vertices, we can compute the length of a longest path in $O(n^3)$ space. Furthermore, in order to compute a longest path, instead of its length only, we have to store for every one of the above $O(n^3)$ computed values a path of $O(n)$ vertices each. Therefore, the total space complexity of Algorithm 2.3 is $O(n^4)$. □

Chapter 3

A matrix representation of interval and proper interval graphs

There are several known characterizations of interval graphs, as well as of proper and unit interval graphs. In particular, an arbitrary graph G is interval if and only if G is chordal and its complement $\overline{G}$ is a comparability graph [57], or equivalently if and only if G is chordal and contains no asteroidal triple (AT) [21]. Furthermore, interval graphs are characterized by the consecutive ones property [50], i.e. the maximal cliques can be linearly ordered such that, for every vertex v of G, the maximal cliques containing v occur consecutively [21, 57]. Namely, in the clique-versus-vertex incidence matrix of any interval graph there is a permutation of its rows, such that the ones in each column appear consecutively. On the other hand, proper interval graphs are characterized as graphs containing no astral triples [73], as well as interval graphs without containing any induced claw $K_{1,3}$ [19, 21]. Very recently, a 2-dimensional structure similar to a matrix, called bubble model, has been introduced as a new representation for proper interval graphs [67].

In this chapter a new characterization of interval and proper interval graphs is presented, which is based on a vertex-versus-vertex zero-one matrix representation of them [P2]. Namely, interval graphs can be represented by the *Normal Interval Representation (NIR)* matrix, while proper interval graphs can be represented by the *Stair Normal Interval Representation (SNIR)* matrix. This matrix representation of a (proper) interval graph G is a special form of its adjacency matrix, according to a specific ordering of the vertices. Although an adjacency matrix of a graph with n vertices needs $O(n^2)$ space in worst case, the whole information of the (S)NIR matrix can be captured in $O(n)$ space. This representation provides insight and may be useful for the efficient formulation and solution of difficult optimization problems. In particular, we illustrate the usefulness of this succinct representation (SNIR) for proper interval graphs by providing in Section 3.2 an optimal $O(n)$ time algorithm for another optimization variant of the Hamiltonian path problem, namely the k-fixed-endpoint path cover problem [P5].

3.1 The NIR and the SNIR matrices

There are several linear $O(n+m)$ time recognition algorithms for interval [20,37,38,65, 78–80,105] and for proper interval graphs [35,36,42,43,97], where n and m are the number of vertices and edges of the input graph, respectively. These algorithms compute also an interval and a proper interval representation, respectively. In an interval representation of an interval graph $G = (V, E)$, where $|V| = n$, all intervals have been assumed to be closed. Furthermore, we can assume without loss of generality that all interval endpoints are integers between 1 and $2n$. On the other hand, if we are given an interval model where endpoints are not all integers, we can sort the endpoints in an increasing order and use the indices of endpoints in the sorted list to construct a new interval model, where the endpoints are restricted to distinct integers between 1 and $2n$. Hence, most researchers on interval graphs are interested in the complexity of problems, where the input graph is given by such a set of intervals [29, 70], which we will call a set of *sorted* intervals. Throughout this chapter, we will assume that such a set of intervals is given.

3.1.1 Interval graphs and the NIR matrix

Consider a numbering of the vertices of G according to their left endpoints; that is, if $I_i = [\ell_i, r_i]$ is the interval that corresponds to vertex $v_i \in V$, where $1 \leq i \leq n$, then $\ell_i < \ell_j$ if and only if $i < j$. An ordering of the vertices according to this numbering is called a *left-end ordering* of G (in contrast to the right-end ordering that has been presented in Chapter 2). We introduce in the next definition a special type of an interval representation [P5], where all intervals are semi-closed and there are exactly $n+1$ different endpoints (instead of $2n$ ones).

Definition 3.1. *An interval representation with n intervals, satisfying the following properties, is a* Normal Interval Representation (NIR)*:*
  1. *all intervals are of the form $[i,j)$, where $i,j \in \mathbb{Z}$ and $0 \leq i < j \leq n$, and*
  2. *exactly one interval begins at i, for every $i \in \{0, 1, \ldots, n-1\}$.*

Lemma 3.1. *Given an interval representation of an interval graph $G = (V, E)$ with sorted intervals, a NIR of G can be computed in $O(n)$ time, where $|V| = n$.*

Proof. The left-end ordering of the intervals according to their left endpoints $\ell_1 < \ell_2 < \ldots < \ell_n$ is given, since the set of intervals are assumed to be sorted. A NIR of G can be computed as follows. First, replace every closed interval $[\ell_i, r_i]$ by the semi-closed interval $[\ell_i, r_i)$. Since initially all endpoints are distinct, the resulting representation with the semi-closed intervals is an intersection model of the same interval graph G. Second, for every right endpoint r_j, where $\ell_i < r_j < \ell_{i+1}$ for some $i \leq n-1$, replace $[\ell_j, r_j)$ by $[\ell_j, \ell_{i+1})$. Also, for every right endpoint r_j, where $\ell_n < r_j$, replace $[\ell_j, r_j)$ by $[\ell_j, \ell_n + 1)$. Since all intervals are semi-closed, no new adjacency is introduced to the interval representation of G by the latter operations. Finally, move bijectively the point ℓ_i to the point $i-1$, for $i = 1, 2, \ldots, n$ and the point $\ell_n + 1$ to the point n. The resulting set of intervals is a NIR of G. Since at every step of the above procedure we operate on each of the n intervals a constant number of times, the running time of this procedure is $O(n)$. □

The next lemma follows from Lemma 3.1.

Lemma 3.2. *An arbitrary graph G is interval if and only if it can be represented by a NIR.*

Proof. Let G be an interval graph. Given an interval representation of G with sorted intervals, a NIR of G can be constructed by the procedure described in the proof of Lemma 3.1. Conversely, consider a NIR R with n intervals, and let $G_R = (V, E)$ be the intersection graph of the semi-closed intervals of R. Then, replace every semi-closed interval $[i-1, j)$ of R, where $1 \leq i \leq n$, by the closed interval $[i-1, j-\frac{1}{i}]$. It is easy to see that the resulting set of closed intervals is an interval representation with $2n$ distinct endpoints of the same graph G_R, and thus, G_R is an interval graph. □

In a particular NIR of an interval graph G, the ordering of the vertices according to the left endpoints of the intervals is called the *vertex ordering* of this NIR. Note that the NIR of G is not unique. For instance, consider two vertices u, v in an interval graph G, for which $N[u] = N[v]$. Then, the left-end ordering of the vertices is not unique, and thus, the resulting NIR of G is also not unique.

Next, we provide a definition of a special type of square matrices, which will be useful in the sequel for the characterization of interval graphs in terms of matrices, cf. Theorem 3.1. Recall first that, given an arbitrary graph $G = (V, E)$ with $|V| = n$ and an ordering $\pi = (v_1, v_2, \ldots, v_n)$ of the vertices of V, the *adjacency matrix* of G with respect to π is a square $n \times n$ zero-one matrix A_G with zero diagonal, such that $A_G(i,j) = 1$ if and only if $v_i v_j \in E$. Note that the adjacency matrix A_G of every (simple, finite, and undirected) graph G is symmetric. Furthermore, a square matrix H is called *lower triangular* if all entries of H above the diagonal are zero, i.e. if $i < j$ then $H(i,j) = 0$. Given an adjacency matrix A_G of a graph G, the *lower triangular part* of A_G is the square zero-one matrix H_G, where $H_G(i,j) = 1$ if and only if $A_G(i,j) = 1$ and $i > j$.

Definition 3.2. *Let H be a square $n \times n$ square zero-one matrix. H is a Normal Interval Representation (NIR) matrix if:*

1. *H is lower triangular with zero diagonal, and*
2. *there is a chain of $x_i \geq 0$ consecutive 1's immediately below the ith diagonal element of H, where $1 \leq i \leq n$, while all remaining elements of the ith column are zero.*

An example of a NIR matrix is given in Figure 3.1(a), where $n = 8$. The next theorem characterizes interval graphs by using the notion of a NIR matrix.

Theorem 3.1. *An arbitrary graph G is interval if and only there exists an ordering π of its vertices, such that the lower triangular part of its adjacency matrix with respect to π is a NIR matrix.*

Proof. Let $G = (V, E)$ be an interval graph with $|V| = n$, and R_G be a NIR of G; note that R_G exists by Lemma 3.2. Let $\pi = (v_1, v_2, \ldots, v_n)$ be the vertex ordering of R_G, and I_i be the interval of R_G that corresponds to vertex v_i, where $1 \leq i \leq n$. Let H_G be the lower triangular part of the adjacency matrix of G with respect to π. We will now prove that H_G is a NIR matrix. Consider two arbitrary vertices $v_i, v_k \in V$, such that $i < k$ and $v_i v_k \in E$. Then, for the interval $I_i = [i-1, j)$ that corresponds to v_i, it holds $j > k - 1$, since otherwise $I_i \cap I_k = \emptyset$, which is a contradiction. Therefore, in particular, $I_i \cap I_\ell \neq \emptyset$ for every $\ell \in \{i+1, i+2, \ldots, k\}$, since $i, i+1, \ldots, k-1 \in [i-1, j) = I_i$. Thus, for every unit entry $H_G(i, k) = 1$ of H_G, where $i < k$, it holds $H_G(i, \ell) = 1$ for every $\ell \in \{i+1, i+2, \ldots, k\}$, i.e. H_G is a NIR matrix.

Conversely, let H be an $n \times n$ NIR matrix and let $G_H = (V, E)$ be the graph with $|V| = n$, such that H is the lower triangular part of the adjacency matrix of G_H. Let $x_i \geq 0$ be the number of consecutive 1's immediately below the ith diagonal element of H. Furthermore, let v_i be the vertex of V that corresponds to the ith diagonal element of H. We will prove that G_H is an interval graph. To this end, we define first a NIR R_H with n intervals as follows. The ith interval I_i of R_H is $I_i = [i-1, i+x_i)$, where $1 \leq i \leq n$. Then, for every pair $\{i, j\}$ of indices, where $1 \leq i < k \leq n$, it holds

$$\begin{aligned} v_i v_k \in E &\Leftrightarrow H(i, k) = 1 \\ &\Leftrightarrow x_i \geq k - i \\ &\Leftrightarrow i + x_i > k - 1 \\ &\Leftrightarrow I_i \cap I_k \neq \emptyset \end{aligned}$$

Thus, R_H is a NIR of G_H, i.e. G_H is an interval graph. This completes the proof. $\square$

Note that, since an interval graph G has not a unique NIR, G has also not a unique NIR matrix. Although an adjacency matrix of an arbitrary graph with n vertices needs $O(n^2)$ space in worst case, we can capture the whole information about an interval graph G using a NIR matrix H_G of G in $O(n)$ space. Indeed, we need just to store the vertex ordering $\pi = (v_1, v_2, \ldots, v_n)$ that corresponds to H_G and the value $i + x_i$ for every vertex v_i. Namely, if $i + x_i = i$, i.e. if $x_i = 0$, then all entries in the ith column of H_G are zero; otherwise, if $i + x_i > i$, then $i + x_i$ indicates the position of the last unit entry in the ith column of H_G. Recall that a NIR R of G can be computed in $O(n)$ time by Lemma 3.1, when an interval representation of G with sorted intervals is given. Then, the intervals in R have the form $[i-1, i+x_i)$, where $i \in \{1, 2, \ldots, n\}$. Thus, the values $i + x_i$, i.e. the whole information of H_G, can be also computed in $O(n)$ time.

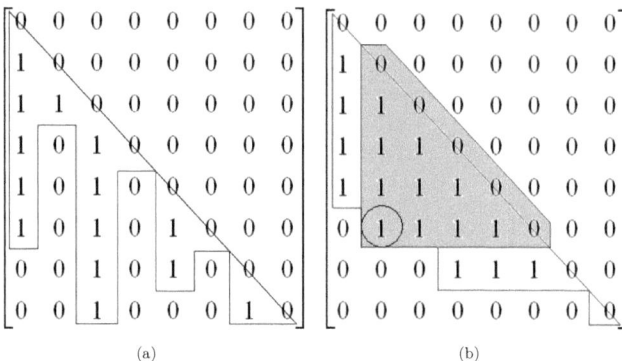

FIGURE 3.1: (a) The NIR matrix H_G of an interval graph G, (b) The SNIR matrix $H_{G'}$ of a proper interval graph G'.

The following lemma characterizes the maximal cliques of an interval graph G in a NIR matrix H_G of G.

Lemma 3.3. *Let $G = (V, E)$ be an interval graph and H_G be a NIR matrix of G. Any maximal clique of G corresponds bijectively to a row of H_G, in which at least one of its unit elements, or its zero diagonal element, does not have any chain of 1's below it.*

Proof. Consider an arbitrary row of H_G; let it be the ith one that corresponds to vertex v_i, in which exactly the i_1th, i_2th, ..., i_rth elements equal one. Note that $j < i$ for every $j \in \{i_1, i_2, \ldots, i_r\}$. Then, the interval I_i intersects the interval I_j in the corresponding NIR of G for every $j \in \{i_1, i_2, \ldots, i_r\}$, since $H_G(i, j) = 1$ for all these values of j. Moreover, all intervals I_j, $j \in \{i_1, i_2, \ldots, i_r\}$, intersect each other also, due to the NIR form of H_G. Thus, the vertex set $Q = \{v_i, v_{i_1}, v_{i_2}, \ldots, v_{i_r}\}$ induces a clique in G.

Consider now the case where the jth element of the ith row of H_G does not have any chain of 1's below it, for some $j \in \{i, i_1, i_2, \ldots, i_r\}$. For the sake of contradiction, suppose that there exists another clique Q' in G, which strictly includes Q, i.e. $Q \subsetneq Q'$. That is, there exists at least one vertex $v_k \in Q' \setminus Q$, where $k \notin \{i, i_1, i_2, \ldots, i_r\}$. Let first $k < i$. Then, since $H_G(i, \ell) = 0$ for every $\ell \in \{1, 2, \ldots, i-1\} \setminus \{i_1, i_2, \ldots, i_r\}$, it follows in particular that $H_G(i, k) = 0$. Thus, $v_i v_k \notin E$, which is a contradiction, since Q' is a clique and $v_i, v_k \in Q'$. Let now $k > i$. Then, since $H_G(\ell, j) = 0$ for every $\ell > i$, it follows in particular that $H_G(k, j) = 0$. Thus, $v_k v_j \notin E$, which is again a contradiction, since Q' is a clique and $v_k, v_j \in Q'$. Therefore, there exists no clique Q' in G, which strictly includes Q, i.e. Q is a maximal clique in G.

Conversely, let $Q = \{v_{i_1}, v_{i_2}, \ldots, v_{i_{|Q|}}\}$ be a maximal clique in G, where $i_1 < i_2 < \ldots < i_{|Q|}$. Then, since Q induces a clique, $I_j \cap I_{i_{|Q|}} \neq \emptyset$, i.e. $H_G(i_{|Q|}, j) = 1$, for every $j \in \{i_1, i_2, \ldots, i_{|Q|-1}\}$. In the case where $i_{|Q|} = n$, clearly none of the i_1th, i_2th, ..., $i_{|Q|}$th elements of the $i_{|Q|}$th row of H_G has any chain of 1's below it. Suppose now that $i_{|Q|} < n$. If $H_G(i_{|Q|+1}, j) = 1$ for every $j \in \{i_1, i_2, \ldots, i_{|Q|}\}$, then $Q' = Q \cup \{v_{|Q|+1}\}$ is a clique in G, which is a contradiction, since Q is a maximal clique by assumption. Thus, there exists at least one index $j \in \{i_1, i_2, \ldots, i_{|Q|}\}$, for which $H_G(i_{|Q|+1}, j) = 0$, i.e. at least one of the unit elements of the $i_{|Q|}$th row of H_G, or its zero diagonal element, does not have any chain of 1's below it in H_G. This completes the lemma. □

For instance, the interval graph G that corresponds the NIR matrix of Figure 3.1(a) has five maximal cliques, which correspond to the 3rd, 4th, 6th, 7th, and 8th rows of the matrix, respectively. These cliques are $Q_1 = \{v_1, v_2, v_3\}$, $Q_2 = \{v_1, v_3, v_4\}$, $Q_3 = \{v_1, v_3, v_5, v_6\}$, $Q_4 = \{v_3, v_5, v_7\}$, and $Q_5 = \{v_3, v_7, v_8\}$.

3.1.2 Proper interval graphs and the SNIR matrix

Consider now the case where G is a proper interval graph. Then, since G is also an interval graph, there exists by Section 3.1.1 a NIR, as well as a NIR matrix H_G of G. We extend now the definition of a NIR (cf. Definition 3.1).

Definition 3.3. *A NIR with n intervals is called a* Stair Normal Interval Representation (SNIR), *if it has the following additional property:*

If for the intervals $[i, j)$ and $[k, \ell)$, $i < k$ holds, then $j \leq \ell$ also holds.

Similarly to Lemmas 3.1 and 3.2, we obtain the following two lemmas.

Lemma 3.4. *Given a proper interval representation of a proper interval graph $G = (V, E)$ with sorted intervals, a SNIR of G can be computed in $O(n)$ time, where $|V| = n$.*

Proof. Let R be the given proper interval representation of G with the sorted intervals. Since G is also an interval graph, we can construct in $O(n)$ time a NIR R_G of G by the procedure described in the proof of Lemma 3.1. We will prove that R_G is also a SNIR. Indeed, let $\pi = (v_1, v_2, \ldots, v_n)$ be the left-end vertex ordering of the sorted intervals in R; note that this ordering coincides with the vertex ordering of R_G. Furthermore, let $I_i = [\ell_i, r_i]$ be the interval in R that corresponds to vertex v_i, where $1 \leq i \leq n$. Consider now two indices i, k, where $1 \leq i < k \leq n$, i.e. $\ell_i < \ell_k$. Then, also $r_i < r_k$ in R. Indeed, otherwise $r_i > r_k$, and thus $I_k \subsetneq I_i$, which is a contradiction, since R is a proper interval representation. Let now $[i-1, r'_i)$ and $[k-1, r'_k)$ be the intervals that correspond to the vertices v_i and v_k in the NIR R_G. Then, it is easy to see by the construction of R_G (cf. the proof of Lemma 3.1) that $r'_i \leq r'_k$, since $r_i < r_k$. Indeed, by this construction, the intervals for v_i and v_k may be "aligned" by their right endpoints in R_G; however, their right endpoints do not change their relative order in comparison to R. Thus, R_G satisfies the condition of Definition 3.3, and thus, R_G is a SNIR. □

Lemma 3.5. *An arbitrary graph G is proper interval if and only if it can be represented by a SNIR.*

Proof. Let G be a proper interval graph. Given a proper interval representation of G with sorted intervals, a SNIR of G can be constructed by Lemma 3.4. Conversely, consider a SNIR R with n intervals, and let $G_R = (V, E)$ be the intersection graph of the semi-closed intervals of R. Then, replace every semi-closed interval $[i-1, j)$ of R, where $1 \leq i \leq n$, by the closed interval $[i-1, j-\frac{1}{i}]$. It is easy to see that the resulting set R' of closed intervals is an interval representation with $2n$ distinct endpoints of the same graph G_R, and thus, G_R is an interval graph. We will now prove that R' is a proper interval representation. Indeed, consider two intervals $[i-1, j)$ and $[k-1, \ell)$ in R, where $i < k$. Then, $j \leq \ell$, since R is a SNIR. If $j < \ell$, then $j - \frac{1}{i} < \ell - \frac{1}{k}$. Otherwise, if $j = \ell$, then again $j - \frac{1}{i} < \ell - \frac{1}{k}$, since $i < k$. Thus, no interval includes another one in R', i.e. R' is a proper interval representation and G_R is a proper interval graph. □

Similarly to Section 3.1.1, in a particular SNIR of a proper interval graph G, the ordering of the vertices according to the left endpoints of the intervals is called the *vertex ordering* of this SNIR. We extend now the definition of a NIR matrix (cf. Definition 3.2).

Definition 3.4. *Let H be a $n \times n$ NIR matrix. H is a* Stair Normal Interval Representation (SNIR) matrix *if it has the following additional property:*

If $i < k$ then $i + x_i \leq k + x_k$.

Intuitively, a SNIR matrix H is a NIR matrix, in which the chains of consecutive 1's are ordered in such a way that H has a stair-shape, as it is illustrated in Figure 3.1(b), where $n = 8$. Similarly to Theorem 3.1, the next theorem characterizes proper interval graphs by using the notion of a SNIR matrix.

Theorem 3.2. *An arbitrary graph G is proper interval if and only there exists an ordering π of its vertices, such that the lower triangular part of its adjacency matrix with respect to π is a SNIR matrix.*

Proof. Let $G = (V, E)$ be a proper interval graph with $|V| = n$, and R_G be a SNIR of G; note that R_G exists by Lemma 3.5. Let $\pi = (v_1, v_2, \ldots, v_n)$ be the vertex ordering of R_G, and $I_i = [i-1, r_i)$ be the interval of R_G that corresponds to vertex v_i, where $1 \leq i \leq n$. Let H_G be the lower triangular part of the adjacency matrix of G with respect to π. Since G is also an interval graph, and since R_G is also a NIR of G, it follows by the proof of Theorem 3.1 that H_G is a NIR matrix. We will now prove that H_G is also a SNIR matrix. For the sake of contradiction, suppose that H_G is not a SNIR matrix, i.e. there exist by Definition 3.4 two indices i, k, where $1 \leq i < k \leq n$, such that $i + x_i > k + x_k$. Then, $v_i v_{i+x_i} \in E$, while $v_k v_{i+x_i} \notin E$. Thus, since both H_G and R_G have the same vertex ordering π, it follows that $r_k \leq i + x_i - 1 < r_i$. That is, $i - 1 < k - 1$ and $r_k < r_i$, i.e. $I_k \subsetneq I_i$, which is a contradiction, since R_G is a SNIR. Thus, H_G is a SNIR matrix of G.

Conversely, let H be an $n \times n$ SNIR matrix and let $G_H = (V, E)$ be the graph with $|V| = n$, such that H is the lower triangular part of the adjacency matrix of G_H. Let $x_i \geq 0$ be the number of consecutive 1's immediately below the ith diagonal element of H. Furthermore, let v_i be the vertex of V that corresponds to the ith diagonal element of H. We will prove that G_H is a proper interval graph. To this end, we define first a SNIR R_H with n intervals as follows. The ith interval I_i of R_H is $I_i = [i-1, i+x_i - \frac{1}{i})$, where $1 \leq i \leq n$. Then, for every pair $\{i, j\}$ of indices, where $1 \leq i < k \leq n$, it holds

$$\begin{aligned} v_i v_k \in E &\Leftrightarrow H(i, k) = 1 \\ &\Leftrightarrow x_i \geq k - i \\ &\Leftrightarrow i + x_i > k - 1 \\ &\Leftrightarrow I_i \cap I_k \neq \emptyset \end{aligned}$$

Thus, R_H is a NIR of G_H, i.e. G_H is an interval graph. We will now prove that R_H is also a SNIR of G_H. Indeed, consider two indices i, k, where $1 \leq i < k \leq n$, and thus $\frac{1}{i} > \frac{1}{k}$. Then, $i + x_i \leq k + x_k$ by Definition 3.4, since H is a SNIR matrix. Therefore, $i + x_i - \frac{1}{i} < k + x_k - \frac{1}{k}$, and thus R_H is a SNIR of G_H, i.e. G_H is a proper interval graph. This completes the proof. □

Similarly to Section 3.1.1, note that both the SNIR and the SNIR matrix of a proper interval graph G are also not unique. Furthermore, since any proper interval graph is also an interval graph, and since any SNIR matrix is also a NIR matrix, we can capture the whole information about a proper interval graph G using a SNIR matrix H_G of G in $O(n)$ space. In particular, this can be done just by storing the vertex ordering $\pi = (v_1, v_2, \ldots, v_n)$ that corresponds to H_G and the positions of the *picks* of H_G, which are defined as follows.

Definition 3.5. *Let G be a proper interval graph and H_G be a SNIR matrix of G. The matrix element $H_G(i, j)$ is called a* pick *of H_G, if the following conditions are satisfied:*

1. $i \geq j$,
2. *if $i > j$ then $H_G(i, j) = 1$,*
3. $H_G(i, k) = 0$, *for every $k \in \{1, 2, \ldots, j-1\}$, and*
4. $H_G(l, j) = 0$, *for every $l \in \{i+1, i+2, \ldots, n\}$.*

Note that all picks of H_G can be computed in $O(n)$ time, since the positions $H_G(i, j)$ of the picks are exactly the positions $H_G(i, i + x_i)$, for some special vertices v_i of G, cf. Section 3.1.1.

Definition 3.6. *Given the pick $H_G(i, j)$ of H_G, the set*

$$\mathcal{S} = \{H_G(k, \ell) \mid j \leq \ell \leq k \leq i\}$$

of matrix entries is the stair *of H_G, which corresponds to this pick.*

In Figure 3.1(b) a stair of the presented SNIR matrix can is drawn dark and the corresponding pick is marked by a circle. Similarly to Lemma 3.3, the following lemma characterizes the maximal cliques of a proper interval graph G in a SNIR matrix H_G of G.

Lemma 3.6. *Let $G = (V, E)$ be a proper interval graph and H_G be a NIR matrix of G. Any maximal clique of G corresponds bijectively to a stair of H_G.*

Proof. Due to Lemma 3.3, every maximal clique of G corresponds bijectively to a row of H_G, in which at least one of its unit elements, or its zero diagonal element, does not have any chain of 1's below it. However, since G is a proper interval graph and due to Definitions 3.5 and 3.6, it follows that such a row corresponds bijectively to a pick of H_G, and therefore also to a stair of it. □

For instance, the proper interval graph G' that corresponds the SNIR matrix $H_{G'}$ of Figure 3.1(b) has four maximal cliques, which correspond to the 5rd, 6th, 7th, and 8th rows of the matrix, respectively. These cliques are $Q_1 = \{v_1, v_2, v_3, v_4, v_5\}$, $Q_2 = \{v_2, v_3, v_4, v_5, v_6\}$, $Q_3 = \{v_4, v_5, v_6, v_7\}$, and $Q_4 = \{v_8\}$.

3.2 The kPC problem on proper interval graphs

In this section we illustrate the usefulness of the SNIR matrix representation of proper interval graphs, by presenting an optimal algorithm for a generalization of the path cover (PC) problem on proper interval graphs, namely the k-fixed-endpoint path cover problem. Except graph theory, the PC problem finds many applications in the area of database design, networks, code optimization and mapping parallel programs to parallel architectures [1, 3, 88, 109].

The PC problem is known to be NP-complete even on the classes of planar graphs [54], bipartite graphs, chordal graphs [57], chordal bipartite graphs, strongly chordal graphs [94], as well as in several classes of intersection graphs [16]. On the other hand, it is solvable in linear $O(n+m)$ time on interval graphs with n vertices and m edges [3]. For the greater class of circular-arc graphs there is an optimal $O(n)$-time approximation algorithm, given a set of n arcs with endpoints sorted [70]. The cardinality of the path cover found by this approximation algorithm is at most one more than the optimal one. Several variants of the Hamiltonian path (HP) and the PC problems are of great interest. The simplest of them are the 1HP and 2HP problems, where the goal is to decide whether G has a Hamiltonian path with one, or two fixed endpoints, respectively. Both problems are NP-hard for general graphs, as a generalization of the HP problem, while 1HP can be solved in polynomial time on interval graphs [7].

The *k-fixed-endpoint path cover (kPC)* problem extends the PC problem as follows. Given a graph G and a set T of k vertices, the goal is to find a path cover of G with minimum cardinality, such that the elements of T are endpoints of these paths. Note that the vertices of $V \setminus T$ are allowed to be endpoints of these paths as well. For $k = 1, 2$, the kPC problem constitutes a direct generalization of the 1HP and 2HP problems, respectively. For the case where the input graph is a cograph on n vertices and m edges, the kPC problem can be solved in $O(n + m)$ time [5].

We present an optimal algorithm for the kPC problem on proper interval graphs with running time $O(n)$ [P5], based on the SNIR matrix H_G that characterizes a proper interval graph G with n vertices, cf. Section 3.1. One of the main properties that we use, is that every maximal clique of G can be represented by one matrix element in H_G, namely the pick of the corresponding stair in H_G, cf. Lemma 3.6. We introduce the notion of a *singular point* in a proper interval graph G on n vertices. An arbitrary vertex of G is called singular point, if it is the unique common vertex of two consecutive maximal cliques. Due to the special structure of H_G, we need to compute only its $O(n)$ picks, in order to capture the complete information of this matrix. Recall that all the picks of the SNIR matrix H_G can be computed in $O(n)$ time (during the construction of H_G itself), when an interval representation of G with sorted intervals is given, cf. Section 3.1.2. Based on this structure, the proposed algorithm detects all singular points of G in $O(n)$ time and then it determines *directly* the paths in an optimal solution, using only the positions of the singular points [P5]. Namely, it turns out that every such path is a Hamiltonian path of a particular subgraph of G with two specific vertices of it as endpoints. Since any algorithm for this problem has to visit at least all n vertices of G, this running time is optimal.

Recently, it has been drawn to our attention that another algorithm has been independently presented for the kPC problem on proper interval graphs with running time $O(n + m)$ [6], where m is the number of edges of the input graph. This algorithm uses a greedy approach to augment the already constructed paths with connect/insert operations, by distinguishing whether these paths have already none, one, or two endpoints in T. The main advantage of the here presented algorithm, besides its running time optimality, is that an optimal solution is constructed directly by the positions of the singular points, which is a structural property of the investigated graph. Given an interval realization of the input graph G, we do not need to visit all its edges, exploiting the special structure of the SNIR matrix.

The rest of this section is organized as follows. First, we introduce in Section 3.2.1 the notion of a singular point in a proper interval graph. In the sequel, we use this notion in Section 3.2.2 to present an algorithm for the 2HP problem, based on the SNIR matrix. This algorithm is then used in Section 3.2.3, in order to derive an algorithm for the kPC problem on proper interval graphs with running time $O(n)$. For simplicity of the presentation, we will refer in the rest of the section to the vertices of a proper interval graph G by $\{1, 2, \ldots, n\}$, instead of $\{v_1, v_2, \ldots, v_n\}$, where $\pi = (v_1, v_2, \ldots, v_n)$ is the vertex ordering of G that corresponds to a SNIR matrix H_G of G.

3.2.1 Singular points in a proper interval graph

Consider a proper interval graph $G = (V, E)$ with n vertices. Let H_G be a SNIR matrix of G. Since G is equivalent to the SNIR matrix H_G, and since H_G specifies a particular ordering of the vertices of G, we identify without loss of generality the vertices of G with their indices in this ordering, i.e. we denote $V = \{1, 2, \ldots, n\}$. For an arbitrary vertex $w \in \{1, 2, \ldots, n\}$ of G, we denote by $s(w)$ and $e(w)$ the adjacent vertices of w with the smallest and greatest index in this ordering, respectively. Due to the stair-shape of H_G, the vertices $s(w)$ and $e(w)$ correspond to the uppermost and lowermost diagonal elements of H_G, which belong to a common stair with w.

Denote now the maximal cliques of G by $Q_1, Q_2, \ldots, Q_m$, $m \leq n$ and suppose that the corresponding pick to Q_i is the matrix element $H_G(a_i, b_i)$, where $i \in \{1, \ldots, m\}$. Since the maximal cliques of G, i.e. the stairs of H_G (cf. Lemma 3.6), are linearly ordered in H_G, it holds that $1 \leq a_1 \leq \ldots \leq a_m \leq n$ and $1 \leq b_1 \leq \ldots \leq b_m \leq n$. Denote for simplicity $a_0 = b_0 = 0$ and $a_{m+1} = b_{m+1} = n+1$. Then, Algorithm 3.1 computes the values $s(w)$ and $e(w)$ for all vertices $w \in \{1, \ldots, n\}$, as it is illustrated in Figure 3.2. Since $m \leq n$, the running time of Algorithm 3.1 is $O(n)$.

Algorithm 3.1 Computation of the values $s(w)$ and $e(w)$ for all vertices w

Input: The SNIR matrix H_G of a proper interval graph G and its picks $H_G(a_i, b_i)$
Output: The values $s(w)$ and $e(w)$ for all vertices $w \in \{1, 2, \ldots, n\}$

1: **for** $i = 0$ to m **do**
2:     **for** $w = a_i + 1$ to a_{i+1} **do**
3:         $s(w) \leftarrow b_{i+1}$
4:     **for** $w = b_i$ to $b_{i+1} - 1$ **do**
5:         $e(w) \leftarrow a_i$

Chapter 3. *A matrix representation of interval and proper interval graphs* 52

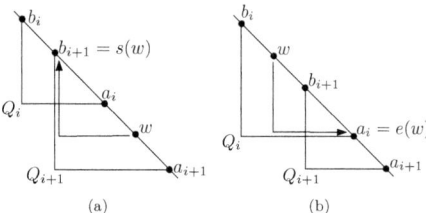

FIGURE 3.2: The computation of the values $s(w)$ and $e(w)$.

The vertices $\{i,\ldots,j\}$ of G, where $i \leq j$, constitute a submatrix $H_{i,j}$ of H_G, which is equivalent to the induced subgraph $G_{i,j}$ by these vertices. Since the proper interval graphs are hereditary, this subgraph remains a proper interval graph as well. In particular, $H_{1,n} = H_G$ is equivalent to $G_{1,n} = G$. In the next definition, we state the notion of a singular point in a proper interval graph. An example of a singular point is illustrated in Figure 3.3.

Definition 3.7. *A vertex w of $G_{i,j}$ is called* singular point *of $G_{i,j}$, if there exist two consecutive cliques Q, Q' of $G_{i,j}$, such that*

$$|Q \cap Q'| = \{w\} \qquad (3.1)$$

Otherwise, w is called regular point *of $G_{i,j}$. The set of all singular points of $G_{i,j}$ is denoted by $S(G_{i,j})$.*

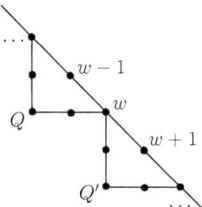

FIGURE 3.3: A singular point w of $G_{i,j}$.

Lemma 3.7. *For every singular point w of $G_{i,j}$, it holds $i + 1 \leq w \leq j - 1$.*

Proof. Since w is a singular point of $G_{i,j}$, there exist two consecutive maximal cliques Q, Q' of $G_{i,j}$ with $Q \cap Q' = \{w\}$. Then, as it is illustrated in Figure 3.3, both Q and Q' contain at least another vertex than w, since otherwise one of them would be included in the other, which is a contradiction. It follows that $i + 1 \leq w \leq j - 1$. □

Definition 3.8. *Consider a connected proper interval graph G and two indices $i \leq j \in \{1,\ldots,n\}$. The submatrix $H_{i,j}$ of H_G is called* two-way matrix, *if all vertices of $G_{i,j}$ are regular points of it. Otherwise, $H_{i,j}$ is called* one-way matrix.

The intuition resulting from Definition 3.8 is the following. If $H_{i,j}$ is an one-way matrix, then $G_{i,j}$ has at least one singular point w. In this case, no vertex among $\{i,\ldots,w-1\}$ is connected to any vertex among $\{w+1,\ldots,j\}$, as it is illustrated in Figure 3.3. Thus, every Hamiltonian path of $G_{i,j}$ passes only once from the vertices $\{i,\ldots,w-1\}$ to the vertices $\{w+1,\ldots,j\}$, through vertex w. Otherwise, if $H_{i,j}$ is a two-way matrix, a Hamiltonian path may pass more than once from $\{i,\ldots,w-1\}$ to $\{w+1,\ldots,j\}$ and backwards, where w is an arbitrary vertex of $G_{i,j}$. The next corollary follows directly from Lemma 3.7.

Corollary 3.1. *An arbitrary vertex w of G is a regular point of the subgraphs $G_{i,w}$ and $G_{w,j}$, for every $i \leq w$ and $j \geq w$.*

3.2.2 The 2HP problem

In this section we solve the 2HP problem on proper interval graphs. In particular, given two fixed vertices u,v of a proper interval graph G, we provide in Section 3.2.2.1 necessary and sufficient conditions for the existence of a Hamiltonian path in G with endpoints u and v. An algorithm with running time $O(n)$ follows directly from these conditions, where n is the number of vertices of G.

3.2.2.1 Necessary and sufficient conditions

Denote by 2HP(G,u,v) the particular instance of the 2HP problem on G with fixed endpoints the vertices u and v of G, where $u,v \in \{1,2,\ldots,n\}$. Observe at first that if G is not connected, then there is no Hamiltonian path at all in G. Also, if G is connected with only two vertices u,v, then there exists trivially a Hamiltonian path with u and v as endpoints. Thus, we assume in the following that G is connected and $n \geq 3$. The next two theorems provide necessary and sufficient conditions for the existence of a Hamiltonian path with endpoints u and v in a connected proper interval graph G. If the conditions of these theorems are satisfied, Algorithm 3.2 constructs such a Hamiltonian path, as it is described in the proofs of these theorems. Note that, in Algorithm 3.2, we use the notation $P \leftarrow P \circ (x)$ to denote the augmentation of a path $P = (y, \ldots, z)$ to the path $P = (y, \ldots, z, x)$.

Theorem 3.3. *Let G be a connected proper interval graph and u, v be two vertices of G, where $v \geq u + 2$. There is a Hamiltonian path in G with u, v as endpoints if and only if the submatrices $H_{1,u+1}$ and $H_{v-1,n}$ of H_G are two-way matrices.*

Proof. Suppose that $H_{1,u+1}$ is an one-way matrix. Then, due to Definition 3.8, $G_{1,u+1}$ has at least one singular point w. Since $G_{1,u+1}$ is connected as an induced subgraph of G, Lemma 3.7 implies that $2 \leq w \leq u$. In order to obtain a contradiction, let P be a Hamiltonian path in G with u and v as endpoints. Suppose first that for the singular point w it holds $w < u$. Then, due to the stair-shape of H_G, the path P has to visit w in order to reach the vertices $\{1, \ldots, w-1\}$. On the other hand, P has to visit w again in order to reach v, since $w < v$. This is a contradiction, since P visits w exactly once as a Hamiltonian path of G. Suppose now that $w = u$. The stair-shape of H_G implies that u has to be connected in P with at least one vertex of $\{1, \ldots, u-1\}$ and with at least one vertex of $\{u+1, \ldots, n\}$. This is also a contradiction, since u is an endpoint of P. Therefore, there exists no Hamiltonian path P of G with u and v as endpoints, if $H_{i,u+1}$ is an one-way matrix. Similarly, we obtain that there exists again no such path P in G, if $H_{v-1,n}$ is an one-way matrix. This completes the necessity part of the proof.

For the sufficiency part, suppose that both $H_{1,u+1}$ and $H_{v-1,n}$ are two-way matrices. Then, Algorithm 3.2 constructs a Hamiltonian path P in G having u and v as endpoints, as follows. In the while-loop of the lines 2-4 of Algorithm 3.2, P starts from vertex u and reaches vertex 1 using sequentially the uppermost diagonal elements, i.e. vertices, of the visited stairs of H_G. Since $H_{1,u+1}$ is a two-way matrix, P does not visit any two consecutive diagonal elements until it reaches vertex 1. In the while-loop of the lines 5-10, P continues visiting all unvisited vertices until vertex $v - 1$. Let t be the actual visited vertex of P during these lines. Since P did not visit any two consecutive diagonal elements until it reached vertex 1 in lines 2-4, at least one of the vertices $t + 1$ and $t + 2$ has not been visited yet. Thus, always one of the lines 7 and 10 is executed.

Next, in the while-loop of the lines 11-13, P starts from vertex $v-1$ and reaches vertex n using sequentially the lowermost diagonal elements of the visited stairs of H_G. During the execution of lines 11-13, since $H_{v-1,n}$ is a two-way matrix, P does not visit any two consecutive diagonal elements until it reaches vertex n. Finally, in the while-loop of the lines 14-18, P continues visiting all unvisited vertices until v. Similarly to the lines 5-10, let t be the actual visited vertex of P. Since P did not visit any two consecutive diagonal elements until it reached vertex n in lines 11-13, at least one of the vertices $t-1$ and $t-2$ has not been visited yet. Thus, always one of the lines 16 and 18 is executed. Figure 3.4(a) illustrates the construction of such a Hamiltonian path by Algorithm 3.2 in a small example. □

Algorithm 3.2 Construction of a Hamiltonian path P in G with u,v as endpoints

Input: The SNIR matrix H_G of a proper interval graph G, all values $s(w)$ and $e(w)$, and two vertices u,v of G, such that the conditions of Theorems 3.3 and 3.3 are satisfied

Output: A Hamiltonian path P of G with u,v as endpoints

1: $t \leftarrow u$; $P \leftarrow (u)$
2: **while** $t > 1$ **do**
3:     $p \leftarrow s(t)$ {the adjacent vertex of t with the smallest index}
4:     $P \leftarrow P \circ (p)$; $t \leftarrow p$
5: **while** $t < v-1$ **do**
6:     **if** $t+1 \notin V(P)$ **then**
7:         $P \leftarrow P \circ (t+1)$; $t \leftarrow t+1$
8:     **else**
9:         **if** $t+2 \notin V(P) \cup \{v\}$ **then**
10:            $P \leftarrow P \circ (t+2)$; $t \leftarrow t+2$
11: **while** $t < n$ **do**
12:     $p \leftarrow e(t)$ {the adjacent vertex of t with the greatest index}
13:     $P \leftarrow P \circ (p)$; $t \leftarrow p$
14: **while** $t > v$ **do**
15:     **if** $t-1 \notin V(P)$ **then**
16:         $P \leftarrow P \circ (t-1)$; $t \leftarrow t-1$
17:     **else**
18:         $P \leftarrow P \circ (t-2)$; $t \leftarrow t-2$
19: **return** P

Theorem 3.4. *Let G be a connected proper interval graph and u be a vertex of G. There is a Hamiltonian path in G with $u, u+1$ as endpoints if and only if H_G is a two-way matrix and either $u \in \{1, n-1\}$ or the vertices $u-1$ and $u+2$ are adjacent.*

Proof. For the necessity part of the proof, assume that G has a Hamiltonian path P with u and $u+1$ as endpoints. Suppose first that H_G is an one-way matrix. Then, at least one of the matrices $H_{1,u+1}$ and $H_{u,n}$ is one-way matrix. Similarly to the proof of Theorem 3.3, there is no Hamiltonian path in G having as endpoints the vertices u and $v = u+1$, which is a contradiction to our assumption.

Suppose now that H_G is a two-way matrix and let $u \in \{2, \ldots, n-2\}$. Then, both vertices $u-1$ and $u+2$ exist in G. Since P starts at u and ends at $u+1$, at least one vertex of $\{1, \ldots, u-1\}$ has to be connected to at least one vertex of $\{u+2, \ldots, n\}$. Thus, due to the stair-shape of H_G, it follows that the vertices $u-1$ and $u+2$ are connected. This completes the necessity part of the proof.

For the sufficiency part, suppose that the conditions of Theorem 3.4 hold. Then, Algorithm 3.2 constructs a Hamiltonian path P in G having u and $u+1$ as endpoints. The only differences from the proof of Theorem 3.3 about the correctness of Algorithm 3.2 are the following. If $u = 1$, the lines 2-10 are not executed at all. In this case, P visits all vertices of G during the execution of lines 11-18, exactly as in the proof of Theorem 3.3. If $u \geq 2$, none of the lines 7 and 10 of Algorithm 3.2 is executed when P visits vertex $t = u - 1$, since in this case $t + 1 = u \in V(P)$ and $t + 2 = u + 1 \in V(P) \cup \{u+1\}$. If $u+1 = n$, then P visits the last vertex $u+1$ in lines 12 and 13. Otherwise, if $u+1 < n$, the vertices $u-1$ and $u+2$ are adjacent, due to the conditions of Theorem 3.4. In this case, P continues visiting all the remaining vertices of G, as in the proof of Theorem 3.3. Figure 3.4(b) illustrates the construction of such a Hamiltonian path by Algorithm 3.2 in a small example. □

Algorithm 3.2 operates on every vertex of G at most twice. Thus, since all values $s(t)$ and $e(t)$ can be computed in $O(n)$ time, its running time is $O(n)$ as well. Figure 3.4 illustrates in a small example the construction by Algorithm 3.2 of a Hamiltonian path with endpoints u and v, for both cases $v \geq u+2$ and $v = u+1$.

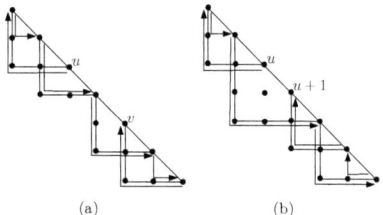

FIGURE 3.4: The construction of a HP with endpoints u, v where (a) $v \geq u + 2$, (b) $v = u + 1$.

3.2.2.2 The decision of 2HP in $O(n)$ time

We can use now the results of Section 3.2.2.1 in order to decide in $O(n)$ time whether a given proper interval graph G has a Hamiltonian path P with two specific endpoints u,v and to construct P, if it exists. The values $s(w)$ and $e(w)$ for all vertices $w \in \{1, \ldots, n\}$ can be computed in $O(n)$ time by Algorithm 3.1. Due to the stair-shape of H_G, the graph G is not connected if and only if there is a vertex $w \in \{1, \ldots, n-1\}$, for which it holds $e(w) = w$ and thus, we can check the connectivity of G in $O(n)$ time. If G is not connected, then it has no Hamiltonian path at all. Finally, a vertex w is singular if and only if $e(w-1) = s(w+1) = w$ and thus, the singular points of G can be computed in $O(n)$ time.

Since the proper interval graphs are hereditary, the subgraphs $G_{1,u+1}$ and $G_{v-1,n}$ of G remain proper interval graphs as well. Thus, if G is connected, we can check in $O(n)$ time whether these graphs have singular points, or equivalently, whether $H_{1,u+1}$ and $H_{v-1,n}$ are two-way matrices. On the other hand, we can check in constant time whether the vertices $u-1$ and $u+2$ are adjacent. Thus, we can decide in $O(n)$ time whether there exists a Hamiltonian path in G with endpoints u,v, due to Theorems 3.3 and 3.4. In the case of non-existence, we output "NO", while otherwise we construct by Algorithm 3.2 the desired Hamiltonian path in $O(n)$ time.

3.2.3 The kPC problem

3.2.3.1 The algorithm

In this section we present Algorithm 3.3, which solves in $O(n)$ the k-fixed-endpoint path cover (kPC) problem on a proper interval graph G with n vertices, for any $k \leq n$. This algorithm uses the characterization of the 2HP problem of the previous section. We assume that for the given set $T = \{t_1, t_2, \ldots, t_k\}$ it holds $t_1 < t_2 < \ldots < t_k$. Denote in the sequel a minimum k-fixed-endpoint path cover of G with respect to the set T by $C(G,T)$. Denote also for simplicity $t_{k+1} = n+1$.

Algorithm 3.3 computes an optimal path cover $C(G,T)$ of G. First, it checks in lines 4-9 the connectivity of G. If G is not connected, the algorithm computes in lines 7-8 recursively the optimal solutions of the first connected component and of the remaining graph.

Algorithm 3.3 Computation of $C(G,T)$ for a proper interval graph G

Input: The SNIR matrix H_G of a proper interval graph G, all values $s(w)$ and $e(w)$, and a set $T = \{t_1, t_2, \ldots, t_k\}$ of vertices of G
Output: A minimum k-fixed-endpoint path cover $C(G,T)$ of G with respect to T

1: **if** $G = \emptyset$ **then**
2:     **return** $\emptyset$
3: Compute the values $s(w)$ and $e(w)$ for every vertex w by Algorithm 3.1
4: $w \leftarrow 1$
5: **while** $w < n$ **do**
6:     **if** $e(w) = w$ **then** $\{G$ is not connected$\}$
7:         $T_1 \leftarrow T \cap \{1, 2, \ldots, w\}$; $T_2 \leftarrow T \setminus T_1$
8:         **return** $C(G_{1,w}, T_1) \cup C(G_{w+1,n}, T_2)$
9:     $w \leftarrow w + 1$
10: **if** $k \leq 1$ **then**
11:     call Algorithm 3.4
12: **if** $t_1 \in S(G)$ **then**
13:     $P_1 \leftarrow (1, 2, \ldots, t_1)$
14:     **return** $\{P_1\} \cup C(G_{t_1+1,n}, T \setminus \{t_1\})$
15: call Algorithm 3.5

It reaches line 10 only if G is connected. In the case where $|T| = k \leq 1$, Algorithm 3.3 calls Algorithm 3.4 as subroutine.

In lines 12-14, Algorithm 3.3 considers the case, where G is connected, $|T| \geq 2$ and t_1 is a singular point of G. Then, Lemma 3.7 implies that $2 \leq t_1 \leq n-1$. Thus, since no vertex among $\{1, \ldots, t_1 - 1\}$ is connected to any vertex among $\{t_1 + 1, \ldots, n\}$ and since $t_1 \in T$, an optimal solution must contain at least two paths. Therefore, it is always optimal to choose in line 13 a path that visits sequentially the first t_1 vertices and then to compute recursively in line 14 an optimal solution in the remaining graph $G_{t_1+1,n}$. Algorithm 3.3 reaches line 15 if G is connected, $|T| \geq 2$ and t_1 is a regular point of G. In this case, it calls Algorithm 3.5 as subroutine.

Algorithm 3.4 computes an optimal path cover $C(G, T)$ of G in the case, where G is connected and $|T| = k \leq 1$. If $k = 0$, then the optimal solution includes clearly only one path, which visits sequentially the vertices $1, 2, \ldots, n$, since G is connected. Let now $k = 1$. If $t_1 \in \{1, n\}$, then the optimal solution is again the single path $(1, 2, \ldots, n)$. Otherwise, suppose that $t_1 \in \{2, \ldots, n-1\}$. In this case, a trivial path cover is that with the paths $(1, 2, \ldots, t_1)$ and $(t_1 + 1, \ldots, n)$. This path cover is not optimal if and only if G has a Hamiltonian path P with $u = t_1$ as one endpoint. The other endpoint v of P lies either in $\{1, \ldots, t_1 - 1\}$ or in $\{t_1 + 1, \ldots, n\}$. If $v \in \{t_1 + 1, \ldots, n\}$, then H_{1, t_1+1}

Algorithm 3.4 Computation of $C(G,T)$, if G is connected and $|T| \leq 1$

Input: The SNIR matrix H_G of a connected proper interval graph G, all values $s(w)$ and $e(w)$, and a set $T = \{t_1, t_2, \ldots, t_k\}$ of $k \leq 1$ vertices of G
Output: A minimum k-fixed-endpoint path cover $C(G,T)$ of G with respect to T

1: **if** $k = 0$ **then**
2:    **return** $\{(1, 2, \ldots, n)\}$
3: **if** $k = 1$ **then**
4:    **if** $t_1 \in \{1, n\}$ **then**
5:      **return** $\{(1, 2, \ldots, n)\}$
6:    **else**
7:      $P_1 \leftarrow 2\text{HP}(G, 1, t_1)$
8:      $P_2 \leftarrow 2\text{HP}(G, t_1, n)$
9:      **if** $P_1 = $ "NO" **then**
10:        **if** $P_2 = $ "NO" **then**
11:          **return** $\{(1, 2, \ldots, t_1), (t_1 + 1, \ldots, n)\}$
12:        **else**
13:          **return** $\{P_2\}$
14:      **else**
15:        **return** $\{P_1\}$

and $H_{v-1,n}$ have to be two-way matrices, due to Theorems 3.3 and 3.4. However, due to Definition 3.8, if $H_{v-1,n}$ is a two-way matrix, then $H_{n-1,n}$ is also a two-way matrix, since $H_{n-1,n}$ is a trivial submatrix of $H_{v-1,n}$.

Thus, if such a Hamiltonian path with endpoints t_1 and v exists, then there exists also one with endpoints t_1 and n by Theorems 3.3 and 3.4. Similarly, if there exists a Hamiltonian path with endpoints $v \in \{1, \ldots, t_1 - 1\}$ and t_1, then there exists also one with endpoints 1 and t_1. Thus, we call the procedures $P_1 = 2\text{HP}(G, 1, t_1)$ and $P_2 = 2\text{HP}(G, t_1, n)$ in lines 7 and 8, respectively. If both outputs are "NO", then the paths $(1, 2, \ldots, t_1)$ and $(t_1 + 1, \ldots, n)$ constitute an optimal solution. Otherwise, we return one of the obtained paths P_1 or P_2 in lines 15 or 13, respectively. Since the running time of Algorithm 3.2 for the 2HP problem is $O(n)$, the running time of Algorithm 3.4 is $O(n)$ as well.

In lines 5-9 and 12-14, Algorithm 3.3 separates G in two subgraphs and computes their optimal solutions recursively. Thus, since the computation of all values $s(w)$ and $e(w)$ can be done in $O(n)$, and since the running time of Algorithms 3.4 and 3.5 (as it will be proved in Section 3.2.3.2) is $O(n)$, we obtain in the following theorem the main result of this section.

Chapter 3. *A matrix representation of interval and proper interval graphs*   60

Algorithm 3.5 Computation of $C(G,T)$, where G is connected, $|T| \geq 2$, $t_1 \notin S(G)$

Input: The SNIR matrix H_G of a connected proper interval graph G, all values $s(w)$ and $e(w)$, and a set $T = \{t_1, t_2, \ldots, t_k\}$ of $k \geq 2$ vertices of G, where $t_1 \notin S(G)$

Output: A minimum k-fixed-endpoint path cover $C(G,T)$ of G with respect to T

1: **if** $\{1, \ldots, t_1 - 1\} \cap S(G) = \emptyset$ **then** $\{e_1 = t_2\}$
2:    **if** $2\mathrm{HP}(G_{1,t_2+1}, t_1, t_2) =$ "NO" **then**
3:      $a \leftarrow t_2$
4:    **else**
5:      **if** $\{t_2 + 1, \ldots, t_3 - 1\} \cap S(G) \neq \emptyset$ **then**
6:        $a \leftarrow \min\{\{t_2 + 1, \ldots, t_3 - 1\} \cap S(G)\}$
7:      **else**
8:        $a \leftarrow t_3 - 1$
9:      $P_1 \leftarrow 2\mathrm{HP}(G_{1,a}, t_1, t_2)$
10:      $C_2 \leftarrow C(G_{a+1,n}, T \setminus \{t_1, t_2\})$
11: **else** $\{e_1 = 1\}$
12:    **if** $2\mathrm{HP}(G_{1,t_1+1}, 1, t_1) =$ "NO" **then**
13:      $a \leftarrow t_1$
14:    **else**
15:      **if** $\{t_1 + 1, \ldots, t_2 - 1\} \cap S(G) \neq \emptyset$ **then**
16:        $a \leftarrow \min\{\{t_1 + 1, \ldots, t_2 - 1\} \cap S(G)\}$
17:      **else**
18:        $a \leftarrow t_2 - 1$
19:      $P_1 \leftarrow 2\mathrm{HP}(G_{1,a}, 1, t_1)$
20:      $C_2 \leftarrow C(G_{a+1,n}, T \setminus \{t_1\})$
21: **return** $\{P_1\} \cup C_2$

Theorem 3.5. *A minimum k-fixed-endpoint path cover of a proper interval graph G with n vertices can be computed by Algorithm 3.3 in $O(n)$ time, given the SNIR matrix H_G of G.*

3.2.3.2   Correctness and complexity of Algorithm 3.5

The correctness of Algorithm 3.5 follows from the technical Lemmas 3.9 and 3.10. To this end, we prove first the auxiliary Lemma 3.8. For the purposes of these proofs, we assume an optimal solution C of G. Denote by P_i the path in C, which has t_i as one endpoint and let e_i be its second endpoint. Observe that, if $e_i = t_j$, then $P_i = P_j$. Furthermore, let ℓ_i be the vertex of P_i with the greatest index in the ordering of H_G. It holds clearly $\ell_i \geq t_i$, for every $i \in \{1, \ldots, k\}$.

Lemma 3.8. *If $e_1 \leq t_1$, then w.l.o.g. $\ell_1 < t_2$ and $e_1 = 1$.*

Proof. At first, suppose that $e_1 = t_1$, i.e. P_1 is a trivial path of one vertex. If $t_1 = 1$, the lemma holds obviously. Otherwise, if $t_1 > 1$, we can extend P_1 by visiting sequentially the vertices $t_1 - 1, \ldots, 1$. Since there is no vertex of T among the vertices $\{1, \ldots, t_1 - 1\}$, the resulting path cover has not greater cardinality than C and $e_1 = 1$.

Let now $e_1 < t_1$. Suppose that $\ell_1 \geq t_2$. Thus, since ℓ_1 is not an endpoint of P_1, it holds that $t_i < \ell_1 < t_{i+1}$ for some $i \in \{2, \ldots, k\}$; recall that $t_{k+1} = n + 1$. Suppose first that $t_i < \ell_1 < \ell_i$, as it is illustrated in Figure 3.5(a). Then, we can clearly transfer to P_i all vertices of P_1 with index between $t_i + 1$ and ℓ_1. The obtained path cover has the same cardinality as C, while the greatest index of the vertices of P_1 is less than t_i.

Suppose now that $t_i < \ell_i < \ell_1$, as it is illustrated in Figure 3.5(b). Since $e_1 < t_1$, the path P_1 is a Hamiltonian path of some subgraph of G_{1,ℓ_1} with endpoints e_1 and t_1. Now, we obtain similarly to the proofs of Theorems 3.3 and 3.4 that H_{t_1-1,ℓ_1} is a two-way matrix, since otherwise the path P_1 would visit two times the same vertex, which is a contradiction. It follows that H_{ℓ_i-1,ℓ_1} is also a two-way matrix, as a submatrix of H_{t_1-1,ℓ_1}. Thus, we can extend P_i by the vertices of P_1 with index between $\ell_i + 1$ and ℓ_1. In the obtained path cover, the greatest index ℓ_1' of the vertices of P_1 is less than ℓ_i. Finally, if $t_i < \ell_1'$, we can obtain, similarly to the above, a new path cover with the same cardinality as C, in which the greatest index of the vertices of P_1 is less than t_i.

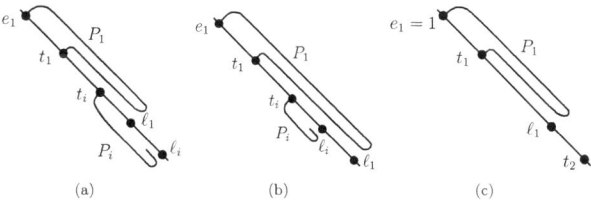

FIGURE 3.5: The case $e_1 \leq t_1$.

It follows now by induction that there is an optimal solution, in which the greatest index ℓ_1 of the vertices of P_1 is less than t_2, i.e. $\ell_1 < t_2$, as it is illustrated in Figure 3.5(c). Then, similarly to above, H_{t_1-1,ℓ_1} is a two-way matrix. Now, Theorems 3.3 and 3.4 imply that G_{1,ℓ_1} has a Hamiltonian path with 1 and t_1 as endpoints. Thus, it is always optimal to choose $P_1 = 2\text{HP}(G_{1,\ell_1}, 1, t_1)$, for some $\ell_1 \in \{t_1, \ldots, t_2 - 1\}$, i.e. $e_1 = 1$. This completes the lemma. □

Lemma 3.9. *If* $\{1, \ldots, t_1\} \cap S(G) = \emptyset$, *then w.l.o.g.* $e_1 = t_2$.

Proof. Suppose at first that $e_1 \leq t_1$. Then, Lemma 3.8 implies that $e_1 = 1$. In particular, the proof of Lemma 3.8 implies that $\ell_1 < t_2$ and that $P_1 = 2\text{HP}(G_{1,\ell_1}, 1, t_1)$, as it is illustrated in Figure 3.6(a). Thus, since P_1 visits all vertices $\{1, 2, \ldots, \ell_1\}$, it holds that

$$|C| = 1 + |C(G_{\ell_1+1,n}, T \setminus \{t_1\})| \tag{3.2}$$

Suppose now that $e_1 > t_1$. Since there are no singular points of G among $\{1, \ldots, t_1\}$, the submatrix H_{1,t_1+1} is a two-way matrix. Then, Theorems 3.3 and 3.4 imply that G_{1,t_2} has a Hamiltonian path with endpoints t_1 and t_2. Thus, we may suppose w.l.o.g. that $P_1 = 2\text{HP}(G_{1,a}, t_1, t_2)$, for an appropriate $a \geq t_2$, as it is illustrated in Figure 3.6(b). Since $P_1 = P_2$, and thus $e_2 = t_1 < t_2$, we obtain similarly to Lemma 3.8 that $a = \ell_2 < t_3$. Since P_1 visits all vertices $\{1, 2, \ldots, a\}$, it follows in this case for the cardinality of C that

$$|C| = 1 + |C(G_{a+1,n}, T \setminus \{t_1, t_2\})| \tag{3.3}$$

Since in (3.2) it holds $\ell_1 < t_2$ and in (3.3) it holds $a \geq t_2$, it follows that $G_{a+1,n}$ is a strict subgraph of $G_{\ell_1+1,n}$. Moreover, since $T \setminus \{t_1, t_2\}$ is a subset of $T \setminus \{t_1\}$, it follows that the quantity in (3.3) is less than or equal to that in (3.2). Thus, we may suppose w.l.o.g. that $e_1 = t_2$. □

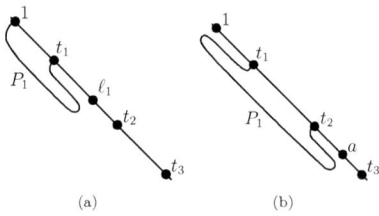

FIGURE 3.6: The case, where there is no singular point of G among $\{1, \ldots, t_1\}$.

Lemma 3.10. *If* $\{1, \ldots, t_1 - 1\} \cap S(G) \neq \emptyset$ *and* $t_1 \notin S(G)$, *then w.l.o.g.* $e_1 = 1$.

Proof. Let $w \in \{1, \ldots, t_1 - 1\}$ be the singular point of G with the smallest index. Due to Lemma 3.7, it holds $w \geq 2$. Then, there is a path P_0 in the optimal solution C, which has an endpoint $t_0 \in \{1, \ldots, w-1\}$. Indeed, otherwise there would be a path visiting vertex w at least twice, which is a contradiction.

Thus, since $\{1, \ldots, t_0\} \cap S(G) = \emptyset$ and since t_0 is an endpoint in the optimal solution C, Lemma 3.9 implies for the other endpoint e_0 of P_0 that $e_0 = t_1$ and therefore $P_0 = P_1$. Thus, since the second endpoint of P_1 is $e_1 = t_0 < t_1$, Lemma 3.8 implies that w.l.o.g. it holds $e_1 = t_0 = 1$, and in particular the proof of Lemma 3.8 implies that $P_1 = 2\mathrm{HP}(G_{1,a}, 1, t_1)$ for some $a \in \{t_1, \ldots, t_2 - 1\}$, as it is illustrated in Figure 3.7. □

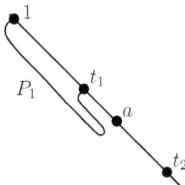

FIGURE 3.7: The case, where there are singular points of G among $\{1, \ldots, t_1 - 1\}$ and t_1 is a regular point of G.

Algorithm 3.5 considers in lines 1-10 the case where there are no singular points of G among $\{1, \ldots, t_1 - 1\}$. Lemma 3.9 implies for this case that $e_1 = t_2$ and, in particular the proof of Lemma 3.9 implies that $P_1 = 2\mathrm{HP}(G_{1,a}, t_1, t_2)$ for some $a \in \{t_2, \ldots t_3 - 1\}$. In order to maximize P_1 as much as possible, we choose the greatest possible value of a, for which $G_{1,a}$ has a Hamiltonian path with endpoints t_1, t_2. Namely, if G_{1,t_2+1} does not have such a Hamiltonian path, we set $a = t_2$ in line 3 of Algorithm 3.5. Suppose now that G_{1,t_2+1} has such a path. In the case, where there is at least one singular point of G among $\{t_2 + 1, \ldots, t_3 - 1\}$, we set a to be this one with the smallest index among them in line 6. Otherwise, we set $a = t_3 - 1$ in line 8. Denote for simplicity $G_{1,n+1} = G$. Then, in the extreme cases $t_3 = t_2 + 1$ or $t_2 = n$, the algorithm sets $a = t_2 = t_3 - 1$.

Next, in lines 11-20, Algorithm 3.5 considers the case, where there is at least one singular point of G among $\{1, \ldots, t_1 - 1\}$. Then, Lemma 3.10 implies that $e_1 = 1$ and, in particular the proof of Lemma 3.10 implies that $P_1 = 2\mathrm{HP}(G_{1,a}, 1, t_1)$, for some

$a \in \{t_1, \ldots, t_2 - 1\}$. In order to maximize P_1 as much as possible, we choose the greatest possible value of a, for which $G_{1,a}$ has a Hamiltonian path with endpoints 1 and t_1. Namely, if G_{1,t_1+1} does not have such a Hamiltonian path, we set $a = t_1$ in line 13 of Algorithm 3.5. Suppose now that G_{1,t_1+1} has such a path. In the case, where there is at least one singular point of G among $\{t_1 + 1, \ldots, t_2 - 1\}$, we set a to be this one with the smallest index among them in line 16. Otherwise, we set $a = t_2 - 1$ in line 18. Note that in the extreme case $t_2 = t_1 + 1$, the algorithm sets $a = t_1 = t_2 - 1$.

Algorithm 3.5 computes P_1 in lines 9 and 19, respectively. Then, it computes recursively the optimum path cover C_2 of the remaining graph in lines 10 and 20, respectively, and it outputs $\{P_1\} \cup C_2$. Thus, since the computation of a 2HP by Algorithm 3.2 can be done in $O(n)$ time, the running time of Algorithm 3.5 is $O(n)$ as well. This implies now the main Theorem 3.5 of this section.

Chapter 4

A new intersection model for tolerance graphs

As already mentioned in Section 1.1, it is of great importance to establish suitable non-trivial intersection models for classes of graphs, since such models may be very useful for the design of efficient algorithms for difficult optimization problems on these graph classes [92]. Such a graph class that admits a very natural intersection model is that of bounded tolerance graphs; namely, it has been proved that a graph is bounded tolerance if and only if it is a parallelogram graph [18,83]. However, this intersection model cannot cope with general tolerance graphs, in which the tolerance of an interval can be greater than its length.

In this chapter we present the first non-trivial intersection model for general tolerance graphs [P3], which generalizes the widely known parallelogram representation of bounded tolerance graphs [18,62,83]. The main idea is to exploit the third dimension in order to capture the information given by unbounded tolerances, and as a result parallelograms are replaced by parallelepipeds. The proposed intersection model is very intuitive and can be efficiently constructed from a given tolerance representation (actually, we show that it can be constructed in linear time).

Apart from being important on its own, this new representation proves to be a powerful tool for designing efficient algorithms for general tolerance graphs. Indeed, using our intersection model, we improve the best existing running times of three problems on tolerance graphs [P3]. We present algorithms to find a minimum coloring and a maximum clique in $O(n \log n)$ time, where n is the number of vertices of the input tolerance graph, which turns out to be optimal. The complexity of the best existing algorithms for these problems was $O(n^2)$ [61,62]. We also present an algorithm to find a maximum weight independent set in $O(n^2)$ time, whereas the complexity of the best known algorithm for this problem was $O(n^3)$ [62]. We note that an $O(n^2 \log n)$ algorithm to find a maximum *cardinality* independent set on a general tolerance graph with n vertices has been proposed in [95], and that [62] refers to an algorithm transmitted by personal communication with running time $O(n^2 \log n)$ to find a maximum weight independent set; to the best of our knowledge, this algorithm has not been published.

It is important to note that the complexity of recognizing tolerance and bounded tolerance graphs has been a challenging open problem [27,62,95] since the introduction of tolerance graphs in 1982 [59]. This is the reason why all existing algorithms on tolerance graphs assumed that the input graph is given along with a tolerance representation of it. We make in this chapter the same assumption as well, while we deal with the recognition of tolerance and bounded tolerance graphs in Chapter 5.

The rest of this chapter is organized as follows. In Section 4.1 we introduce the new three-dimensional intersection model of tolerance graphs. In Section 4.2 we present a canonical representation of tolerance graphs, which is a special case of the new intersection model, and then we show how this canonical representation can be used in order to obtain optimal algorithms for finding a minimum coloring and a maximum clique in a tolerance graph. The running time optimality of these algorithms is being discussed in Section 4.2.4. In Section 4.3 we present our algorithm for finding a maximum weight independent set in tolerance graphs, which is also based on the new intersection model.

4.1 A new intersection model

One of the most natural representations of bounded tolerance graphs is given by parallelograms between two parallel lines in the Euclidean plane [18,62,83]. In this section we extend this representation to a three-dimensional representation of general tolerance graphs. Given a tolerance graph $G = (V, E)$ along with a tolerance representation of it, recall that vertex $v_i \in V$ corresponds to an interval $I_i = [a_i, b_i]$ on the real line with

Chapter 4. *A new intersection model for tolerance graphs* 67

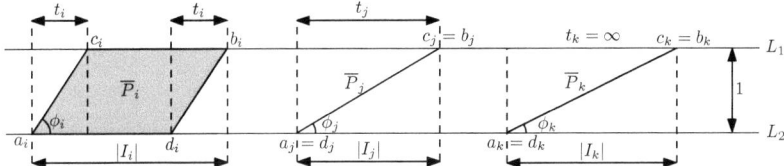

FIGURE 4.1: Parallelograms $\overline{P}_i$ and $\overline{P}_j$ correspond to bounded vertices v_i and v_j, respectively, whereas $\overline{P}_k$ corresponds to an unbounded vertex v_k.

a tolerance $t_i \geq 0$. Without loss of generality we may assume that $t_i > 0$ for every vertex v_i [62].

Definition 4.1. *Given a tolerance representation of a tolerance graph $G = (V, E)$, vertex v_i is bounded if $t_i \leq |I_i|$. Otherwise, v_i is unbounded. V_B and V_U are the sets of bounded and unbounded vertices in V, respectively. Clearly $V = V_B \cup V_U$.*

We can also assume without loss of generality that $t_i = \infty$ for any unbounded vertex v_i, since if v_i is unbounded, then the intersection of any other interval with I_i is strictly smaller than t_i. Let L_1 and L_2 be two parallel lines at distance one in the Euclidean plane.

Definition 4.2. *Given an interval $I_i = [a_i, b_i]$ with tolerance t_i, $\overline{P}_i$ is the parallelogram defined by the points c_i, b_i in L_1 and a_i, d_i in L_2, where $c_i = \min\{b_i, a_i + t_i\}$ and $d_i = \max\{a_i, b_i - t_i\}$. The slope ϕ_i of $\overline{P}_i$ is $\phi_i = \arctan\left(\frac{1}{c_i - a_i}\right)$.*

An example is depicted in Figure 4.1, where $\overline{P}_i$ and $\overline{P}_j$ correspond to bounded vertices v_i and v_j, and $\overline{P}_k$ corresponds to an unbounded vertex v_k. Observe that when vertex v_i is bounded, the values c_i and d_i coincide with the *tolerance points* defined in [48, 62, 71], and $\phi_i = \arctan\left(\frac{1}{t_i}\right)$. On the other hand, when vertex v_i is unbounded, the values c_i and d_i coincide with the endpoints b_i and a_i of I_i, respectively, and $\phi_i = \arctan\left(\frac{1}{|I_i|}\right)$. Observe also that in both cases $t_i = b_i - a_i$ and $t_i = \infty$, parallelogram $\overline{P}_i$ is reduced to a line segment (c.f. $\overline{P}_j$ and $\overline{P}_k$ in Figure 4.1). Since $t_i > 0$ for every vertex v_i, it follows that $0 < \phi_i < \frac{\pi}{2}$. Furthermore, we can assume without loss of generality that all points a_i, b_i, c_i, d_i and all slopes ϕ_i are distinct [48, 62, 71].

Observation 4.1. *Let $v_i \in V_U, v_j \in V_B$. Then $|I_i| < t_j$ if and only if $\phi_i > \phi_j$.*

We are now ready to give the main definition of this chapter.

Chapter 4. A new intersection model for tolerance graphs   68

Definition 4.3. Let $G = (V, E)$ be a tolerance graph with a tolerance representation $\{I_i = [a_i, b_i], t_i \mid i = 1, \ldots, n\}$. For every $i = 1 \ldots, n$, P_i is the parallelepiped in $\mathbb{R}^3$ defined as follows:

(a) If $t_i \leq b_i - a_i$ (v_i is bounded), then $P_i = \{(x, y, z) \in \mathbb{R}^3 \mid (x, y) \in \overline{P}_i,\ 0 \leq z \leq \phi_i\}$.

(b) If $t_i > b_i - a_i$ (v_i is unbounded), then $P_i = \{(x, y, z) \in \mathbb{R}^3 \mid (x, y) \in \overline{P}_i,\ z = \phi_i\}$.

The set of parallelepipeds $\{P_i \mid i = 1, \ldots, n\}$ is a parallelepiped representation of G.

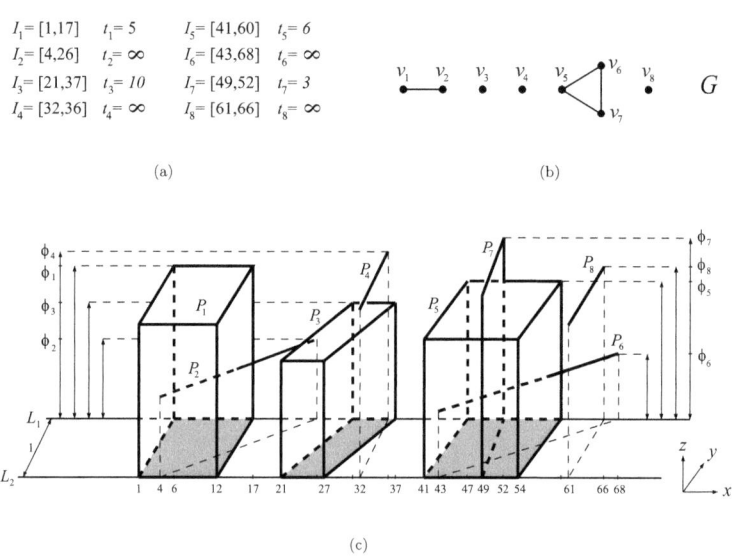

FIGURE 4.2: The intersection model for tolerance graphs: (a) a set of intervals $I_i = [a_i, b_i]$ and tolerances t_i, $i = 1, \ldots, 8$, (b) the corresponding tolerance graph G and (c) a parallelepiped representation of G.

Observe that for each interval I_i, the parallelogram $\overline{P}_i$ of Definition 4.2 (see also Figure 4.1) coincides with the projection of the parallelepiped P_i on the plane $z = 0$. An example of the construction of these parallelepipeds is given in Figure 4.2, where a set of eight intervals with their associated tolerances is given in Figure 4.2(a). The corresponding tolerance graph G is depicted in Figure 4.2(b), while the parallelepiped representation is illustrated in Figure 4.2(c). In the case $t_i < b_i - a_i$, the parallelepiped P_i is three-dimensional, c.f. P_1, P_3, and P_5, while in the border case $t_i = b_i - a_i$ it degenerates to a two-dimensional rectangle, c.f. P_7. In these two cases, each P_i corresponds

Chapter 4. *A new intersection model for tolerance graphs* 69

to a bounded vertex v_i. In the remaining case $t_i = \infty$ (that is, v_i is unbounded), the parallelepiped P_i degenerates to a one-dimensional line segment above plane $z = 0$, c.f. P_2, P_4, P_6, and P_8.

We prove now that these parallelepipeds form a three-dimensional intersection model for the class of tolerance graphs (namely, that every tolerance graph G can be viewed as the intersection graph of the corresponding parallelepipeds P_i).

Theorem 4.1. *Let $G = (V, E)$ be a tolerance graph with a tolerance representation $\{I_i = [a_i, b_i], t_i \mid i = 1, \ldots, n\}$. Then for every $i \neq j$, $v_i v_j \in E$ if and only if $P_i \cap P_j \neq \emptyset$.*

Proof. We distinguish three cases according to whether vertices v_i and v_j are bounded or unbounded:

(a) Both vertices are bounded, that is $t_i \leq b_i - a_i$ and $t_j \leq b_j - a_j$. It follows from [62] that $v_i v_j \in E(G)$ if and only if $\overline{P}_i \cap \overline{P}_j \neq \emptyset$. However, due to the definition of the parallelepipeds P_i and P_j, in this case $P_i \cap P_j \neq \emptyset$ if and only if $\overline{P}_i \cap \overline{P}_j \neq \emptyset$ (c.f. P_1 and P_3, or P_5 and P_7, in Figure 4.2).

(b) Both vertices are unbounded, that is $t_i = t_j = \infty$. Since no two unbounded vertices are adjacent, $v_i v_j \notin E(G)$. On the other hand, the line segments P_i and P_j lie on the disjoint planes $z = \phi_i$ and $z = \phi_j$ of $\mathbb{R}^3$, respectively, since we assumed that the slopes ϕ_i and ϕ_j are distinct. Thus, $P_i \cap P_j = \emptyset$ (c.f. P_2 and P_4).

(c) One vertex is unbounded (that is, $t_i = \infty$) and the other is bounded (that is, $t_j \leq b_j - a_j$). If $\overline{P}_i \cap \overline{P}_j = \emptyset$, then $v_i v_j \notin E$ and $P_i \cap P_j = \emptyset$ (c.f. P_1 and P_6). Suppose that $\overline{P}_i \cap \overline{P}_j \neq \emptyset$. We distinguish two cases:

  (i) $\phi_i < \phi_j$. It is easy to check that $|I_i \cap I_j| \geq t_j$ and thus $v_i v_j \in E$. Since $\overline{P}_i \cap \overline{P}_j \neq \emptyset$ and $\phi_i < \phi_j$, then necessarily the line segment P_i intersects the parallelepiped P_j on the plane $z = \phi_i$, and thus $P_i \cap P_j \neq \emptyset$ (c.f. P_1 and P_2).

  (ii) $\phi_i > \phi_j$. Clearly $|I_i \cap I_j| < t_i = \infty$. Furthermore, since $\phi_i > \phi_j$, Observation 4.1 implies that $|I_i \cap I_j| \leq |I_i| < t_j$. It follows that $|I_i \cap I_j| < \min\{t_i, t_j\}$, and thus $v_i v_j \notin E$. On the other hand, $z = \phi_i$ for all points $(x, y, z) \in P_i$, while $z \leq \phi_j < \phi_i$ for all points $(x, y, z) \in P_j$, and therefore $P_i \cap P_j = \emptyset$ (c.f. P_3 and P_4). □

Clearly, for each $v_i \in V$ the parallelepiped P_i can be constructed in constant time. Therefore,

Lemma 4.1. *Given a tolerance representation of a tolerance graph G with n vertices, a parallelepiped representation of G can be constructed in $O(n)$ time.*

4.2 Coloring and Clique Algorithms in $O(n \log n)$

In this section we present optimal $O(n \log n)$ algorithms for constructing a minimum coloring and a maximum clique in a tolerance graph $G = (V, E)$ with n vertices, given a parallelepiped representation of G. These algorithms improve the best known running time $O(n^2)$ of these problems on tolerance graphs [61, 62]. First, we introduce a canonical representation of tolerance graphs in Section 4.2.1, and then we use it to obtain the algorithms for the minimum coloring and the maximum clique problems in Section 4.2.2. Finally, we discuss the optimality of both algorithms in Section 4.2.4.

4.2.1 A canonical representation

We associate with every vertex v_i of G the point $p_i = (x_i, y_i)$ in the Euclidean plane, where $x_i = b_i$ and $y_i = \frac{\pi}{2} - \phi_i$. Since all endpoints of the parallelograms $\overline{P}_i$ and all slopes ϕ_i are distinct, all coordinates of the points p_i are distinct as well. Similarly to [61, 62], we state the following two definitions.

Definition 4.4. *An unbounded vertex $v_i \in V_U$ of a tolerance graph G is called* inevitable *(for a certain parallelepiped representation), if replacing P_i by $\{(x, y, z) \mid (x, y) \in P_i, 0 \leq z \leq \phi_i\}$ creates a new edge in G. Otherwise, v_i is called* evitable.

Note here that, given an arbitrary unbounded vertex $v_i \in V_U$, replacing P_i by $\{(x, y, z) \mid (x, y) \in P_i, 0 \leq z \leq \phi_i\}$ in a parallelepiped representation of G is equivalent with replacing in the corresponding tolerance representation of G the infinite tolerance $t_i = \infty$ of v_i by the finite tolerance $t_i = |I_i|$, i.e. with making v_i a bounded vertex.

Definition 4.5. *Let $v_i \in V_U$ be an inevitable unbounded vertex of a tolerance graph G (for a certain parallelepiped representation). A vertex v_j is called a* hovering vertex *of v_i if $a_j < a_i$, $b_i < b_j$, and $\phi_i > \phi_j$.*

It is now easy to see that, by Definition 4.5, if v_j is a hovering vertex of v_i, then $v_i v_j \notin E$. Note that, in contrast to [61], in Definition 4.4, an isolated unbounded vertex v_i might be also inevitable, while in Definition 4.5, a hovering vertex might be also unbounded. The next two lemmas follow by Definitions 4.4 and 4.5.

Lemma 4.2. *Let $v_i \in V_U$ be an inevitable unbounded vertex of the tolerance graph G (for a certain parallelepiped representation). Then, there exists a hovering vertex v_j of v_i.*

Proof. Since v_i is an inevitable unbounded vertex, replacing P_i by $\{(x,y,z) \mid (x,y) \in P_i, 0 \leq z \leq \phi_i\}$ creates a new edge in G; let $v_i v_j$ be such an edge. Then, clearly $\overline{P}_i \cap \overline{P}_j \neq \emptyset$. We will prove that v_j is a hovering vertex of v_i. Otherwise, $\phi_i < \phi_j$, $a_j > a_i$, or $b_i > b_j$. Suppose first that $\phi_i < \phi_j$. If $v_j \in V_U$, then v_i remains not connected to v_j after the replacement of P_i by $\{(x,y,z) \mid (x,y) \in P_i, 0 \leq z \leq \phi_i\}$, since $\phi_i < \phi_j$, which is a contradiction. If $v_j \in V_B$, then v_i is connected to v_j also before the replacement of P_i, since $\phi_i < \phi_j$ and $\overline{P}_i \cap \overline{P}_j \neq \emptyset$, which is again a contradiction. Thus, $\phi_i > \phi_j$. Suppose now that $a_j > a_i$ or $b_i > b_j$. Then, since $\phi_i > \phi_j$, it is easy to see that in both cases $\overline{P}_i \cap \overline{P}_j = \emptyset$, which is a contradiction. Thus, $a_j < a_i$, $b_i < b_j$, and $\phi_i > \phi_j$, i.e. v_j is a hovering vertex of v_i by Definition 4.5. □

Lemma 4.3. *Let $v_i \in V_U$ be an inevitable unbounded vertex of a tolerance graph G and v_j be a hovering vertex of v_i (in a certain parallelepiped representation of G). Then, $N(v_i) \subseteq N(v_j)$.*

Proof. Consider an arbitrary inevitable unbounded vertex $v_i \in V_U$ and a hovering vertex v_j of v_i. Then, $a_j < a_i$, $b_i < b_j$, and $\phi_i > \phi_j$ by Definition 4.5. Thus, in particular, $\overline{P}_i \cap \overline{P}_j \neq \emptyset$. If $N(v_i) = \emptyset$, then the lemma clearly holds. Otherwise, consider a vertex $v_k \in N(v_i)$. It follows that $v_k \in V_B$, since $v_i \in V_U$ and no two unbounded vertices are adjacent in G. Furthermore, since $v_i v_k \in E$, it follows that $\overline{P}_i \cap \overline{P}_k \neq \emptyset$ and $\phi_k > \phi_i$. Then, it is easy to see that also $\overline{P}_j \cap \overline{P}_k \neq \emptyset$, and that $\phi_k > \phi_i > \phi_j$. Thus, $P_j \cap P_k \neq \emptyset$, i.e. $v_j v_k \in E$, since v_k is a bounded vertex. That is, $v_k \in N(v_j)$ for every $v_k \in N(v_i)$, and thus the lemma follows. □

Definition 4.6. *A parallelepiped representation of a tolerance graph G is called canonical if every unbounded vertex is inevitable.*

For example, in the tolerance graph depicted in Figure 4.2, v_4 and v_8 are inevitable unbounded vertices, v_3 and v_6 are hovering vertices of v_4 and v_8, respectively, while v_2

and v_6 are evitable unbounded vertices. Therefore, this representation is not canonical for the graph G. However, if we replace P_i by $\{(x,y,z) \mid (x,y) \in P_i, 0 \le z \le \phi_i\}$ for $i = 2, 6$, we get a canonical representation for G.

In the following, we present an algorithm that constructs a canonical representation of a given tolerance graph G.

Definition 4.7. Let $\alpha = (x_\alpha, y_\alpha)$ and $\beta = (x_\beta, y_\beta)$ be two points in the plane. Then α dominates β if $x_\alpha > x_\beta$ and $y_\alpha > y_\beta$. Given a set A of points, the point $\gamma \in A$ is called an extreme point of A if there is no point $\delta \in A$ that dominates γ. $Ex(A)$ is the set of the extreme points of A.

Given a tolerance graph $G = (V, E)$ with the set $V = \{v_1, v_2, \ldots, v_n\}$ of vertices (and its parallelepiped representation), we can assume without loss of generality that $a_i < a_j$ whenever $i < j$. Recall that with every vertex v_i we associated the point $p_i = (x_i, y_i)$, where $x_i = b_i$ and $y_i = \frac{\pi}{2} - \phi_i$, respectively. We define for every $i = 1, 2, \ldots, n$ the set $A_i = \{p_1, p_2, \ldots, p_i\}$ of the points associated with the first i vertices of G.

Lemma 4.4. Let $v_i \in V_U$ be an unbounded vertex of a tolerance graph G. Then:

(a) If $p_i \in Ex(A_i)$ then v_i is evitable.

(b) If $p_i \notin Ex(A_i)$ and point p_j dominates p_i for some bounded vertex $v_j \in V_B$ with $j < i$ then v_i is inevitable and v_j is a hovering vertex of v_i.

Proof. (a) Assume, to the contrary, that v_i is inevitable. By Lemma 4.2 there is a hovering vertex v_j of v_i. But then, $x_i = b_i < b_j = x_j$ and $y_i = \frac{\pi}{2} - \phi_i < \frac{\pi}{2} - \phi_j = y_j$, while $a_j < a_i$, i.e. $j < i$. Therefore $p_j \in A_i$ and p_j dominates p_i, which is a contradiction, since $p_i \in Ex(A_i)$. Thus, v_i is evitable.

(b) Suppose that p_j dominates p_i, for some vertex $v_j \in V_B$ with $j < i$. The ordering of the vertices implies $a_j < a_i$, while $x_i < x_j$ and $y_i < y_j$ imply $b_i < b_j$ and $\phi_i > \phi_j$. Thus, v_i is inevitable and v_j is a hovering vertex of v_i. □

The following theorem shows that, given a parallelepiped representation of a tolerance graph G, we can construct in $O(n \log n)$ a canonical representation of G. This result is crucial for the time complexity analysis of the algorithms of Section 4.2.2.

Theorem 4.2. *Every parallelepiped representation of a tolerance graph G with n vertices can be transformed by Algorithm 4.1 to a canonical representation of G in $O(n \log n)$ time.*

Proof. We describe and analyze Algorithm 4.1 that generates a canonical representation of G. First, we sort the vertices $v_1, v_2, \ldots, v_n$ of G such that $a_i < a_j$ whenever $i < j$. Then, we process sequentially all vertices v_i of G. The bounded and the inevitable unbounded vertices will not be changed, while the evitable unbounded vertices will be replaced by bounded ones. At step i we update the set $Ex(A_i)$ of the extreme points of A_i (note that the set A_i itself remains unchanged during the algorithm). For two points p_{i_1}, p_{i_2} of $Ex(A_i)$, $x_{i_1} > x_{i_2}$ if and only if $y_{i_1} < y_{i_2}$. We store the elements of $Ex(A_i)$ in a list P, in which the points p_j are sorted increasingly according to their x values (or, equivalently, decreasingly according to their y values). Due to Lemma 4.4(a), and since during the algorithm the evitable unbounded vertices of G are replaced by bounded ones, after the process of vertex v_i, all points in the list P correspond to bounded vertices of G in the current parallelepiped representation.

We distinguish now the following cases:

Case 1. v_i is bounded. If there exists a point of P that dominates p_i then $p_i \notin Ex(A_i)$. Thus, we do not change P, and we continue to the process of v_{i+1}. If no point of P dominates p_i then $p_i \in Ex(A_i)$. Thus, we add p_i to P and we remove from P all points that are dominated by p_i.

Case 2. v_i is unbounded. If there exists a point $p_j \in P$ that dominates p_i then $p_i \notin Ex(A_i)$, while Lemma 4.4(b) implies that v_i is inevitable and v_j is a hovering vertex of v_i. Thus, similarly to Case 1, we do not change P, and we continue to the process of v_{i+1}. If no point of P dominates p_i then $p_i \in Ex(A_i)$. Thus, we add the point p_i to P and remove from P all points that are dominated by p_i. In this case, v_i is evitable by Lemma 4.4(a). Hence, we replace P_i by $\{(x, y, z) \mid (x, y) \in P_i, 0 \leq z \leq \phi_i\}$ in the current parallelepiped representation of G and we consider from now on v_i as a bounded vertex.

It follows that after the process of each vertex v_i (either bounded or unbounded) the list P stores the points of $Ex(A_i)$. Furthermore, at every iteration of the algorithm, all points of the list P correspond to bounded vertices in the current parallelepiped representation of G.

Chapter 4. *A new intersection model for tolerance graphs* 74

Algorithm 4.1 Construction of a canonical representation of a tolerance graph G
Input: A parallelepiped representation R of a given tolerance graph G with n vertices
Output: A canonical representation R' of G

1: Sort the vertices of G, such that $a_i < a_j$ whenever $i < j$
2: $\ell_0 \leftarrow \min\{x_i \mid 1 \leq i \leq n\}$; $r_0 \leftarrow \max\{x_i \mid 1 \leq i \leq n\}$
3: $p_s \leftarrow (\ell_0 - 1, \frac{\pi}{2})$; $p_t \leftarrow (r_0 + 1, 0)$
4: $P \leftarrow (p_s, p_t)$; $R' \leftarrow R$
5: **for** $i = 1$ to n **do**
6:     Find the point $p_j \in P$ having the smallest x_j with $x_j > x_i$
7:     **if** $y_j < y_i$ **then** {no point of P dominates p_i}
8:         Find the point $p_k \in P$ having the greatest x_k with $x_k < x_i$
9:         Find the point $p_\ell \in P$ having the greatest y_ℓ with $y_\ell < y_i$
10:         **if** $x_k \geq x_\ell$ **then**
11:             Replace points $p_\ell, p_{\ell+1} \ldots, p_k$ by point p_i in the list P
12:         **else**
13:             Insert point p_i between points p_k and p_ℓ in the list P
14:         **if** $v_i \in V_U$ **then** {v_i is an evitable unbounded vertex}
15:             Replace P_i by $\{(x, y, z) \mid (x, y) \in P_i, 0 \leq z \leq \phi_i\}$ in R'
16:     **else** {$y_j > y_i$; p_j dominates p_i}
17:         **if** $v_i \in V_U$ **then** {v_i is an inevitable unbounded vertex}
18:             Associate v_j to v_i as a hovering vertex of v_i
19: **return** R'

The processing of vertex v_i is done by executing three binary searches in the list P as follows. Let $\ell_0 = \min\{x_i \mid 1 \leq i \leq n\}$ and $r_0 = \max\{x_i \mid 1 \leq i \leq n\}$. For convenience, we add two dummy points $p_s = (\ell_0 - 1, \frac{\pi}{2})$ and $p_t = (r_0 + 1, 0)$. First, we find the point $p_j \in P$ with the smallest value x_j, such that $x_j > x_i$ (see Figure 4.3). Note that $p_i \in Ex(A_i)$ if and only if $y_j < y_i$. If $y_j > y_i$ then p_j dominates p_i (see Figure 4.3(a)). Thus, if $v_i \in V_U$, Lemma 4.4(b) implies that v_i is an inevitable unbounded vertex and v_j is a hovering vertex of v_i; note that v_j is a bounded vertex in the current parallelepiped representation of G. In the opposite case $y_j < y_i$, we have to add p_i to P. In order to remove from P all points that are dominated by p_i, we execute binary search two more times. In particular, we find the points p_k and p_ℓ of P with the greatest values x_k and y_ℓ, respectively, such that $x_k < x_i$ and $y_\ell < y_i$ (see Figure 4.3(b)). If there are some points of P that are dominated by p_i, then p_k and p_ℓ have the greatest and smallest values x_k and x_ℓ among them, respectively, and $x_k \geq x_\ell$. In this case, we replace all points $p_\ell, p_{\ell+1}, \ldots, p_k$ by the point p_i in the list P. Otherwise, if no point of P is dominated by p_i, then $x_k < x_\ell$. In this case, we remove no point from P and we insert p_i between p_k and p_ℓ in P.

Finally, after processing all vertices v_i of G, we return a canonical representation of the

Chapter 4. *A new intersection model for tolerance graphs* 75

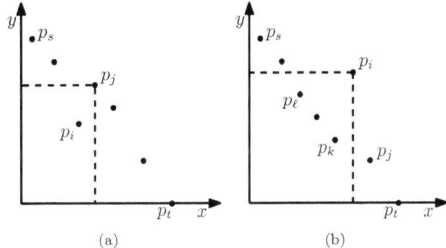

FIGURE 4.3: The cases where the associated point p_i to the currently processed vertex v_i is (a) dominated by the point p_j in A_i and (b) an extreme point of the set A_i.

given tolerance graph G, in which every vertex that remains unbounded has a hovering vertex assigned to it. Since the processing of every vertex can be done in $O(\log n)$ time by executing three binary searches, and since the sorting of the vertices can be done in $O(n \log n)$ time, the running time of Algorithm 4.1 is $O(n \log n)$. □

4.2.2 Minimum coloring

In the next theorem we present an optimal $O(n \log n)$ algorithm for computing a minimum coloring of a tolerance graph G with n vertices, given a parallelepiped representation of G. The informal description of the algorithm is identical to the one in [61], which has running time $O(n^2)$; the difference is in the fact that we use our new representation, in order to improve the time complexity.

Algorithm 4.2 Minimum coloring of a tolerance graph G

Input: A parallelepiped representation of a given tolerance graph G
Output: A minimum coloring of G

1: Construct a canonical representation of G by Algorithm 4.1, where a hovering vertex is associated with every inevitable unbounded vertex
2: Color $G[V_B]$ by the algorithm of [47]
3: **for** every inevitable unbounded vertex $v_i \in V_U$ **do**
4:     Assign to v_i the same color as its hovering vertex in $G[V_B]$

Theorem 4.3. *A minimum coloring of a tolerance graph G with n vertices can be computed in $O(n \log n)$ time.*

Proof. We present Algorithm 4.2 that computes a minimum coloring of G. Given a parallelepiped representation of G, we construct a canonical representation of G in $O(n \log n)$

time by Algorithm 4.1. V_B and V_U are the sets of bounded and inevitable unbounded vertices of G in the latter representation, respectively. In particular, Algorithm 4.1 associates a hovering vertex $v_j \in V_B$ with every inevitable unbounded vertex $v_i \in V_U$. We find a minimum proper coloring of the bounded tolerance graph $G[V_B]$ in $O(n \log n)$ time using the algorithm of [47]. Finally, we associate with every inevitable unbounded vertex $v_i \in V_U$ the same color as that of its hovering vertex $v_j \in V_B$ in the coloring of $G[V_B]$.

Consider an arbitrary inevitable unbounded vertex $v_i \in V_U$ and its hovering vertex $v_j \in V_B$. Consider also a vertex v_k of G, such that $v_i v_k \in E$. Then, $v_k \in V_B$, since no two unbounded vertices are adjacent in G. Furthermore, $v_j v_k \in E$ by Lemma 4.3. It follows that v_k does not have the same color as v_j in the proper coloring of $G[V_B]$, and thus the resulting coloring of G is proper. Finally, since both colorings of $G[V_B]$ and of G have the same number of colors, it follows that this proper coloring of G is minimum. Since the coloring of $G[V_B]$ can be done in $\mathcal{O}(n \log n)$ time and the coloring of all inevitable unbounded vertices $v_i \in V_U$ can be done in $O(n)$ time, Algorithm 4.2 returns a minimum proper coloring G in $O(n \log n)$ time. □

4.2.3 Maximum clique

In the next theorem we prove that a maximum clique of a tolerance graph G with n vertices can be computed in optimal $O(n \log n)$ time, given a parallelepiped representation of G. This theorem follows from Theorem 4.2 and from the clique algorithm presented in [47], and it improves the best known $O(n^2)$ running time mentioned in [61].

Theorem 4.4. *A maximum clique of a tolerance graph G with n vertices can be computed in $O(n \log n)$ time.*

Proof. We compute first a canonical representation of G in $O(n \log n)$ time by Algorithm 4.1. The proof of Theorem 4.3 implies that $\chi(G) = \chi(G[V_B])$, where $\chi(H)$ denotes the chromaric number of a given graph H. Since tolerance graphs are perfect graphs [60], $\omega(G) = \chi(G)$ and $\omega(G[V_B]) = \chi(G[V_B])$, where $\omega(H)$ denotes the clique number of a given graph H. It follows that $\omega(G) = \omega(G[V_B])$. We compute now a maximum clique Q of the bounded tolerance graph $G[V_B]$ in $O(n \log n)$ time. This can be done by the algorithm presented in [47] that computes a maximum clique in a trapezoid graph, since

Chapter 4. A new intersection model for tolerance graphs   77

bounded tolerance graphs are trapezoid graphs [62]. Since $\omega(G) = \omega(G[V_B])$, Q is a maximum clique of G as well. □

4.2.4 Optimality of the running time

In this section we use permutation graphs [62]. Given a sequence $S = a_1, a_2, \ldots, a_n$ of numbers, a *subsequence* of S is a sequence $S' = a_{i_1}, a_{i_2}, \ldots, a_{i_k}$, where $a_{i_j} \in S$ for every $j \in \{1, 2, \ldots, k\}$, and $1 \leq i_1 < i_2 < \ldots < i_k \leq n$. S' is called an *increasing subsequence* of S, if $a_{i_1} < a_{i_2} < \ldots < a_{i_k}$. Clearly, increasing subsequences in a permutation graph G correspond to independent sets of G, while increasing subsequences in the complement $\overline{G}$ of G correspond to cliques of G, where $\overline{G}$ is also a permutation graph. Since $\Omega(n \log n)$ is a lower time bound for computing the length of a longest increasing subsequence in a permutation [47, 49], the same lower time bound holds for computing a maximum clique and a maximum independent set in a permutation graph G. Furthermore, since permutation graphs are perfect graphs [57], the chromatic number $\chi(G)$ of a permutation graph G equals the clique number $\omega(G)$ of G. Thus, $\Omega(n \log n)$ is a lower time bound for computing the chromatic number of a permutation graph. Finally, since the class of permutation graphs is a subclass of tolerance graphs [62], the same lower bounds hold for tolerance graphs. It follows that the algorithms described in Theorems 4.3 and 4.4 for computing a minimum coloring and a maximum clique in tolerance graphs are optimal.

4.3 Weighted Independent Set Algorithm in $O(n^2)$

In this section we present an algorithm for computing a maximum weight independent set in a tolerance graph $G = (V, E)$ with n vertices in $O(n^2)$ time, given a parallelepiped representation of G, and a weight $w(v_i) > 0$ for every vertex v_i of G. The proposed algorithm improves the running time $O(n^3)$ of the one presented in [62]. In the following, consider as above the partition of the vertex set V into the sets V_B and V_U of bounded and unbounded vertices of G, respectively.

Similarly to [62], we add two isolated bounded vertices v_s and v_t to G with weights $w(v_s) = w(v_t) = 0$, such that the corresponding parallelepipeds P_s and P_t lie completely to the left and to the right of all other parallelepipeds of G, respectively. Since both v_s

and v_t are bounded vertices, we augment the set V_B by the vertices v_s and v_t. In particular, we define the set of vertices $V'_B = V_B \cup \{v_s, v_t\}$ and the tolerance graph $G' = (V', E)$, where $V' = V'_B \cup V_U$. Since $G'[V'_B]$ is a bounded tolerance graph, it is a cocomparability graph as well [60, 62]. A transitive orientation of the comparability graph $\overline{G'[V'_B]}$ can be obtained by directing each edge according to the upper left endpoints c_i of the parallelograms $\overline{P}_i$. Formally, let $(V'_B, \prec)$ be the partial order defined on the bounded vertices V'_B, such that $v_i \prec v_j$ if and only if $v_i v_j \notin E$ and $c_i < c_j$. Recall that a *chain* of elements in a partial order is a set of mutually comparable elements in this order [45].

Observation 4.2 ([62]). *The independent sets of $G[V_B]$ are in one-to-one correspondence with the chains in the partial order $(V'_B, \prec)$ from v_s to v_t.*

For the sequel, recall that for every unbounded vertex $v_k \in V_U$ the parallelepiped P_k degenerates to a line segment, while the upper endpoints b_k and c_k of the parallelogram $\overline{P}_k$ coincide, i.e. $b_k = c_k$.

Definition 4.8. *For every $v_i, v_j \in V'_B$ with $v_i \prec v_j$, $L_i(j) = \{v_k \in V_U \mid b_i < b_k < c_j, v_i v_k \notin E\}$ and its weight $w(L_i(j)) = \sum_{v \in L_i(j)} w(v)$.*

Definition 4.9. *For every $v_j \in V'_B$, $R_j = \{v_k \in V_U \mid c_j < b_k < b_j, v_j v_k \notin E\}$ and its weight $w(R_j) = \sum_{v \in R_j} w(v)$.*

For every pair of bounded vertices $v_i, v_j \in V'_B$ with $v_i \prec v_j$, the set $L_i(j)$ consists of those unbounded vertices $v_k \in V_U$, for which $v_i v_k \notin E$ and whose upper endpoint $b_k = c_k$ of $\overline{P}_k$ lies between $\overline{P}_i$ and $\overline{P}_j$. Furthermore, $v_j v_k \notin E$ for every vertex $v_k \in L_i(j)$. Indeed, in the case where $\overline{P}_k \cap \overline{P}_j \neq \emptyset$, it holds $\phi_k > \phi_j$, since $b_k = c_k < c_j$, and thus $P_k \cap P_j = \emptyset$. Similarly, the set R_j consists of those unbounded vertices $v_k \in V_U$, for which $v_j v_k \notin E$ and whose upper endpoint $b_k = c_k$ of $\overline{P}_k$ lies between the upper endpoints c_j and b_j of $\overline{P}_j$. Furthermore, $v_i v_k \notin E$ for every vertex $v_k \in R_j$ as well. Indeed, since $v_j v_k \notin E$, it follows that $\phi_k > \phi_j$, and thus, $\overline{P}_i \cap \overline{P}_k = \emptyset$ and $P_i \cap P_k = \emptyset$. In particular, in the example of Figure 4.4, $L_1(2) = \{v_3, v_5\}$ and $R_2 = \{v_6\}$. In this figure, the line segments that correspond to the unbounded vertices v_4 and v_7, respectively, are drawn with dotted lines to illustrate the fact that $v_4 v_1 \in E$ and $v_7 v_2 \in E$.

Definition 4.10 ([62]). *For every $v_i, v_j \in V'_B$ with $v_i \prec v_j$, $S(v_i, v_j) = \{v_k \in V_U \mid v_i v_k, v_j v_k \notin E, b_i < b_k < b_j\}$.*

Chapter 4. A new intersection model for tolerance graphs   79

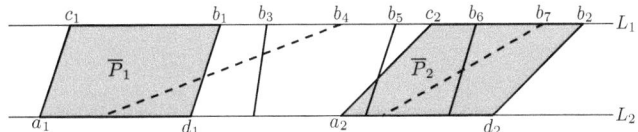

FIGURE 4.4: The parallelograms $\overline{P}_i$, $i = 1, 2, \ldots, 7$ of a tolerance graph with the sets $V_B = \{v_1, v_2\}$ and $V_U = \{v_3, v_4, \ldots, v_7\}$ of bounded and unbounded vertices, respectively. In this graph, $L_1(2) = \{v_3, v_5\}$, $R_2 = \{v_6\}$ and $S(v_1, v_2) = \{v_3, v_5, v_6\}$.

Observation 4.3. *For every pair of bounded vertices $v_i, v_j \in V'_B$ with $v_i \prec v_j$,*

$$S(v_i, v_j) = L_i(j) \cup R_j$$

Furthermore, $L_i(j) \subseteq L_i(\ell)$ for every triple $\{v_i, v_j, v_\ell\}$ of bounded vertices, where $v_i \prec v_j$, $v_i \prec v_\ell$, and $c_j < c_\ell$.

In particular, in the example of Figure 4.4, $S(v_1, v_2) = L_1(2) \cup R_2 = \{v_3, v_5, v_6\}$.

Lemma 4.5 ([62]). *Given a tolerance graph G with a set of positive weights for the vertices of G, any maximum weight independent set of G consists of a chain of bounded vertices $v_{x_1} \prec v_{x_2} \prec \ldots \prec v_{x_k}$ together with the union of the sets $\cup \{S(v_{x_i}, v_{x_{i+1}}) \mid i = 0, 1, \ldots, k\}$, where $v_{x_0} = v_s$ and $v_{x_{k+1}} = v_t$.*

Now, using Lemma 4.5 and Observation 4.3, we can present Algorithm 4.3 for the maximum weight independent set on tolerance graphs.

Theorem 4.5. *A maximum weight independent set of a tolerance graph G with n vertices can be computed in $O(n^2)$ time.*

Proof. We present Algorithm 4.3 that computes the value of a maximum weight independent set of G. A slight modification of Algorithm 4.3 returns a maximum weight independent set of G, instead of its value. First, we construct the partial order $(V'_B, \prec)$ defined on the bounded vertices $V'_B = V_B \cup \{v_s, v_t\}$, such that $v_i \prec v_j$ whenever $v_i v_j \notin E$ and $c_i < c_j$. This can be done in $O(n^2)$ time. Then, we sort the bounded vertices of V'_B, such that $c_i < c_j$ whenever $i < j$. This can be done in $O(n \log n)$ time. As a preprocessing step, we compute for every bounded vertex $v_j \in V'_B$ the set R_j and its weight $w(R_j)$ in linear $O(n)$ time by visiting at most all unbounded vertices $v_k \in V_U$. Thus, all values $w(R_j)$ are computed in $O(n^2)$ time.

Algorithm 4.3 Maximum weight independent set of a tolerance graph G

Input: A parallelepiped representation of a given tolerance graph G
Output: The value of a maximum weight independent set of G

1: Add the dummy bounded vertices v_s, v_t to G, such that P_s and P_t lie completely to the left and to the right of all other parallelepipeds of G, respectively
2: $V'_B \leftarrow V_B \cup \{v_s, v_t\}$
3: Construct the partial order $(V'_B, \prec)$ of the bounded vertices V'_B
4: Sort the bounded vertices V'_B, such that $c_i < c_j$ whenever $i < j$
5: **for** $j = 1$ to $|V'_B|$ **do**
6: $\quad W(v_j) \leftarrow 0$
7: $\quad$ Compute the value $w(R_j)$
8: **for** $i = 1$ to $|V'_B|$ **do** {initialization}
9: $\quad$ **for** every $v_j \in V'_B$ with $v_i \prec v_j$ **do**
10: $\quad\quad$ Update the value $w(L_i(j))$
11: $\quad\quad$ **if** $W(v_j) < (w(v_j) + w(R_j)) + W(v_i) + w(L_i(j))$ **then**
12: $\quad\quad\quad$ $W(v_j) \leftarrow (w(v_j) + w(R_j)) + W(v_i) + w(L_i(j))$
13: **return** $W(v_t)$

We associate with each bounded vertex $v_j \in V'_B$ a cumulative weight $W(v_j)$ defined as follows:

$$W(v_s) = 0$$
$$W(v_j) = (w(v_j) + w(R_j)) + \max_{v_i \prec v_j}\{W(v_i) + w(L_i(j))\}, \text{ for every } v_j \in V'_B \setminus \{v_s\}$$

The cumulative weight $W(v_j)$ of an arbitrary bounded vertex $v_j \in V'_B$ equals the maximum weight of an independent set S of vertices v_k (both bounded and unbounded), for which $b_k \leq b_j$ and $v_j \in S$. Initially all values $W(v_j)$ are set to zero.

In the main part of Algorithm 4.3, we process sequentially all bounded vertices $v_i \in V'_B$. For every such vertex v_i, we update sequentially the cumulative weights $W(v_j)$ for all bounded vertices $v_j \in V'_B$ with $v_i \prec v_j$ by comparing the current value of $W(v_j)$ with the value $(w(v_j) + w(R_j)) + W(v_i) + w(L_i(j))$, and by storing the greatest of them in $W(v_j)$. After all bounded vertices of V'_B have been processed, the value of the maximum weight independent set of G is stored in $W(v_t)$, due to Lemma 4.5 and Observation 4.3.

While processing the bounded vertex v_i, we compute the values $w(L_i(j))$ sequentially for every j, where $v_i \prec v_j$, as follows. Let v_{j_1}, v_{j_2} be two bounded vertices that are visited consecutively by the algorithm, during the process of vertex v_i. Then, due to Observation 4.3, we compute the value $w(L_i(j_2))$ by adding to the previous value $w(L_i(j_1))$

the weights of all unbounded vertices $v_k \in V_U$, for which $v_k v_i \notin E$, and whose upper endpoints $b_k = c_k$ lie between c_{j_1} and c_{j_2}.

Since we visit all bounded and all unbounded vertices of the graph at most once during the process of v_i, this can be done in $O(n)$ time. Thus, since there are in total at most $n+2$ bounded vertices $v_i \in V'_B$, Algorithm 4.3 returns the value of the maximum weight independent set of G in $O(n^2)$ time. Finally, observe that, storing at every step of Algorithm 4.3 the independent sets that correspond to the values $W(v_i)$, and removing at the end the vertices v_s and v_t, the algorithm returns at the same time a maximum weight independent set of G, instead of its value. $\square$

Chapter 5

The recognition of tolerance and bounded tolerance graphs

Although tolerance and bounded tolerance graphs have been studied extensively, the recognition problems for both these classes have been the most fundamental open problems since their introduction in 1982 [27, 57, 62]. Therefore, all existing algorithms assume that, along with the input tolerance graph, a tolerance representation of it is given. The only result about the complexity of recognizing tolerance and bounded tolerance graphs is that they have a (non-trivial) polynomial sized tolerance representation, hence the problems of recognizing tolerance and bounded tolerance graphs are in the class NP [66]. Recently, a linear time recognition algorithm for the subclass of *bipartite tolerance* graphs has been presented in [27]. Furthermore, the class of trapezoid graphs (which strictly contains parallelogram, i.e. bounded tolerance, graphs [103]) can be also recognized in polynomial time [90, 107]. On the other hand, the recognition of max-tolerance graphs is known to be NP-hard [75]. Unfortunately, the structure of max-tolerance graphs differs significantly from that of tolerance graphs (max-tolerance graphs are not even perfect, as they can contain induced C_5's [75]), so the technique used in [75] does not carry over to tolerance graphs.

Since very few subclasses of perfect graphs are known to be NP-hard to recognize (for instance, perfectly orderable graphs [93] or EPT graphs [58]), it was believed that the recognition of tolerance graphs was polynomial. Furthermore, as bounded tolerance graphs, which are equivalent to parallelogram graphs [18, 83], constitute a natural subclass of trapezoid graphs and share a very similar structure with them, and since the recognition of trapezoid graphs is well known to be polynomial [90, 107], it was plausible that their recognition was also polynomial.

In this chapter, we establish the complexity of recognizing tolerance and bounded tolerance graphs. Namely, we prove that both problems are surprisingly NP-complete [P4], by providing a reduction from the monotone-Not-All-Equal-3-SAT (monotone-NAE-3-SAT) problem. Consider a boolean formula ϕ in conjunctive normal form with three literals in every clause (3-CNF), which is monotone, i.e. no variable is negated. The formula ϕ is called NAE-satisfiable if there exists a truth assignment of the variables of ϕ, such that every clause has at least one true variable and one false variable. Given a monotone 3-CNF formula ϕ, we construct a trapezoid graph H_ϕ, which is parallelogram, i.e. bounded tolerance, if and only if ϕ is NAE-satisfiable. Moreover, we prove that the constructed graph H_ϕ is tolerance if and only if it is bounded tolerance [P4]. Thus, since the recognition of tolerance and of bounded tolerance graphs are in the class NP [66], it follows that these problems are both NP-complete. Actually, our results imply that the recognition problems remain NP-complete even if the given graph is trapezoid, since the constructed graph H_ϕ is trapezoid.

For our reduction we extend the notion of an acyclic orientation of permutation and trapezoid graphs. Our main tool is a new algorithm that transforms a given trapezoid graph into a permutation graph by splitting some specific vertices, while preserving this new acyclic orientation property [P4]. One of the main advantages of this algorithm is that the constructed permutation graph does not depend on any particular trapezoid representation of the input graph G.

The rest of this chapter is organized as follows. We first present in Section 5.1 several properties of permutation and trapezoid graphs, as well as the algorithm Split-U, which constructs a permutation graph from a trapezoid graph. In Section 5.2 we present the reduction of the monotone-NAE-3-SAT problem to the recognition of bounded tolerance graphs. In Section 5.3 we prove that this reduction can be extended to the recognition of general tolerance graphs.

5.1 Trapezoid graphs and representations

In this section we first introduce (in Section 5.1.1) the notion of an *acyclic representation* of permutation and of trapezoid graphs. This is followed (in Section 5.1.2) by some structural properties of trapezoid graphs, which will be used in the sequel for the splitting algorithm Split-U. Given a trapezoid graph G and a vertex subset U of G with certain properties, this algorithm constructs a permutation graph $G^{\#}(U)$ with $2|U|$ vertices, which is independent on any particular trapezoid representation of the input graph G.

Whenever we deal with a trapezoid (resp. permutation and bounded tolerance, i.e. parallelogram) graph, we will consider without loss of generality a trapezoid (resp. permutation and parallelogram) representation, in which all endpoints of the trapezoids (resp. line segments and parallelograms) are distinct [48, 62, 71]. Given a permutation graph P along with a permutation representation R, we may not distinguish in the following between a vertex of P and the corresponding line segment in R, whenever it is clear from the context. Furthermore, with a slight abuse of notation, we will refer in the sequel to the line segments of a permutation representation just as *lines*.

5.1.1 Acyclic permutation and trapezoid representations

Let $P = (V, E)$ be a permutation graph and R be a permutation representation of P. For a vertex $u \in V$, denote by $\theta_R(u)$ the angle of the line of u with L_2 in R. The class of permutation graphs is the intersection of comparability and cocomparability graphs [57]. Thus, given a permutation representation R of P, we can define two partial orders $(V, <_R)$ and $(V, \ll_R)$ on the vertices of P [57]. Namely, for two vertices u and v of G, $u <_R v$ if and only if $uv \in E$ and $\theta_R(u) < \theta_R(v)$, while $u \ll_R v$ if and only if $uv \notin E$ and u lies to the left of v in R. The partial order $(V, <_R)$ implies a transitive orientation Φ_R of P, such that $\langle uv \rangle \in \Phi_R$ whenever $u <_R v$.

Let $G = (V, E)$ be a trapezoid graph, and R be a trapezoid representation of G, where for any vertex $u \in V$, the trapezoid corresponding to u in R is denoted by T_u. Since trapezoid graphs are also cocomparability graphs [57], we can similarly define the partial order $(V, \ll_R)$ on the vertices of G, such that $u \ll_R v$ if and only if $uv \notin E$ and T_u lies completely to the left of T_v in R. In this case, we may denote also $T_u \ll_R T_v$, instead of $u \ll_R v$.

In a given trapezoid representation R of a trapezoid graph G, we denote by $l(T_u)$ and $r(T_u)$ the left and the right line of T_u in R, respectively. Similarly to the case of permutation graphs, we use the relation $\ll_R$ for the lines $l(T_u)$ and $r(T_u)$, e.g. $l(T_u) \ll_R r(T_v)$ means that the line $l(T_u)$ lies to the left of the line $r(T_v)$ in R. Moreover, if the trapezoids of all vertices of a subset $S \subseteq V$ lie completely to the left (resp. right) of the trapezoid T_u in R, we write $R(S) \ll_R T_u$ (resp. $T_u \ll_R R(S)$). Note that there are several trapezoid representations of a particular trapezoid graph G. Given one such representation R, we can obtain another one R' by *vertical axis flipping* of R, i.e. R' is the mirror image of R along an imaginary line perpendicular to L_1 and L_2. Moreover, we can obtain another representation R'' of G by *horizontal axis flipping* of R, i.e. R'' is the mirror image of R along an imaginary line parallel to L_1 and L_2. We will use extensively these two basic operations throughout this chapter. To simplify the presentation, we use throughout this chapter $\{u_i^1, u_i^2\}_{i=1}^n$ to denote the set of n unordered pairs $\{u_1^1, u_1^2\}, \{u_2^1, u_2^2\}, \ldots, \{u_n^1, u_n^2\}$.

Definition 5.1. Let P be a permutation graph with $2n$ vertices $\{u_1^1, u_1^2, u_2^1, u_2^2, \ldots, u_n^1, u_n^2\}$. Let R be a permutation representation and Φ_R be the corresponding transitive orientation of P. The simple directed graph F_R is obtained by merging u_i^1 and u_i^2 into a single vertex u_i, for every $i = 1, 2, \ldots, n$, where the arc directions of F_R are implied by the corresponding directions in Φ_R. Then,

1. R is an acyclic permutation representation with respect to $\{u_i^1, u_i^2\}_{i=1}^n$ if F_R has no directed cycle,

2. P is an acyclic permutation graph with respect to $\{u_i^1, u_i^2\}_{i=1}^n$, if P has an acyclic representation R with respect to $\{u_i^1, u_i^2\}_{i=1}^n$.

In Figure 5.1 we show an example of a permutation graph P with six vertices in Figure 5.1(a), a permutation representation R of P in Figure 5.1(b), the transitive orientation Φ_R of P in Figure 5.1(c), and the corresponding simple directed graph F_R in Figure 5.1(d). In the figure, the pairs $\{u_i^1, u_i^2\}_{i=1}^3$ are grouped inside ellipses. In this example, R is not an acyclic permutation representation with respect to $\{u_i^1, u_i^2\}_{i=1}^3$, since F_R has a directed cycle of length two. However, note that, by exchanging the lines u_1^1 and u_2^1 in R, the resulting permutation representation R' is acyclic with respect to $\{u_i^1, u_i^2\}_{i=1}^3$, and thus P is acyclic with respect to $\{u_i^1, u_i^2\}_{i=1}^3$.

Chapter 5. *The recognition of tolerance and bounded tolerance graphs* 87

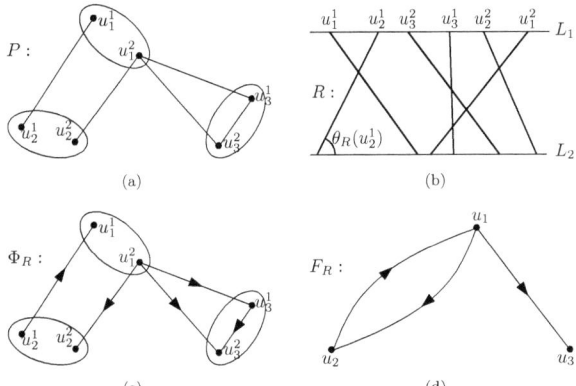

FIGURE 5.1: (a) A permutation graph P, (b) a permutation representation R of P,
(c) the transitive orientation Φ_R of P, and
(d) the corresponding simple directed graph F_R.

Definition 5.2. *Let G be a trapezoid graph with n vertices and R be a trapezoid representation of G. Let P be the permutation graph with $2n$ vertices corresponding to the left and right lines of the trapezoids in R, R_P be the permutation representation of P induced by R, and $\{u_i^1, u_i^2\}$ be the vertices of P that correspond to the same vertex u_i of G, $i = 1, 2, \ldots, n$. Then,*

1. *R is an acyclic trapezoid representation, if R_P is an acyclic permutation representation with respect to $\{u_i^1, u_i^2\}_{i=1}^n$,*

2. *G is an acyclic trapezoid graph, if it has an acyclic representation R.*

The next lemma follows easily from Definitions 5.1 and 5.2.

Lemma 5.1. *Any parallelogram graph is an acyclic trapezoid graph.*

Proof. Let G be a parallelogram graph with n vertices $\{u_1, u_2, \ldots, u_n\}$ and R be a parallelogram representation of G. That is, R is a trapezoid representation of G, such that the left and right lines $l(T_{u_i})$ and $r(T_{u_i})$ of the trapezoid T_{u_i}, $i = 1, 2, \ldots, n$, are parallel in R, i.e. $\theta_R(l(T_{u_i})) = \theta_R(r(T_{u_i}))$. Let P be the permutation graph with $2n$ vertices $\{u_1^1, u_1^2, u_2^1, u_2^2, \ldots, u_n^1, u_n^2\}$ corresponding to the left and right lines of the trapezoids of G in R, i.e. the vertices u_i^1 and u_i^2 correspond to $l(T_{u_i})$ and $r(T_{u_i})$, $i = 1, 2, \ldots, n$, respectively. Let R_P be the permutation representation of P induced by R, and Φ_{R_P} be the corresponding transitive orientation of the permutation graph P. Recall that, for two intersecting lines a, b in R_P, it holds $\langle ab \rangle \in \Phi_{R_P}$ whenever $\theta_R(a) < \theta_R(b)$. It follows that for any $i = 1, 2, \ldots, n$, the pair $\{u_i^1, u_i^2\}$ of vertices in P has incoming arcs from (resp. outgoing arcs to) vertices of other pairs $\{u_j^1, u_j^2\}$ in Φ_{R_P}, which have smaller (resp. greater) angle with the line L_2 in R_P. Thus, the simple directed graph F_{R_P} defined in Definition 5.1 has no directed cycles, and therefore R_P is an acyclic permutation representation with respect to $\{u_i^1, u_i^2\}_{i=1}^n$, i.e. R is an acyclic trapezoid representation of G by Definition 5.2. □

5.1.2 Structural properties of trapezoid graphs

In the following, we state some definitions concerning an arbitrary simple undirected graph $G = (V, E)$, which are useful for our analysis. Although these definitions apply to any graph, we will use them only for trapezoid graphs. Similar definitions, for the restricted case where the graph G is connected, were studied in [30]. For a vertex subset $U \subseteq V$, $N(U) = \bigcup_{u \in U} N(u) \setminus U$. If $N(U) \subseteq N(W)$ for two vertex subsets U and W, then U is said to be *neighborhood dominated* by W. Clearly, the relationship of neighborhood domination is transitive.

Let $C_1, C_2, \ldots, C_\omega$, $\omega \geq 1$, be the connected components of $G \setminus N[u]$ and $V_i = V(C_i)$, $i = 1, 2, \ldots, \omega$. For simplicity of the presentation, we will identify in the sequel the component C_i and its vertex set V_i, $i = 1, 2, \ldots, \omega$. For $i = 1, 2, \ldots, \omega$, the *neighborhood domination closure* of V_i with respect to u is the set $D_u(V_i) = \{V_p \mid N(V_p) \subseteq N(V_i), p = 1, 2, \ldots, \omega\}$ of connected components of $G \setminus N[u]$. A component V_i is called a *master component* of u if $|D_u(V_i)| \geq |D_u(V_j)|$ for all $j = 1, 2, \ldots, \omega$. The *closure complement* of the neighborhood domination closure $D_u(V_i)$ is the set $D_u^*(V_i) = \{V_1, V_2, \ldots, V_\omega\} \setminus D_u(V_i)$. Finally, for a subset $S \subseteq \{V_1, V_2, \ldots, V_\omega\}$, a component $V_j \in S$ is called *maximal* if there is no component $V_k \in S$ such that $N(V_j) \subsetneq N(V_k)$.

Intuitively, if G is a trapezoid graph and R is a trapezoid representation of G, one can think of a master component V_i of u as the first connected component of $G \setminus N[u]$ to the right, or to the left of T_u in R. For example, consider the trapezoid graph G with vertex set $\{u, u_1, u_2, u_3, v_1, v_2, v_3, v_4\}$, which is given by the trapezoid representation R of Figure 5.2. The connected components of $G \setminus N[u] = \{v_1, v_2, v_3, v_4\}$ are $V_1 = \{v_1\}$, $V_2 = \{v_2\}$, $V_3 = \{v_3\}$, and $V_4 = \{v_4\}$.

Then, $N(V_1) = \{u_1\}$, $N(V_2) = \{u_1, u_3\}$, $N(V_3) = \{u_2, u_3\}$, and $N(V_4) = \{u_3\}$. Hence, $D_u(V_1) = \{V_1\}$, $D_u(V_2) = \{V_1, V_2, V_4\}$, $D_u(V_3) = \{V_3, V_4\}$, and $D_u(V_4) = \{V_4\}$; thus, V_2 is the only master component of u. Furthermore, $D_u^*(V_1) = \{V_2, V_3, V_4\}$, $D_u^*(V_2) = \{V_3\}$, $D_u^*(V_3) = \{V_1, V_2\}$, and $D_u^*(V_4) = \{V_1, V_2, V_3\}$.

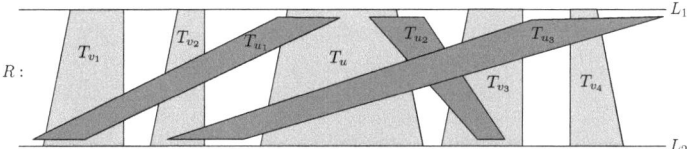

FIGURE 5.2: A trapezoid representation R of a trapezoid graph G.

Lemma 5.2. *Let G be a simple graph, u be a vertex of G, and let $V_1, V_2, \ldots, V_\omega$, $\omega \geq 1$, be the connected components of $G \setminus N[u]$. If V_i is a master component of u, such that $D_u^*(V_i) \neq \emptyset$, then $D_u^*(V_j) \neq \emptyset$ for every component V_j of $G \setminus N[u]$.*

Proof. Since V_i is a master component, and since $D_u^*(V_i) \neq \emptyset$, it follows that $|D_u(V_j)| \leq |D_u(V_i)| < \omega$ for every connected component $V_j \in \{V_1, V_2, \ldots, V_\omega\}$. Therefore, $|D_u(V_j)| < \omega$, and thus, $D_u^*(V_j) \neq \emptyset$ as well. □

In the following we investigate several properties of trapezoid graphs, in order to derive the vertex-splitting algorithm Split-U in Section 5.1.3.

Remark 5.1. *Similar properties of trapezoid graphs have been studied in [30], leading to another vertex-splitting algorithm, called Split-All. However, the algorithm proposed in [30] is incorrect, since it is based on an incorrect property[1], as was also verified by [31]. In the sequel of this section, we present new definitions and properties. In the cases where a similarity arises with those of [30], we refer to it specifically.*

The next lemma, which has been stated in Observation 3.1(4) in [30] (without a proof), will be used in our analysis below. For the sake of completeness, we present in the following its proof.

---

[1]In Observation 3.1(5) of [30], it is claimed that for an arbitrary trapezoid representation R of a connected trapezoid graph G, where V_i is a master component of u such that $D_u^*(V_i) \neq \emptyset$ and $R(V_i) \ll_R T_u$, it holds $R(D_u(V_i)) \ll_R T_u \ll_R R(D_u^*(V_i))$. However, the first part of the latter inequality is not true. For instance, in the trapezoid graph G of Figure 5.2, $V_2 = \{v_2\}$ is a master component of u, where $D_u^*(V_2) = \{V_3\} = \{\{v_3\}\} \neq \emptyset$ and $R(V_2) \ll_R T_u$. However, $V_4 = \{v_4\} \in D_u(V_2)$ and $T_u \ll_R T_{v_4}$, and thus, $R(D_u(V_2)) \not\ll_R T_u$.

Chapter 5. *The recognition of tolerance and bounded tolerance graphs* 90

Lemma 5.3. *Let R be a trapezoid representation of a trapezoid graph G, and V_i be a master component of a vertex u of G, such that $R(V_i) \ll_R T_u$. Then, $T_u \ll_R R(V_j)$ for every component $V_j \in D_u^*(V_i)$.*

Proof. Suppose otherwise that $R(V_j) \ll_R T_u$, for some $V_j \in D_u^*(V_i)$. Consider first the case where $R(V_j) \ll_R R(V_i) \ll_R T_u$. Then, since V_i lies between V_j and T_u in R, all trapezoids that intersect T_u and V_j, must also intersect V_i. Thus, $N(V_j) \subseteq N(V_i)$, i.e. $V_j \in D_u(V_i)$, which is a contradiction, since $V_j \in D_u^*(V_i)$. Consider now the case where $R(V_i) \ll_R R(V_j) \ll_R T_u$. Then, we obtain similarly that $N(V_i) \subseteq N(V_j)$, and thus, $D_u(V_i) \subseteq D_u(V_j)$. Since $V_j \in D_u(V_j) \setminus D_u(V_i)$, it follows that $|D_u(V_i)| < |D_u(V_j)|$. This is a contradiction to the assumption that V_i is a master component of u. Thus, $T_u \ll_R R(V_j)$ for every $V_j \in D_u^*(V_i)$. □

In the following two definitions, we partition the neighbors $N(u)$ of a vertex u in a trapezoid graph G into four possibly empty sets. In the first definition, these sets depend on the graph G itself and on two particular connected components V_i and V_j of $G \setminus N[u]$, while in the second one, they depend on a particular trapezoid representation R of G.

Definition 5.3. *Let G be a trapezoid graph, and u be a vertex of G. Let V_i be a master component of u, such that $D_u^*(V_i) \neq \emptyset$, and V_j be a maximal component of $D_u^*(V_i)$. Then, the vertices of $N(u)$ are partitioned into four possibly empty sets:*

1. *$N_0(u, V_i, V_j)$: vertices not adjacent to either V_i or V_j,*
2. *$N_1(u, V_i, V_j)$: vertices adjacent to V_i but not to V_j,*
3. *$N_2(u, V_i, V_j)$: vertices adjacent to V_j but not to V_i,*
4. *$N_{12}(u, V_i, V_j)$: vertices adjacent to both V_i and V_j.*

Definition 5.4. *Let G be a trapezoid graph, R be a representation of G, and u be a vertex of G. Denote by $D_1(u, R)$ and $D_2(u, R)$ the sets of trapezoids of R that lie completely to the left and to the right of T_u in R, respectively. Then, the vertices of $N(u)$ are partitioned into four possibly empty sets:*

1. *$N_0(u, R)$: vertices not adjacent to either $D_1(u, R)$ or $D_2(u, R)$,*
2. *$N_1(u, R)$: vertices adjacent to $D_1(u, R)$ but not to $D_2(u, R)$,*
3. *$N_2(u, R)$: vertices adjacent to $D_2(u, R)$ but not to $D_1(u, R)$,*
4. *$N_{12}(u, R)$: vertices adjacent to both $D_1(u, R)$ and $D_2(u, R)$.*

Chapter 5. *The recognition of tolerance and bounded tolerance graphs* 91

Now, the following lemma connects the last two definitions; in particular, it states that, if $R(V_i) \ll_R T_u$, then the partitions of the set $N(u)$ defined in Definitions 5.3 and 5.4 coincide. This lemma will enable us to define in the sequel a partition of the set $N(u)$, independently of any trapezoid representation R of G, and regardless of any particular connected components V_i and V_j of $G \setminus N[u]$, cf. Definition 5.6.

Lemma 5.4. *Let G be a trapezoid graph, R be a representation of G, and u be a vertex of G. Let V_i be a master component of u, such that $D_u^*(V_i) \neq \emptyset$, and let V_j be a maximal component of $D_u^*(V_i)$. If $R(V_i) \ll_R T_u$, then $N_X(u, V_i, V_j) = N_X(u, R)$ for every $X \in \{0, 1, 2, 12\}$.*

Proof. Since $D_u^*(V_i) \neq \emptyset$ and $R(V_i) \ll_R T_u$, it follows by Lemma 5.3 that $T_u \ll_R R(V_j)$, i.e. $V_j \in D_2(u, R)$. Suppose that a component $V_\ell \neq V_j$ is the leftmost one of $D_2(u, R)$ in R, i.e. $T_u \ll_R R(V_\ell) \ll_R R(V_j)$. Since V_ℓ lies between T_u and V_j in R, all trapezoids that intersect T_u and V_j, must also intersect V_ℓ, and thus, $N(V_j) \subseteq N(V_\ell)$. It follows that $V_\ell \in D_u^*(V_i)$, i.e. $V_\ell \notin D_u(V_i)$, since otherwise $V_j \in D_u(V_i)$, which is a contradiction. Furthermore, since V_j is a maximal component of $D_u^*(V_i)$, and since $N(V_j) \subseteq N(V_\ell)$, it follows that $N(V_j) = N(V_\ell)$, i.e. $N_X(u, V_i, V_j) = N_X(u, V_i, V_\ell)$ for every $X \in \{0, 1, 2, 12\}$.

Suppose that a component $V_k \neq V_i$ is the rightmost one of $D_1(u, R)$ in R, i.e. $R(V_i) \ll_R R(V_k) \ll_R T_u$. Then, $V_k \in D_u(V_i)$, since otherwise $T_u \ll_R R(V_k)$ by Lemma 5.3, which is a contradiction. Thus, $N(V_k) \subseteq N(V_i)$. Furthermore, since V_k lies between V_j and T_u in R, all trapezoids that intersect T_u and V_j, must also intersect V_k, and thus, $N(V_i) \subseteq N(V_k)$. Therefore, $N(V_i) = N(V_k)$, i.e. $N_X(u, V_i, V_\ell) = N_X(u, V_k, V_\ell)$ for every $X \in \{0, 1, 2, 12\}$, and thus, $N_X(u, V_i, V_j) = N_X(u, V_k, V_\ell)$ for every $X \in \{0, 1, 2, 12\}$.

Consider now a vertex $v \in N(u)$, and recall that V_k (resp. V_ℓ) is the rightmost (resp. leftmost) component of $D_1(u, R)$ (resp. $D_2(u, R)$) in R. Thus, if T_v intersects at least one component of $D_1(u, R)$ (resp. $D_2(u, R)$), then T_v intersects also with V_k (resp. V_ℓ). On the other hand, if T_v does not intersect any component of $D_1(u, R)$ (resp. $D_2(u, R)$), then T_v clearly does not intersect V_k (resp. V_ℓ), since $V_k \subseteq D_1(u, R)$ (resp. $V_j \subseteq D_2(u, R)$). It follows that $N_X(u, V_k, V_\ell) = N_X(u, R)$, and thus, $N_X(u, V_i, V_j) = N_X(u, R)$ for every $X \in \{0, 1, 2, 12\}$. This proves the lemma. □

Note that, given a trapezoid representation R of G, we may assume in Lemma 5.4 without loss of generality that $R(V_i) \ll_R T_u$, by possibly performing a vertical axis flipping of R.

Thus, we can state now the following definition of the sets δ_u and δ_u^*, regardless of the choice the components V_i and V_j of u.

Definition 5.5. *Let G be a trapezoid graph, u be a vertex of G, and V_i be an arbitrarily chosen master component of u. Then, $\delta_u = V_i$ and*

1. *if $D_u^*(V_i) = \emptyset$, then $\delta_u^* = \emptyset$,*
2. *if $D_u^*(V_i) \neq \emptyset$, then $\delta_u^* = V_j$, for an arbitrarily chosen maximal component $V_j \in D_u^*(V_i)$.*

From now on, whenever we speak about δ_u and δ_u^*, we assume that these arbitrary choices of V_i and V_j have been already made. Now, we are ready to define the following partition of the set $N(u)$, which will be used for the vertex splitting in Algorithm Split-U, cf. Definition 5.7.

Definition 5.6. *Let G be a trapezoid graph and u be a vertex of G. The vertices of $N(u)$ are partitioned into four possibly empty sets:*

1. *$N_0(u)$: vertices not adjacent to either δ_u or δ_u^*,*
2. *$N_1(u)$: vertices adjacent to δ_u but not to δ_u^*,*
3. *$N_2(u)$: vertices adjacent to δ_u^* but not to δ_u,*
4. *$N_{12}(u)$: vertices adjacent to both δ_u and δ_u^*.*

The next corollary follows now from Lemma 5.4 and Definitions 5.5 and 5.6.

Corollary 5.1. *Let G be a trapezoid graph, R be a representation of G, and u be a vertex of G with $\delta_u^* \neq \emptyset$. Let V_i be the master component of u that corresponds to δ_u. If $R(V_i) \ll_R T_u$, then $N_X(u) = N_X(u, R)$ for every $X \in \{0, 1, 2, 12\}$.*

In the following, we state two auxiliary lemmas that will be used in the proof of Theorem 5.1.

Lemma 5.5. *Let G be a trapezoid graph and u be a vertex of G. Then, $N_2(u) \cup N_{12}(u) = \emptyset$ if and only if $\delta_u^* = \emptyset$.*

Proof. Suppose first that $\delta_u^* = \emptyset$. Then, clearly there exists no vertex $v \in N(u)$ adjacent to δ_u^*, and thus, $N_2(u) \cup N_{12}(u) = \emptyset$. Conversely, suppose that $N_2(u) \cup N_{12}(u) = \emptyset$, and assume that $\delta_u^* \neq \emptyset$. Let $\delta_u = V_i$ and $\delta_u^* = V_j$, where V_i is a master component of u and V_j is a maximal component of $D_u^*(V_i)$. If $N(V_j) = \emptyset$, then clearly $N(V_j) \subseteq N(V_i)$, and thus, $V_j \in D_u(V_i)$, which is a contradiction. Thus, $N(V_j) \neq \emptyset$, i.e. some vertices of $N(u)$ are adjacent to some vertices of V_j. Since $\delta_u^* = V_j$, it follows by Definition 5.6 that $N_2(u) \cup N_{12}(u) \neq \emptyset$, which is a contradiction. Thus, $\delta_u^* = \emptyset$. □

Lemma 5.6. *Let G be a trapezoid graph and u be a vertex of G. If $\delta_u^* \neq \emptyset$, then $N_1(u) \cup N_{12}(u) \neq \emptyset$.*

Proof. Suppose that $\delta_u^* \neq \emptyset$. Let V_i be the master component that corresponds to δ_u, and V_j be the maximal component of $D_u^*(V_i)$ that corresponds to δ_u^*. Assume that $N_1(u) \cup N_{12}(u) = \emptyset$, i.e. no neighbor of u is adjacent to any vertex $v \in V_i$. It follows that $N(V_i) = \emptyset$. On the other hand, since $\delta_u^* \neq \emptyset$, we obtain by Lemma 5.5 that $N_2(u) \cup N_{12}(u) \neq \emptyset$. That is, some neighbors of u are adjacent to some vertices of V_j, i.e. $N(V_j) \neq \emptyset$. Therefore, $N(V_i) = \emptyset \subsetneq N(V_j)$, and thus, $D_u(V_i) \subsetneq D_u(V_j)$, i.e. $|D_u(V_i)| < |D_u(V_j)|$. This is a contradiction, since V_i is a master component of u. Thus, $N_1(u) \cup N_{12}(u) \neq \emptyset$. □

5.1.3 A splitting algorithm

We define now the splitting of a vertex u of a trapezoid graph G, where $\delta_u^* \neq \emptyset$. Note that this splitting operation does not depend on any trapezoid representation of G. Intuitively, if the graph G was given along with a specific trapezoid representation R, this would have meant that we replace the trapezoid T_u in R by its two lines $l(T_u)$ and $r(T_u)$.

Definition 5.7. *Let G be a trapezoid graph and u be a vertex of G, where $\delta_u^* \neq \emptyset$. The graph $G^\#(u)$ obtained by the vertex splitting of u is defined as follows:*

1. $V(G^\#(u)) = V(G) \setminus \{u\} \cup \{u_1, u_2\}$, where u_1 and u_2 are the two new vertices.
2. $E(G^\#(u)) = E[V(G)\setminus\{u\}] \cup \{u_1 x \mid x \in N_1(u)\} \cup \{u_2 x \mid x \in N_2(u)\} \cup \{u_1 x, u_2 x \mid x \in N_{12}(u)\}$.

The vertices u_1 and u_2 are the derivatives *of vertex u.*

We state now the notion of a standard trapezoid representation with respect to a particular vertex, which will be used in the proof of Theorem 5.1.

Algorithm 5.1 Split-U

Input: A trapezoid graph G and a vertex subset $U = \{u_1, u_2, \ldots, u_k\}$, such that $\delta_{u_i}^* \neq \emptyset$ for all $i = 1, 2, \ldots, k$

Output: The permutation graph $G^\#(U)$

1: $\overline{U} \leftarrow V(G) \setminus U$; $H_0 \leftarrow G$
2: **for** $i = 1$ to k **do**
3:     $H_i \leftarrow H_{i-1}^\#(u_i)$ $\{H_i$ is obtained by the vertex splitting of u_i in $H_{i-1}\}$
4: $G^\#(U) \leftarrow H_k[V(H_k) \setminus \overline{U}]$ {remove from H_k all unsplitted vertices}
5: **return** $G^\#(U)$

Definition 5.8. Let G be a trapezoid graph and u be a vertex of G, where $\delta_u^* \neq \emptyset$. A trapezoid representation R of G is standard with respect to u, if the following properties are satisfied:

1. $l(T_u) \ll_R R(N_0(u) \cup N_2(u))$,
2. $R(N_0(u) \cup N_1(u)) \ll_R r(T_u)$.

Now, given a trapezoid graph G and a vertex subset $U = \{u_1, u_2, \ldots, u_k\}$, such that $\delta_{u_i}^* \neq \emptyset$ for every $i = 1, 2, \ldots, k$, Algorithm Split-U returns a graph $G^\#(U)$ by splitting every vertex of U exactly once. At every step, Algorithm Split-U splits a vertex of U, and finally, it removes all vertices of the set $V(G) \setminus U$, which have not been split.

Remark 5.2. As mentioned in Remark 5.1, a similar algorithm, called Split-All, was presented in [30]. We would like to emphasize here the following four differences between the two algorithms. First, that Split-All gets as input a sibling-free graph G (two vertices u, v of a graph G are called siblings, if $N[u] = N[v]$; G is called sibling-free if G has no pair of sibling vertices), while our Algorithm Split-U gets as an input any graph (though, we will use it only for trapezoid graphs), which may contain pairs of sibling vertices. Second, Split-All splits all the vertices of the input graph, while Split-U splits only a subset of them, which satisfy a special property. Third, the order of vertices that are split by Split-All depends on a certain property (inclusion-minimal neighbor set), while Split-U splits the vertices in an arbitrary order. Last, the main difference between these two algorithms is that they perform a different vertex splitting operation at every step, since Definitions 5.5 and 5.6 do not comply with the corresponding Definitions 4.1 and 4.2 of [30].

Chapter 5. *The recognition of tolerance and bounded tolerance graphs* 95

Theorem 5.1. *Let G be a trapezoid graph and $U = \{u_1, u_2, \ldots, u_k\}$ be a vertex subset of G, such that $\delta_{u_i}^* \neq \emptyset$ for every $i = 1, 2, \ldots, k$. Then, the graph $G^\#(U)$ obtained by Algorithm Split-U, is a permutation graph with $2k$ vertices. Furthermore, if G is acyclic, then $G^\#(U)$ is acyclic with respect to $\{u_i^1, u_i^2\}_{i=1}^k$, where u_i^1 and u_i^2 are the derivatives of u_i, $i = 1, 2, \ldots, k$.*

Proof. Let R be a trapezoid representation of G. In order to prove that the graph $G^\#(U)$ constructed by Algorithm Split-All is a permutation graph, we will construct from R a permutation representation $R^\#(U)$ of $G^\#(U)$. To this end, we will construct sequentially, for every $i = 1, 2, \ldots, k$, a standard trapezoid representation of H_{i-1} with respect to u_i, in which all derivatives u_j^1, u_j^2, $1 \leq j \leq i-1$, are represented by trivial trapezoids, i.e. lines.

Let $u = u_1$. If R is not a standard representation with respect to u, we construct first from R a trapezoid representation R' of G that satisfies the first condition of Definition 5.8. Then, we construct from R' a trapezoid representation R'' of G that satisfies also the second condition of Definition 5.8, i.e. R'' is a standard trapezoid representation R' of G with respect to u.

Let V_i be the master component of u that corresponds to δ_u. By possibly performing a vertical axis flipping of R, we may assume w.l.o.g. that $R(V_i) \ll_R T_u$. Furthermore, the sets $N_0(u)$, $N_1(u)$, $N_2(u)$, and $N_{12}(u)$ coincide by Corollary 5.1 with the sets $N_0(u, R)$, $N_1(u, R)$, $N_2(u, R)$, and $N_{12}(u, R)$, respectively. Recall that, by Definition 5.4, $D_1(u, R)$ and $D_2(u, R)$ denote the sets of trapezoids of R that lie completely to the left and to the right of T_u in R, respectively.

Let p_x and q_x be the endpoints on L_1 and L_2, respectively, of the left line $l(T_x)$ of an arbitrary trapezoid T_x in R. Suppose that $N_0(u) \cup N_2(u) \neq \emptyset$. Let p_v and q_w be the leftmost endpoints on L_1 and L_2, respectively, of the trapezoids of $N_0(u) \cup N_2(u)$, and suppose that $p_v < p_u$ and $q_w < q_u$. Note that, possibly, $v = w$. Then, all vertices x, for which T_x has an endpoint between p_v and p_u on L_1 (resp. between q_w and q_u on L_2) are adjacent to u. Indeed, suppose otherwise that $T_x \cap T_u = \emptyset$, for such a vertex x. Then, $T_x \ll_R T_u$, i.e. $x \in D_1(u, R)$, since T_x has an endpoint to the left of T_u in R. Furthermore, since $T_v \cap T_u \neq \emptyset$ (resp. $T_w \cap T_u \neq \emptyset$), it follows that $T_x \cap T_v \neq \emptyset$ (resp. $T_x \cap T_w \neq \emptyset$). However, since $x \in D_1(u, R)$, it follows that $v \in N_1(u, R) \cup N_{12}(u, R) = N_1(u) \cup N_{12}(u)$ (resp. $w \in N_1(u, R) \cup N_{12}(u, R) = N_1(u) \cup N_{12}(u)$), which is a contradiction.

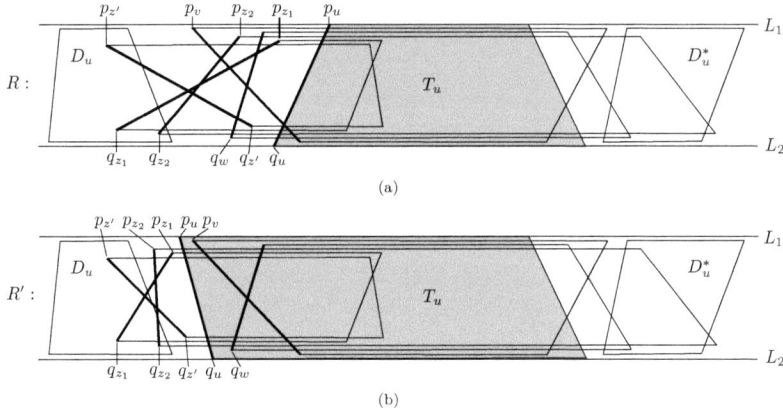

FIGURE 5.3: The movement of the left line $l(T_u)$ of the trapezoid T_u, in order to construct a standard trapezoid representation with respect to u.

Consider now a vertex $z \in N_1(u) \cup N_{12}(u)$ with $l(T_z) \ll_R l(T_u)$, where $p_v < p_z < p_u$. Then, $q_z < q_w$. Indeed, suppose otherwise that $q_w < q_z$ (recall that all endpoints are assumed to be distinct). Then, since $z \in N_1(u) \cup N_{12}(u)$, there exists a vertex $x \in D_1(u, R)$, i.e. with $T_x \ll_R T_u$, such that $T_z \cap T_x \neq \emptyset$. Since $v, w \in N_0(u) \cup N_2(u)$, it follows that $T_v \cap T_x = \emptyset$ and $T_w \cap T_x = \emptyset$, and thus, $T_x \ll_R T_v$ and $T_x \ll_R T_w$. Therefore, since $p_v < p_z$ and $q_w < q_z$, we obtain that $T_x \ll_R T_z$, and thus, $T_z \cap T_x = \emptyset$, which is a contradiction. It follows that $q_z < q_w$. Moreover, z is adjacent to all vertices x in G, whose trapezoid T_x has an endpoint on L_1 between p_v and p_z, including p_v. Indeed, otherwise, $T_x \ll_R T_z$, and thus, $T_x \ll_R T_u$, since $l(T_z) \ll_R l(T_u)$. This is however a contradiction, since $x \in N(u)$, as we have proved above. Similarly, if $q_w < q_z < q_u$, then $p_z < p_v$ and z is adjacent to all vertices x in G, whose trapezoid T_x has an endpoint on L_2 between q_w and q_z, including q_w.

We construct now from R a new trapezoid representation R' of G as follows. First, for all vertices $z \in N_1(u) \cup N_{12}(u)$ with $l(T_z) \ll_R l(T_u)$, for which $p_v < p_z < p_u$ (and thus $q_z < q_w$), we move the endpoint p_z of $l(T_z)$ directly before p_v on L_1. In the sequel, for all vertices $z' \in N_1(u) \cup N_{12}(u)$ with $l(T_{z'}) \ll_R l(T_u)$, for which $q_w < q_{z'} < q_u$ (and thus $p_z < p_v$), we move the endpoint $q_{z'}$ of $l(T_{z'})$ directly before q_w on L_2. During the movement of all these lines $l(T_z)$ (resp. $l(T_{z'})$), we keep the same relative positions of their endpoints p_z on L_1 (resp. $q_{z'}$ on L_2) as in R, and thus we introduce no new line intersection among the lines of the trapezoids of G. Since all these vertices z (resp. z')

are adjacent to all vertices x of G, whose trapezoid T_x has an endpoint on L_1 (resp. L_2) between p_v and p_z, including p_v (resp. between q_w and q_z, including q_w), these movements do not remove any adjacency from, and do not add any new adjacency to G.

Finally, we move both endpoints p_u and q_u of $l(T_u)$ directly before p_v and q_w on L_1 and L_2, respectively. Since u is adjacent to all vertices x, for which T_x has an endpoint between p_v and p_u on L_1, or between q_w and q_u on L_2 in R, the resulting representation R' is a trapezoid representation of G, in which the first condition of Definition 5.8 is satisfied. Since we moved all lines $l(T_z)$ and $l(T_{z'})$ to the left of T_v and T_w, R' has no additional line intersections than R. Moreover, note that for any line intersection of two lines a and b in R', the relative position of the endpoints of a and b on L_1 and L_2 remains the same as in R. In the case where $p_v > p_u$ (resp. $q_w > q_u$) we replace in the above construction p_v by p_u (resp. q_w by q_u), while in the case where $N_0(u) \cup N_2(u) = \emptyset$, we define $R' = R$. An example of the construction of R' is given in Figure 5.3. In this example, $v \in N_0(u)$, $w \in N_2(u)$, $z_1, z' \in N_1(u)$ and $z_2 \in N_{12}(u)$.

If R' is not a standard trapezoid representation with respect to u, then we move $r(T_u)$ to the right (similarly to the above), obtaining thus a trapezoid representation R'' of G, in which the second condition of Definition 5.8 is satisfied. Since during the construction of R'' from R' only the line $r(T_u)$, and other lines that lie completely to the right of $r(T_u)$, are moved to the right, the first condition of Definition 5.8 is satisfied for R'' as well. Thus, R'' is a standard representation of G with respect to u. Similarly to R', R'' has no additional line intersections than R. Moreover, for any line intersection of two lines a and b in R'', the relative position of the endpoints of a and b on L_1 and L_2 remains the same as in R.

Since R'' is standard with respect to u, the left line $l(T_u)$ of T_u in R'' intersects exactly with those trapezoids T_z, for which $z \in N_1(u) \cup N_{12}(u)$. On the other hand, the right line $r(T_u)$ of T_u in R'' intersects exactly with those trapezoids T_z, for which $z \in N_2(u) \cup N_{12}(u)$. Thus, if we replace in R'' the trapezoid T_u by the two trivial trapezoids (lines) $l(T_u)$ and $r(T_u)$, we obtain a trapezoid representation $R^{\#}(u)$ of the graph $G^{\#}(u)$ defined in Definition 5.7.

Consider now a vertex $v \in \{u_2, u_3, \ldots, u_k\}$. Due to the assumption, $\delta_v^* \neq \emptyset$ in G, before the vertex splitting of u, and thus, $N_2(v) \cup N_{12}(v) \neq \emptyset$ and $N_1(v) \cup N_{12}(v) \neq \emptyset$ in G by Lemmas 5.5 and 5.6. We will prove that $\delta_v^* \neq \emptyset$ in the trapezoid graph $G^{\#}(u)$ as well, after the vertex splitting of u. Due to Lemma 5.5, it suffices to show that $N_2(v) \cup N_{12}(v) \neq \emptyset$ in $G^{\#}(u)$. Let V_i be the master component of v in G that corresponds to δ_v, before the vertex splitting of u. We may assume w.l.o.g. that $R''(V_i) \ll_{R''} T_v$, by possibly performing a vertical axis flipping of R''. By Corollary 5.1, $N_1(v) \cup N_{12}(v) = N_1(v, R'') \cup N_{12}(v, R'')$ and $N_2(v) \cup N_{12}(v) = N_2(v, R'') \cup N_{12}(v, R'')$, i.e. these are the sets of neighbors of v in G, whose trapezoids intersect with the trapezoids of $D_1(v, R'')$ and $D_2(v, R'')$ in R'', respectively. Since $N_1(v, R'') \cup N_{12}(v, R'') \neq \emptyset$ and $N_2(v, R'') \cup N_{12}(v, R'') \neq \emptyset$ in G, and since $R^{\#}(u)$ is obtained from R'' by replacing the trapezoid T_u with the lines $l(T_u)$ and $r(T_u)$, it follows easily that $N_1(v, R^{\#}(u)) \cup N_{12}(v, R^{\#}(u)) \neq \emptyset$ and $N_2(v, R^{\#}(u)) \cup N_{12}(v, R^{\#}(u)) \neq \emptyset$ as well. Let V_k be the master component of v in $G^{\#}(u)$ that corresponds to δ_v, after the vertex splitting of u. If V_k lies to the left (resp. right) of T_v in $R^{\#}(u)$, then $N_2(v) \cup N_{12}(v)$ in $G^{\#}(u)$ equals to $N_2(v, R^{\#}(u)) \cup N_{12}(v, R^{\#}(u))$ (resp. to $N_1(v, R^{\#}(u)) \cup N_{12}(v, R^{\#}(u))$, by performing a vertical axis flipping of $R^{\#}(u)$). Therefore, $N_2(v) \cup N_{12}(v) \neq \emptyset$, and thus, $\delta_v^* \neq \emptyset$ in $G^{\#}(u)$, after the vertex splitting of u.

Applying iteratively the above construction for $u = u_i$, $i = 2, 3, \ldots, k$, i.e. by splitting sequentially all vertices of U exactly once, we obtain after k vertex splittings, and after removing from the resulting graph the vertices of $\overline{U} = V(G) \setminus U$, a trapezoid representation $R^{\#}(U)$ of the graph $G^{\#}(U)$ returned by Algorithm Split-U. Since every trapezoid T_u, $u \in U$, has been replaced by two trivial trapezoids, i.e. lines, in $R^{\#}(U)$, it follows that $G^{\#}(U)$ is a permutation graph with $2k$ vertices, and $R^{\#}(U)$ is a permutation representation of $G^{\#}(U)$.

Finally, suppose that R is an acyclic trapezoid representation of G. According to Definition 5.2, let P be the permutation graph with $2n$ vertices corresponding to the left and right lines of the trapezoids in R, R_P be the permutation representation of P induced by R, and $\{u_i^1, u_i^2\}$ be the vertices of P that correspond to the same vertex u_i of G, $i = 1, 2, \ldots, n$. Since R is an acyclic trapezoid representation of G, it follows by Definition 5.2 that R_P is an acyclic permutation representation with respect to $\{u_i^1, u_i^2\}_{i=1}^n$. That is, the simple directed graph F_{R_P} obtained (according to Definition 5.1) by merging u_i^1 and u_i^2 in P into a single vertex u_i, for every $i = 1, 2, \ldots, n$, has no directed cycle.

Since, during the construction of $R^{\#}(U)$, the trapezoid representation obtained after every vertex splitting has no additional line intersections than the previous one, it follows that $R^{\#}(U)$ has no additional line intersections than R. Moreover, for any line intersection of two lines a and b in $R^{\#}(U)$, the relative position of the endpoints of a and b on

L_1 and L_2 remains the same as in R. Thus, the simple directed graph $F_{R^{\#}(U)}$ obtained (according to Definition 5.1) by merging u_i^1 and u_i^2 in $G^{\#}(U)$ into a single vertex u_i, for every $i = 1, 2, \ldots, k$, is a subdigraph of F_{R_P}. Therefore, since F_{R_P} has no directed cycle, $F_{R^{\#}(U)}$ has no directed cycle as well, i.e. $G^{\#}(U)$ is an acyclic permutation graph with respect to $\{u_i^1, u_i^2\}_{i=1}^k$. This completes the theorem. □

5.2 The recognition of bounded tolerance graphs

In this section we provide a reduction from the *monotone-Not-All-Equal-3-SAT (monotone-NAE-3-SAT)* problem to the problem of recognizing whether a given graph is a bounded tolerance graph. A boolean formula ϕ is called *monotone* if no variable in ϕ is negated. Given a (monotone) boolean formula ϕ in conjunctive normal form with three literals in each clause (3-CNF), ϕ is *NAE-satisfiable* if there is a truth assignment of ϕ, such that every clause contains at least one true literal and at least one false one. The **NAE-3-SAT** problem, i.e. the problem of deciding whether an arbitrary given 3-CNF formula ϕ is NAE-satisfiable is known to be NP-complete [104]. We can assume w.l.o.g. that each clause has three distinct literals. Furthermore, it is easy to prove that the problem remains NP-complete, even if the given formula ϕ is restricted to be monotone. Namely, to reduce NAE-3-SAT to monotone-NAE-3-SAT, replace each variable x by two variables x_0 and x_1 (depending on whether x appears negated or not), add variables x_2, x_3, x_4, and add the clauses $(x_0 \vee x_1 \vee x_2)$, $(x_0 \vee x_1 \vee x_3)$, $(x_0 \vee x_1 \vee x_4)$, and $(x_2 \vee x_3 \vee x_4)$.

Given a monotone 3-CNF formula ϕ, we construct in polynomial time a trapezoid graph H_ϕ, such that H_ϕ is a bounded tolerance graph if and only if ϕ is NAE-satisfiable. To this end, we construct first a permutation graph P_ϕ and a trapezoid graph G_ϕ.

5.2.1 The permutation graph P_ϕ

Consider a monotone 3-CNF formula $\phi = \alpha_1 \wedge \alpha_2 \wedge \ldots \wedge \alpha_k$ with k clauses and n boolean variables $x_1, x_2, \ldots, x_n$, such that $\alpha_i = (x_{r_{i,1}} \vee x_{r_{i,2}} \vee x_{r_{i,3}})$ for $i = 1, 2, \ldots, k$, where $1 \leq r_{i,1} < r_{i,2} < r_{i,3} \leq n$. We construct the permutation graph P_ϕ, along with a permutation representation R_P of P_ϕ, as follows. Let L_1 and L_2 be two parallel lines and let $\theta(\ell)$ denote the angle of the line ℓ with L_2 in R_P. For every clause α_i, $i = 1, 2, \ldots, k$, we correspond to each of the literals, i.e. variables, $x_{r_{i,1}}$, $x_{r_{i,2}}$, and $x_{r_{i,3}}$, a pair of intersecting lines with endpoints on L_1 and L_2. Namely, we correspond to the variable $x_{r_{i,1}}$ the pair $\{a_i, c_i\}$, to $x_{r_{i,2}}$ the pair $\{e_i, b_i\}$ and to $x_{r_{i,3}}$ the pair $\{d_i, f_i\}$, respectively, such that $\theta(a_i) > \theta(c_i)$, $\theta(e_i) > \theta(b_i)$, $\theta(d_i) > \theta(f_i)$, and such that the lines a_i, c_i lie completely to the left of e_i, b_i in R_P, and e_i, b_i lie completely to the left of d_i, f_i in R_P, as it is illustrated in Figure 5.4. Denote the lines that correspond to the variable $x_{r_{i,j}}$, $j = 1, 2, 3$, by $\ell_{i,j}^1$ and $\ell_{i,j}^2$, respectively, such that $\theta(\ell_{i,j}^1) > \theta(\ell_{i,j}^2)$. That is, $(\ell_{i,1}^1, \ell_{i,1}^2) = (a_i, c_i)$, $(\ell_{i,2}^1, \ell_{i,2}^2) = (e_i, b_i)$, and $(\ell_{i,3}^1, \ell_{i,3}^2) = (d_i, f_i)$. Note that no line of a pair $\{\ell_{i,j}^1, \ell_{i,j}^2\}$ intersects with a line of another pair $\{\ell_{i',j'}^1, \ell_{i',j'}^2\}$.

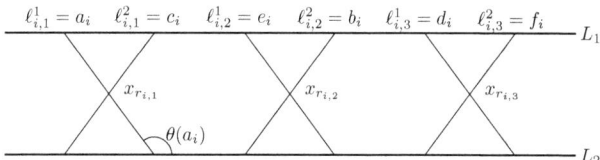

FIGURE 5.4: The six lines of the permutation graph P_ϕ, which correspond to the clause $\alpha_i = (x_{r_{i,1}} \vee x_{r_{i,2}} \vee x_{r_{i,3}})$ of the boolean formula ϕ.

Denote by S_p, $p = 1, 2, \ldots, n$, the set of pairs $\{\ell_{i,j}^1, \ell_{i,j}^2\}$ that correspond to the variable x_p, i.e. $r_{i,j} = p$. We order the pairs $\{\ell_{i,j}^1, \ell_{i,j}^2\}$ such that any pair of S_{p_1} lies completely to the left of any pair of S_{p_2}, whenever $p_1 < p_2$, while the pairs that belong to the same set S_p are ordered arbitrarily. For two consecutive pairs $\{\ell_{i,j}^1, \ell_{i,j}^2\}$ and $\{\ell_{i',j'}^1, \ell_{i',j'}^2\}$ in S_p, where $\{\ell_{i,j}^1, \ell_{i,j}^2\}$ lies to the left of $\{\ell_{i',j'}^1, \ell_{i',j'}^2\}$, we add a pair $\{u_{i,j}^{i',j'}, v_{i,j}^{i',j'}\}$ of parallel lines that intersect both $\ell_{i,j}^1$ and $\ell_{i',j'}^1$, but no other line. Note that $\theta(\ell_{i,j}^1) > \theta(u_{i,j}^{i',j'})$ and $\theta(\ell_{i',j'}^1) > \theta(u_{i,j}^{i',j'})$, while $\theta(u_{i,j}^{i',j'}) = \theta(v_{i,j}^{i',j'})$. This completes the construction. Denote the resulting permutation graph by P_ϕ, and the corresponding permutation representation of P_ϕ by R_P. Observe that P_ϕ has n connected components, which are called *blocks*, one for each variable $x_1, x_2, \ldots, x_n$.

An example of the construction of P_ϕ and R_P from ϕ with $k = 3$ clauses and $n = 4$ variables is illustrated in Figure 5.5. In this figure, the lines $u_{i,j}^{i',j'}$ and $v_{i,j}^{i',j'}$ are drawn in bold.

The formula ϕ has $3k$ literals, and thus the permutation graph P_ϕ has $6k$ lines $\ell_{i,j}^1, \ell_{i,j}^2$ in R_P, one pair for each literal. Furthermore, two lines $u_{i,j}^{i',j'}, v_{i,j}^{i',j'}$ correspond to each pair of consecutive pairs $\{\ell_{i,j}^1, \ell_{i,j}^2\}$ and $\{\ell_{i',j'}^1, \ell_{i',j'}^2\}$ in R_P, except for the case where these pairs of lines belong to different variables, i.e. when $r_{i,j} \neq r_{i',j'}$. Therefore, since ϕ

has n variables, there are $2(3k-n) = 6k-2n$ lines $u_{i,j}^{i',j'}, v_{i,j}^{i',j'}$ in R_P. Thus, R_P has in total $12k - 2n$ lines, i.e. P_ϕ has $12k - 2n$ vertices. In the example of Figure 5.5, $k = 3$, $n = 4$, and thus, P_ϕ has 28 vertices.

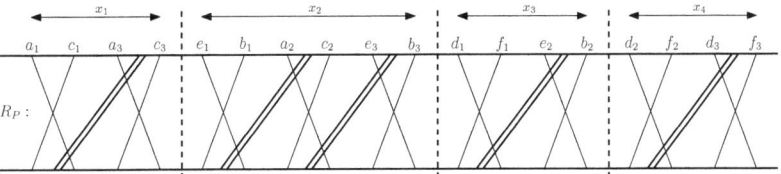

FIGURE 5.5: The permutation representation R_P of the permutation graph P_ϕ for $\phi = \alpha_1 \wedge \alpha_2 \wedge \alpha_3 = (x_1 \vee x_2 \vee x_3) \wedge (x_2 \vee x_3 \vee x_4) \wedge (x_1 \vee x_2 \vee x_4)$.

Let $m = 6k - n$, where $2m$ is the number of vertices in P_ϕ. We group the lines of R_P, i.e. the vertices of P_ϕ, into pairs $\{u_i^1, u_i^2\}_{i=1}^m$, as follows. For every clause α_i, $i = 1, 2, \ldots, k$, we group the lines $a_i, b_i, c_i, d_i, e_i, f_i$ into the three pairs $\{a_i, b_i\}$, $\{c_i, d_i\}$, and $\{e_i, f_i\}$. The remaining lines are grouped naturally according to the construction; namely, every two lines $\{u_{i,j}^{i',j'}, v_{i,j}^{i',j'}\}$ constitute a pair.

Lemma 5.7. *If the permutation graph P_ϕ is acyclic with respect to $\{u_i^1, u_i^2\}_{i=1}^m$ then the formula ϕ is NAE-satisfiable.*

Proof. Suppose that P_ϕ is acyclic with respect to $\{u_i^1, u_i^2\}_{i=1}^m$, and let R_0 be an acyclic permutation representation of P_ϕ with respect to $\{u_i^1, u_i^2\}_{i=1}^m$. Then, in particular, R_0 is acyclic with respect to $\{a_i, b_i\}, \{c_i, d_i\}, \{e_i, f_i\}$, for every $i = 1, 2, \ldots, k$. We will construct a truth assignment of the variables $x_1, x_2, \ldots, x_n$ that NAE-satisfies ϕ, as follows. For every $i = 1, 2, \ldots, k$, we define $x_{r_{i,1}} = 1$ if and only if $\theta(c_i) < \theta(a_i)$ in R_0, $x_{r_{i,2}} = 1$ if and only if $\theta(b_i) < \theta(e_i)$ in R_0, and $x_{r_{i,3}} = 1$ if and only if $\theta(f_i) < \theta(d_i)$ in R_0.

Note that this assignment is consistent; that is, all variables $x_{r_{i,j}}$ that correspond to the same x_k are assigned the same value. Indeed, the existence of the lines $u_{i,j}^{i',j'}, v_{i,j}^{i',j'}$ (cf. the bold lines in Figure 5.6(a)) forces all pairs of crossing lines $\{\ell_{i,j}^1, \ell_{i,j}^2\}$ in the same block to correspond to either 0 or 1 in the assignment.

Now, we show that in each clause α_i, $i = 1, 2, \ldots, k$, there exists at least one true and at least one false variable. For an arbitrary index $i = 1, 2, \ldots, k$, let P_i be the subgraph induced by the vertices $a_i, b_i, c_i, d_i, e_i, f_i$ in P_ϕ, and R_i be the permutation representation of P_i, which is induced by R_0. According to Definition 5.1, we construct the simple directed graph F_{R_i} by merging into a single vertex each of the pairs $\{a_i, b_i\}$, $\{c_i, d_i\}$ and $\{e_i, f_i\}$ of vertices of P_i. The arc directions of F_{R_i} are implied by the corresponding directions in Φ_{R_i} (or equivalently, in Φ_{R_0}). Then, since R_0 is acyclic with respect to $\{a_i, b_i\} \cup \{c_i, d_i\} \cup \{e_i, f_i\}$, so is R_i. Thus, it follows by Definition 5.1 that F_{R_i} has no directed cycle. Therefore, the edges $c_i a_i$, $b_i e_i$, and $f_i d_i$ of P_ϕ take such directions in Φ_{R_0} that it does not hold simultaneously $\langle c_i a_i \rangle, \langle b_i e_i \rangle, \langle f_i d_i \rangle \in \Phi_{R_0}$, or $\langle a_i c_i \rangle, \langle e_i b_i \rangle, \langle d_i f_i \rangle \in \Phi_{R_0}$. That is, it does not hold simultaneously $\theta(c_i) < \theta(a_i)$, $\theta(b_i) < \theta(e_i)$, and $\theta(f_i) < \theta(d_i)$, or $\theta(a_i) < \theta(c_i)$, $\theta(e_i) < \theta(b_i)$, and $\theta(d_i) < \theta(f_i)$ in R_0, respectively. Then, by the definition of the above truth assignment, it follows that it does not hold simultaneously $x_{r_{i,1}} = x_{r_{i,2}} = x_{r_{i,3}} = 1$, or $x_{r_{i,1}} = x_{r_{i,2}} = x_{r_{i,3}} = 0$, and therefore, the clause $\alpha_i = (x_{r_{i,1}} \vee x_{r_{i,2}} \vee x_{r_{i,3}})$ is NAE-satisfied. Finally, since this holds for every $i = 1, 2, \ldots, k$, ϕ is NAE-satisfiable. $\square$

For the formula ϕ of Figure 5.5, an example of an acyclic permutation representation R_0 of P_ϕ with respect to $\{u_i^1, u_i^2\}_{i=1}^m$, along with the corresponding transitive orientation Φ_{R_0} of P_ϕ, is illustrated in Figure 5.6. This transitive orientation corresponds to the NAE-satisfying truth assignment $(x_1, x_2, x_3, x_4) = (1, 1, 0, 0)$ of ϕ. Similarly to Figure 5.5, the lines $u_{i,j}^{i',j'}$ and $v_{i,j}^{i',j'}$ are drawn in bold in Figure 5.6(a). Furthermore, for better visibility, the vertices that correspond to these lines are grouped in shadowed ellipses in Figure 5.6(b), while the arcs incident to them are drawn dashed.

5.2.2 The trapezoid graphs G_ϕ and H_ϕ

Let $\{u_i^1, u_i^2\}_{i=1}^m$ be the pairs of vertices in the constructed permutation graph P_ϕ and R_P be its permutation representation. We construct now from P_ϕ the trapezoid graph G_ϕ with m vertices $\{u_1, u_2, \ldots, u_m\}$, as follows. We replace in the permutation representation R_P for every $i = 1, 2, \ldots, m$ the lines u_i^1 and u_i^2 by the trapezoid T_{u_i}, which has u_i^1 and u_i^2 as its left and right lines, respectively. Let R_G be the resulting trapezoid representation of G_ϕ.

Finally, we construct from G_ϕ the trapezoid graph H_ϕ with $7m$ vertices, by adding to every trapezoid T_{u_i}, $i = 1, 2, \ldots, m$, six parallelograms $T_{u_{i,1}}, T_{u_{i,2}}, \ldots, T_{u_{i,6}}$ in the trapezoid representation R_G, as follows. Let ε be the smallest distance in R_G between two different endpoints on L_1, or on L_2. The right (resp. left) line of $T_{u_{1,1}}$ lies to the right (resp. left) of u_1^1, and it is parallel to it at distance $\frac{\varepsilon}{2}$. The right (resp. left) line

Chapter 5. *The recognition of tolerance and bounded tolerance graphs* 103

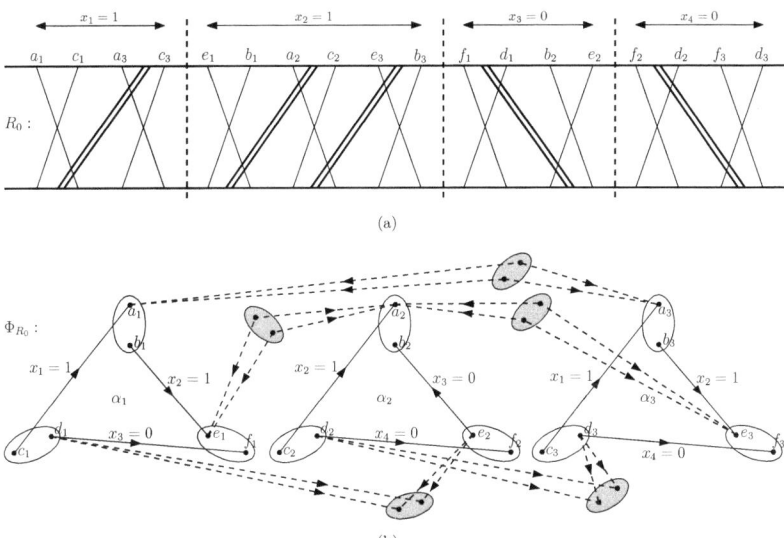

FIGURE 5.6: The NAE-satisfying truth assignment $(x_1, x_2, x_3, x_4) = (1, 1, 0, 0)$ of the formula ϕ of Figure 5.5: (a) an acyclic permutation representation R_0 of P_ϕ and (b) the corresponding transitive orientation Φ_{R_0} of P_ϕ.

of $T_{u_{1,2}}$ lies to the left of u_1^1, and it is parallel to it at distance $\frac{\varepsilon}{4}$ (resp. $\frac{3\varepsilon}{4}$). Moreover, the right (resp. left) line of $T_{u_{1,3}}$ lies to the left of u_1^1, and it is parallel to it at distance $\frac{3\varepsilon}{8}$ (resp. $\frac{7\varepsilon}{8}$). Similarly, the left (resp. right) line of $T_{u_{1,4}}$ lies to the left (resp. right) of u_1^2, and it is parallel to it at distance $\frac{\varepsilon}{2}$. The left (resp. right) line of $T_{u_{1,5}}$ lies to the right of u_1^2, and it is parallel to it at distance $\frac{\varepsilon}{4}$ (resp. $\frac{3\varepsilon}{4}$). Finally, the right (resp. left) line of $T_{u_{1,6}}$ lies to the right of u_1^2, and it is parallel to it at distance $\frac{3\varepsilon}{8}$ (resp. $\frac{7\varepsilon}{8}$), as illustrated in Figure 5.7.

After adding the parallelograms $T_{u_{1,1}}, T_{u_{1,2}}, \ldots, T_{u_{1,6}}$ to a trapezoid T_{u_1}, we update the smallest distance ε between two different endpoints on L_1, or on L_2 in the resulting representation, and we continue the construction iteratively for all $i = 2, \ldots, m$. Denote by H_ϕ the resulting trapezoid graph with $7m$ vertices, and by R_H the corresponding trapezoid representation. Note that in R_H, between the endpoints of the parallelograms $T_{u_{i,1}}$, $T_{u_{i,2}}$, and $T_{u_{i,3}}$ (resp. $T_{u_{i,4}}$, $T_{u_{i,5}}$, and $T_{u_{i,6}}$) on L_1 and L_2, there are no other endpoints of H_ϕ, except those of u_i^1 (resp. u_i^2), for every $i = 1, 2, \ldots, m$. Furthermore, note that R_H is standard with respect to u_i, for every $i = 1, 2, \ldots, m$. The following

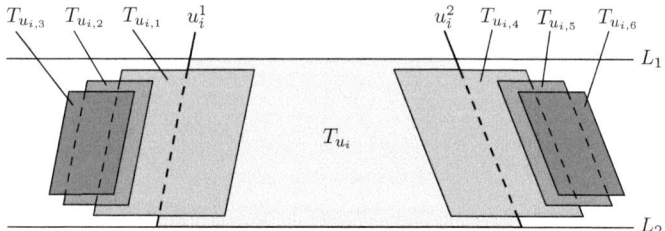

FIGURE 5.7: The addition of the six parallelograms $T_{u_{i,1}}, T_{u_{i,2}}, \ldots, T_{u_{i,6}}$ to the trapezoid T_{u_i}, $i = 1, 2, \ldots, m$, in the construction of the trapezoid graph H_ϕ from G_ϕ.

auxiliary lemma is crucial in the proof of Theorem 5.2.

Lemma 5.8. *In the trapezoid graph H_ϕ, $\delta^*_{u_i} \neq \emptyset$ for every $i = 1, 2, \ldots, m$.*

Proof. Let $i \in \{1, 2, \ldots, m\}$. Recall that, by Definition 5.4, $D_1(u_i, R_H)$ (resp. $D_2(u_i, R_H)$) denotes the set of trapezoids of H_ϕ that lie completely to the left (resp. to the right) of T_{u_i} in R_H. In particular, $T_{u_{i,2}}, T_{u_{i,3}} \in D_1(u_i, R_H)$ and $T_{u_{i,5}}, T_{u_{i,6}} \in D_2(u_i, R_H)$. By the construction of R_H, it is easy to see that $T_{u_{i,2}} \cup T_{u_{i,3}}$ (resp. $T_{u_{i,5}} \cup T_{u_{i,6}}$) is the rightmost (resp. leftmost) connected component of $D_1(u_i, R_H)$ (resp. $D_2(u_i, R_H)$). Thus, $N(V_k) \subseteq N(\{u_{i,2}, u_{i,3}\})$ (resp. $N(V_\ell) \subseteq N(\{u_{i,5}, u_{i,6}\})$), for every connected component V_k (resp. V_ℓ) of $D_1(u_i, R_H)$ (resp. $D_2(u_i, R_H)$). Let V_p be the master component of u_i, such that $D_{u_i} = V_p$. Then, either $V_p = \{u_{i,2}, u_{i,3}\}$, or $V_p = \{u_{i,5}, u_{i,6}\}$. In the case where $V_p = \{u_{i,2}, u_{i,3}\}$, we have $u_{i,4} \in N(\{u_{i,5}, u_{i,6}\}) \nsubseteq N(V_p)$, and thus $\{u_{i,5}, u_{i,6}\} \in \delta^*_{u_i}$. In the case where $V_p = \{u_{i,5}, u_{i,6}\}$, we have $u_{i,1} \in N(\{u_{i,2}, u_{i,3}\}) \nsubseteq N(V_p)$, and thus, $\{u_{i,2}, u_{i,3}\} \in \delta^*_{u_i}$. This proves the lemma. □

Theorem 5.2. *The formula ϕ is NAE-satisfiable if and only if the trapezoid graph H_ϕ is a bounded tolerance graph.*

Proof. Since a graph is a bounded tolerance graph if and only if it is a parallelogram graph [18, 83], it suffices to prove that ϕ is NAE-satisfiable if and only if the trapezoid graph H_ϕ is a parallelogram graph.

($\Leftarrow$) Suppose that H_ϕ is a parallelogram graph, and let $U = \{u_1, u_2, \ldots, u_m\}$. Then, H_ϕ is an acyclic trapezoid graph by Lemma 5.1. Consider the permutation graph $H_\phi^\#(U)$ with $2m$ vertices, which is obtained by Algorithm Split-U on H_ϕ. Starting with the trapezoid representation R_H of H_ϕ, we obtain by the construction of Theorem 5.1 a permutation representation $R_H^\#(U)$ of $H_\phi^\#(U)$. Note that, since R_H is a standard trapezoid representation of H_ϕ with respect to every u_i, $i = 1, 2, \ldots, m$, the line u_i^1 (resp. u_i^2) of T_{u_i} is not moved during the construction of $R_H^\#(U)$ from R_H, for every $i = 1, 2, \ldots, m$. Therefore, $H_\phi^\#(U) = P_\phi$. On the other hand, since by Lemma 5.8 $\delta_{u_i}^* \neq \emptyset$ for every vertex $u_i \in U$, and since H_ϕ is an acyclic trapezoid graph, Theorem 5.1 implies that $H_\phi^\#(U) = P_\phi$ is an acyclic permutation graph with respect to $\{u_i^1, u_i^2\}_{i=1}^m$. Thus, ϕ is NAE-satisfiable by Lemma 5.7.

($\Rightarrow$) Conversely, suppose that ϕ has a NAE-satisfying truth assignment τ. We will construct first a permutation representation R_0 of P_ϕ, and then two trapezoid representations R_0' and R_0'' of G_ϕ and H_ϕ, respectively, as follows. Similarly to the representation R_P, the representation R_0 has n blocks, i.e. connected components, one for each variable $x_1, x_2, \ldots, x_n$. R_0 is obtained from R_P by performing a horizontal axis flipping of every block, which corresponds to a variable $x_p = 0$ in the truth assignment τ. Every other block, which corresponds to a variable $x_p = 1$ in the assignment τ, remains the same in R_0, as in R_P. Thus, $\theta(\ell_{i,j}^1) > \theta(\ell_{i,j}^2)$ if $x_{r_{i,j}} = 1$ in τ, and $\theta(\ell_{i,j}^1) < \theta(\ell_{i,j}^2)$ if $x_{r_{i,j}} = 0$ in τ, for every pair $\{\ell_{i,j}^1, \ell_{i,j}^2\}$ of lines in R_0 (which correspond to the literal $x_{r_{i,j}}$ of the clause α_i in ϕ). An example of the construction of this representation R_0 of P_ϕ for the truth assignment $\tau = (1, 1, 0, 0)$ is illustrated in Figure 5.6(a).

Since τ is a NAE-satisfying truth assignment of ϕ, at least one literal is true and at least one is false in τ in every clause α_i, $i = 1, 2, \ldots, k$. Thus, there are six possible truth assignments for every clause, namely $(1, 1, 0)$, $(1, 0, 1)$, $(0, 1, 1)$, $(0, 0, 1)$, $(0, 1, 0)$, and $(1, 0, 0)$. For the first three ones, we can assign appropriate angles to the lines a_i, b_i, c_i, d_i, e_i, and f_i in the representation R_0, such that the relative positions of all endpoints in L_1 and L_2 remain unchanged, and such that a_i is parallel to b_i, c_i is parallel to d_i, and e_i is parallel to f_i, as illustrated in Figure 5.8. The last three truth assignments of α_i are the complement of the first three ones. Thus, by performing a horizontal axis flipping of the blocks in Figure 5.8, to which the lines a_i, b_i, c_i, d_i, e_i, and f_i belong, it is easy to see that for these assignments, we can also assign appropriate angles to these lines in the representation R_0, such that the relative positions of all endpoints in L_1 and L_2 remain unchanged, and such that a_i is parallel to b_i, c_i is parallel to d_i, and e_i is parallel to f_i.

Recall that for every two consecutive pairs $\{\ell_{i,j}^1, \ell_{i,j}^2\}$ and $\{\ell_{i',j'}^1, \ell_{i',j'}^2\}$ of lines in R_P (resp. R_0), which belong to the same block, i.e. where $r_{i,j} = r_{i',j'}$, there are two parallel

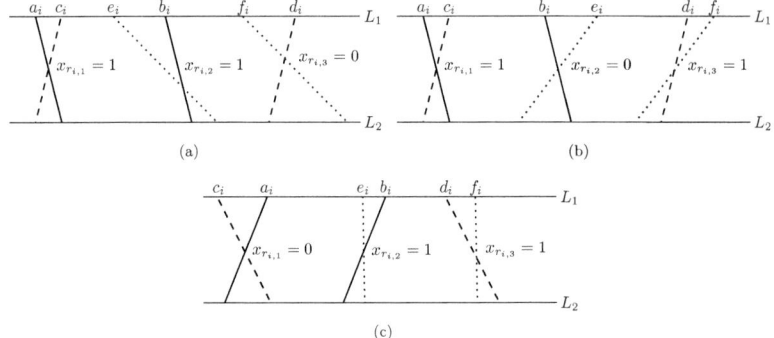

FIGURE 5.8: The relative positions of the lines a_i, b_i, c_i, d_i, e_i, and f_i for the truth assignments (a) $(1,1,0)$, (b) $(1,0,1)$, and (c) $(0,1,1)$ of the clause α_i.

lines $u_{i,j}^{i',j'}, v_{i,j}^{i',j'}$ that intersect both $\ell_{i,j}^1$ and $\ell_{i',j'}^1$. Thus, after assigning the appropriate angles to the lines $\{\ell_{i,j}^1, \ell_{i,j}^2\}$, $i = 1, 2, \ldots, k$, $j = 1, 2, 3$, we can clearly assign the appropriate angles to the lines $u_{i,j}^{i',j'}, v_{i,j}^{i',j'}$, such that the relative positions of all endpoints in L_1 and L_2 remain unchanged, and such that $u_{i,j}^{i',j'}$ remains parallel to $v_{i,j}^{i',j'}$. Summarizing, the lines u_i^1 and u_i^2 are parallel in R_0, for every $i = 1, 2, \ldots, m$.

We construct now the trapezoid representation R_0' of G_ϕ from the permutation representation R_0, by replacing for every $i = 1, 2, \ldots, m$ the lines u_i^1 and u_i^2 by the trapezoid T_{u_i}, which has u_i^1 and u_i^2 as its left and right lines, respectively. Since R_0 is obtained by performing horizontal axis flipping of some blocks of R_P, and then changing the angles of the lines, while respecting the relative positions of the endpoints, R_0' is indeed another trapezoid representation of G_ϕ than R_G. Since u_i^1 is now parallel to u_i^2 for every $i = 1, 2, \ldots, m$, it follows clearly that R_0' is a parallelogram representation, and thus, G_ϕ is a parallelogram graph.

Finally, we construct the trapezoid representation R_0'' of H_ϕ from R_0', similarly to the construction of R_H from R_G. Namely, we add for every trapezoid T_{u_i}, $i = 1, 2, \ldots, m$, six parallelograms $T_{u_{i,1}}, T_{u_{i,2}}, \ldots, T_{u_{i,6}}$, resulting in a trapezoid graph with $7m$ vertices. Since in R_0'' the parallelograms $T_{u_{i,1}}$, $T_{u_{i,2}}$, and $T_{u_{i,3}}$ (resp. $T_{u_{i,4}}$, $T_{u_{i,5}}$, and $T_{u_{i,6}}$) are sufficiently close to the left line u_i^1 (resp. right line u_i^2) of T_{u_i}, $i = 1, 2, \ldots, m$, and since between the endpoints of the parallelograms $T_{u_{i,1}}$, $T_{u_{i,2}}$, and $T_{u_{i,3}}$ (resp. $T_{u_{i,4}}$, $T_{u_{i,5}}$, and $T_{u_{i,6}}$) on L_1 and L_2, there are no other endpoints, it follows that R_0'' is indeed another trapezoid representation of H_ϕ than R_H. Finally, since R_0' is a parallelogram representation, and since $T_{u_{i,1}}, T_{u_{i,2}}, \ldots, T_{u_{i,6}}$, $i = 1, 2, \ldots, m$, are all parallelograms, R_0'' is also a parallelogram representation, and thus, H_ϕ is a parallelogram graph. □

Therefore, since monotone-NAE-3-SAT is NP-complete, the problem of recognizing bounded tolerance graphs is NP-hard. Moreover, since the recognition of bounded tolerance graphs lies in NP [66], we can summarize our results as follows.

Theorem 5.3. *Given a graph G, it is NP-complete to decide whether it is a bounded tolerance graph.*

5.3 The recognition of tolerance graphs

In this section we show that the reduction from the monotone-NAE-3-SAT problem to the problem of recognizing bounded tolerance graphs presented in Section 5.2, can be extended to the problem of recognizing general tolerance graphs. Consider now a monotone 3-CNF formula ϕ and the trapezoid graph H_ϕ constructed from ϕ in Section 5.2.2.

Lemma 5.9. *In the trapezoid graph H_ϕ, there are no two vertices u and v, such that $uv \notin E(H_\phi)$ and $N(v) \subseteq N(u)$ in H_ϕ.*

Proof. The proof is done by investigating all cases for a pair of non-adjacent vertices u, v. First, observe that, by the construction of H_ϕ from G_ϕ, we have $N[u_{i,2}] = N[u_{i,3}]$, $N[u_{i,1}] = N[u_{i,2}] \cup \{u_i\}$, $N[u_{i,5}] = N[u_{i,6}]$, and $N[u_{i,4}] = N[u_{i,5}] \cup \{u_i\}$.

Consider first two vertices u_i and u_k in H_ϕ, for some $i, k = 1, 2, \ldots, m$ and $i \neq k$. Then, by the construction of H_ϕ from G_ϕ, and since u_i and u_k are non-adjacent, $u_{i,1} \in N(u_i) \setminus N(u_k)$ and $u_{k,1} \in N(u_k) \setminus N(u_i)$. Consider next the vertices u_i and $u_{k,j}$, for some $i, k = 1, 2, \ldots, m$ and $j = 1, 2, \ldots, 6$. If $i = k$, then $j \in \{2, 3, 5, 6\}$, since $u_{i,1}, u_{i,4} \in N(u_i)$. In the case where $j \in \{2, 3\}$, we have $u_{i,4} \in N(u_i) \setminus N(u_{k,j})$ and $u_{k,5-j} \in N(u_{k,j}) \setminus N(u_i)$, while in the case where $j \in \{5, 6\}$, we have $u_{i,1} \in N(u_i) \setminus N(u_{k,j})$ and $u_{k,11-j} \in N(u_{k,j}) \setminus N(u_i)$. Suppose that $i \neq k$. Then, it follows by the construction of H_ϕ from G_ϕ that $u_{i,1} \in N(u_i) \setminus N(u_{k,j})$. Furthermore, if $j \in \{1, 2, 3\}$ (resp. $j \in \{4, 5, 6\}$), then $u_{k,j'} \in N(u_{k,j}) \setminus N(u_i)$ for any index $j' \in \{1, 2, 3\} \setminus \{j\}$ (resp. $j' \in \{4, 5, 6\} \setminus \{j\}$).

Consider finally the vertices $u_{i,\ell}$ and $u_{k,j}$, for some $i,k = 1,2,\ldots,m$ and $\ell, j = 1,2,\ldots,6$. If $i = k$, then w.l.o.g. $\ell \in \{1,2,3\}$ and $j \in \{4,5,6\}$, since $u_{i,\ell}$ and $u_{k,j}$ are non-adjacent. In this case, $u_{i,\ell'} \in N(u_{i,\ell}) \setminus N(u_{k,j})$ and $u_{k,j'} \in N(u_{k,j}) \setminus N(u_{i,\ell})$, for all indices $\ell' \in \{1,2,3\} \setminus \{\ell\}$ and $j' \in \{4,5,6\} \setminus \{j\}$. Suppose that $i \neq k$. If $j \in \{1,2,3\}$ (resp. $j \in \{4,5,6\}$), let j' be any index of $\{1,2,3\} \setminus \{j\}$ (resp. $\{4,5,6\} \setminus \{j\}$). Similarly, if $\ell \in \{1,2,3\}$ (resp. $\ell \in \{4,5,6\}$), let ℓ' be any index of $\{1,2,3\} \setminus \{\ell\}$ (resp. $\{4,5,6\} \setminus \{\ell\}$). Then, it follows by the construction of H_ϕ from G_ϕ that $u_{i,\ell'} \in N(u_{i,\ell}) \setminus N(u_{k,j})$ and $u_{k,j'} \in N(u_{k,j}) \setminus N(u_{i,\ell})$.

Therefore, for all possible choices of non-adjacent vertices u,v in the trapezoid graph H_ϕ, we have $N(u) \setminus N(v) \neq \emptyset$ and $N(v) \setminus N(u) \neq \emptyset$, which proves the lemma. □

Lemma 5.10. *If H_ϕ is a tolerance graph then it is a bounded tolerance graph.*

Proof. Suppose that H_ϕ is a tolerance graph, and consider a parallelepiped representation R of H_ϕ. Due to Theorem 4.2, we may assume w.l.o.g. that R is canonical, cf. Section 4.2.1. If R has no unbounded vertices, then we are done. Otherwise, there exists at least one inevitable unbounded vertex v in R, which has a hovering vertex u by Lemma 4.2, where $uv \notin E(H_\phi)$. Then, $N(v) \subseteq N(u)$ in H_ϕ by Lemma 4.3, which contradicts Lemma 5.9. Thus, there exists no unbounded vertex in R, i.e. H_ϕ is a bounded tolerance graph. □

We can state now the following theorem, which is implied by Theorem 5.2 and Lemma 5.10.

Theorem 5.4. *The formula ϕ is NAE-satisfiable if and only if H_ϕ is a tolerance graph.*

Proof. Suppose that ϕ is NAE-satisfiable. Then, by Theorem 5.2, H_ϕ is a bounded tolerance graph, and thus, H_ϕ is a tolerance graph. Suppose conversely that H_ϕ is a tolerance graph. Then, by Lemma 5.10, H_ϕ is a bounded tolerance graph. Thus, ϕ is NAE-satisfiable by Theorem 5.2. □

Therefore, since monotone-NAE-3-SAT is NP-complete, the problem of recognizing tolerance graphs is NP-hard. Moreover, since the recognition of tolerance graphs lies in NP [66], and since H_ϕ is a trapezoid graph, we obtain the following theorem.

Theorem 5.5. *Given a graph G, it is NP-complete to decide whether it is a tolerance graph. The problem remains NP-complete even if the given graph G is known to be a trapezoid graph.*

Chapter 6

Preemptive scheduling of equal-length jobs

One of the most natural applications of both interval and tolerance graphs is that of scheduling and resource allocation, cf. Sections 1.2 and 1.3. In this chapter, we investigate a scheduling problem from the algorithmic point of view. Namely, we consider the scheduling of n jobs $J_1, J_2, \ldots, J_n$ on a single machine. At an arbitrary moment the machine can serve at most one job J_i, while all jobs need the same processing time p (or equivalently, they all have equal length p); however, a positive weight w_i is assigned to job J_i. Furthermore, every job J_i has a release time r_i, after which J_i is available to be processed. In our model, we consider preemptive scheduling, that is, the execution of a job J_i may be interrupted for the execution of another job J_j, while the execution of J_i will be resumed later on. A schedule $\mathcal{S}$ of the jobs is called feasible, if every job J_i starts not earlier than its release time r_i. In a particular feasible schedule we denote by C_i the completion time of job J_i, i.e. the time point at which the execution of J_i finishes. The objective is to find a feasible preemptive schedule of the given n jobs that minimizes the weighted sum $\sum_{i=1}^{n} w_i C_i$ of the completion times.

Preemptive scheduling has attracted many research efforts. Several problems, which are NP-hard in the general case, admit polynomial algorithms under the assumption of equal-length jobs. In particular, the problem of minimizing the sum of completion times on identical parallel machines is known to be polynomially solvable for equal-length jobs [12,68], while it is unary NP-hard for arbitrary processing times [12]. The problem of maximizing the weighted throughput, or equivalently of minimizing the weighted number of late jobs on a single machine, is NP-hard [53] and pseudo-polynomially solvable [84] in the general case. On the contrary, its restriction to equal-length jobs is solvable in polynomial time in the preemptive, as well as in the non-preemptive case [10, 13]. For the problem of minimizing the total tardiness there is also a polynomial algorithm for equal-length jobs [112]. Furthermore, minimizing the sum of completion times [8] or the number of late jobs [9, 84] on a single machine can be done in polynomial time also for arbitrary processing times. More detailed complexity results on machine scheduling can be found in [22, 23].

In the non-preemptive case, the problems of minimizing the number of late jobs on a single machine [52] and minimizing the sum of the completion times on identical parallel machines [106] are polynomial for equal-length jobs, while the corresponding problems in the general case are both NP-hard, also on a single machine [85]. Moreover, polynomial time algorithms have been presented in [44] for the case of equal-length jobs on uniform parallel machines.

The complexity status of the problem we focus on in this chapter has been stated as an open question in the general case, where there are arbitrarily many different weights w_i [11, 12, 14, 23]. On the contrary, the complexity status of most of the closely related problems is already known. In particular, the non-preemptive version of this problem is known to be polynomially solvable on a fixed number of identical parallel machines [11]. On the other hand, the preemptive version of this problem is known to be NP-hard if the processing times are arbitrary on a single machine [82], or even for equal processing times on identical parallel machines [87].

In this chapter we present the first polynomial algorithm for the case where there is a constant number k of different weight values, i.e. $w_i \in \{\alpha_j\}_{j=1}^k$ [P6]. The running time of the presented algorithm is $O((\frac{n}{k}+1)^k n^8)$, while its space complexity is $O((\frac{n}{k}+1)^k n^6)$. These results provide evidence that the problem under consideration could admit a polynomial solution even in the case of arbitrarily many different weights.

Several real-life applications of this problem can be found, even in the case of a constant number of different weights. In the context of service management, vehicles may arrive to a garage in predefined appointments for regular check. This process is preemptive, since the check of one vehicle can be interrupted by the check of another one, while the service time of each vehicle is the same in a regular check. In addition, special purpose vehicles, such as ambulances, have higher priority, i.e. weight, than others. Similar situations may occur in the design of operating systems, where, for instance, system processes are of higher priority than user processes.

The rest of this chapter is organized as follows. In Section 6.1 we provide some properties of an optimal schedule, in order to determine the possible start and completion times of the jobs. By using these results, we construct a polynomial dynamic programming algorithm in Section 6.2.

6.1 Properties of an optimal schedule

In this section we provide some properties of an optimal preemptive schedule $\mathcal{S}$, in order to determine the set of all possible start and completion times of the n jobs in $\mathcal{S}$. For every job J_i let r_i be its release time and C_i be its completion time in $\mathcal{S}$. As a first step, we prove the following lemma, which will be used several times in the remaining part of this chapter.

Lemma 6.1. *For every job J_i that is at least partially executed in an optimal schedule $\mathcal{S}$ in the time interval $[r_k, C_k)$, where $i \neq k$, it holds $C_i < C_k$.*

Proof. The proof will be done by contradiction. Suppose that job J_i is partially executed in at least one time interval $I \subset [r_k, C_k)$ and that $C_i > C_k$, as it is illustrated in Figure 6.1. Since J_k is completed at time C_k in $\mathcal{S}$, there is a sufficient small positive $\varepsilon \leq |I|$, such that J_k is executed during the interval $[C_k - \varepsilon, C_k)$. We can exchange now a part of length ε of the interval I with the interval $[C_k - \varepsilon, C_k)$. In this modified schedule $\mathcal{S}'$, the completion time of J_k becomes at most $C_k - \varepsilon$, while the completion times of all other jobs remain the same. This is a contradiction to the assumption that $\mathcal{S}$ is optimal. It follows that $C_i < C_k$. □

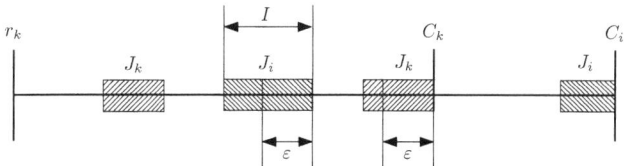

FIGURE 6.1: The impossible case $C_i > C_k$, where job J_i is partially executed in $[r_k, C_k)$.

The following lemma restricts the possible values of the makespan $C_{\max}$ of any optimal schedule, i.e. the completion time of the last completed job.

Lemma 6.2. *The makespan $C_{\max}$ in an optimal schedule $\mathcal{S}$ equals*

$$C_{\max} = r_i + \ell p$$

for some $i, \ell \in \{1, 2, \ldots, n\}$.

Proof. Let t be the end of the last idle period in $\mathcal{S}$, i.e. the machine is working continuously between t and $C_{\max}$. Let also that job J_i is executed directly after t, for some $i \in \{1, 2, \ldots, n\}$. Then, t equals the release time r_i of J_i, since otherwise J_i could be scheduled to complete earlier, resulting thus to a better schedule, which is a contradiction. Furthermore, every job J_k that is at least partially executed after t, has release time $r_k \geq t$, since otherwise J_k could be scheduled to complete earlier, which is again a contradiction. Thus, since the machine is working continuously between t and $C_{\max}$, it holds that $C_{\max} = r_i + \ell p$, where $\ell \in \{1, 2, \ldots, n\}$ is the number of jobs executed in the interval $[t, C_{\max})$. □

Now, the next lemma determines the possible start and completion times of the jobs $J_1, J_2, \ldots, J_n$ in $\mathcal{S}$.

Lemma 6.3. *The start and completion times of the jobs in an optimal schedule $\mathcal{S}$ take values from the set*

$$T = \{r_i + \ell p \mid 1 \leq i \leq n, 0 \leq \ell \leq n\} \qquad (6.1)$$

Proof. Consider an arbitrary job J_k and let $\mathcal{J} = \{J_i \mid C_i \leq C_k\}$ be the set of all jobs that are completed not later than J_k in $\mathcal{S}$. Consider now a job $J_m \notin \mathcal{J}$. Then, Lemma 6.1 implies that no part of J_m is executed at all in any time interval $[r_i, C_i)$, where $J_i \in \mathcal{J}$, since otherwise it would be $C_m < C_i \leq C_k$, i.e. $J_m \in \mathcal{J}$, which is a contradiction. It follows that the completion time C_k of job J_k remains the same if we remove from schedule $\mathcal{S}$ all jobs $J_m \notin \mathcal{J}$.

Thus, it holds due to Lemma 6.2 that $C_k = r_i + \ell p$, for some $J_i \in \mathcal{J}$ and $\ell \in \{1, 2, \ldots, |\mathcal{J}|\}$. Since $|\mathcal{J}| \leq n$, it follows that for the completion time of an arbitrary job J_k it holds $C_k \in T$. Furthermore, due to the optimality of $\mathcal{S}$, an arbitrary job

J_i starts either at its release time r_i, or at the completion time C_k of another job J_k. Thus, all start points of the jobs belong to T as well. □

6.2 The dynamic programming algorithm

In this section we propose a polynomial dynamic programming algorithm that computes the value of an optimal preemptive schedule on a single machine, where the weights of the jobs take k possible values $\{\alpha_i \mid 1 \leq i \leq k\}$, with $\alpha_1 > \ldots > \alpha_k > 0$. We partition the jobs into k sets $\mathcal{J}^i = \{J_1^i, J_2^i, \ldots, J_{n_i}^i\}$, $i \in \{1, \ldots, k\}$, such that job J_ℓ^i has weight α_i for every $\ell \in \{1, \ldots, n_i\}$. Assume without loss of generality that for every i, the jobs J_ℓ^i are sorted with respect to ℓ in non-decreasing order according to their release times r_ℓ^i, i.e.

$$r_1^i \leq r_2^i \leq \ldots \leq r_{n_i}^i \qquad (6.2)$$

6.2.1 Definitions and boundary conditions

We now introduce the sets and variables needed for the dynamic programming algorithm, which is presented in Section 6.2.3. These sets and variables will be linked together in Section 6.2.2. Intuitively, the dynamic programming algorithm considers an interval $[y, z)$ and a set Q of jobs that can be scheduled completely in this interval. Then, the decomposition scheme followed by the algorithm relies on a particular time point $s \in (y, z)$ that allows us to split the problem into two subproblems, namely into the intervals $[y, s)$ and $[s, z)$. Roughly speaking, this time point s is the start point in an optimal schedule of the lightest job of Q (or of a suitable subset of Q, in some cases) with the greatest release time.

Let

$$\mathbf{t} = (t_k, t_{k-1}, \ldots, t_1) \qquad (6.3)$$

be a vector $\mathbf{t} \in \mathbb{N}_0^k$, where for its coordinates it holds $0 \leq t_i \leq n_i$ for every $i \in \{1, \ldots, k\}$. Let $\mathcal{P}(\mathbf{t}) = \{i \mid t_i > 0, 1 \leq i \leq k\}$ be the set of indices that correspond to strictly positive coordinates of $\mathbf{t}$. For every vector $\mathbf{t} \neq \mathbf{0} = (0, \ldots, 0)$ and every $i \in \mathcal{P}(\mathbf{t})$ define the vectors

$$\mathbf{t}'_i = (t_k, \ldots, t_{i+1}, t_i - 1, t_{i-1}, \ldots, t_1) \tag{6.4}$$

$$\mathbf{t}''_i = (0, \ldots, 0, t_i, t_{i-1}, \ldots, t_1) \tag{6.5}$$

and let

$$\mathbf{t}_{\max} = \max \mathcal{P}(\mathbf{t}) \tag{6.6}$$

be the maximum index i, for which $t_i > 0$. Furthermore, let

$$\mathcal{R} = \{r^i_\ell \mid 1 \leq i \leq k, 1 \leq \ell \leq n_i\} \tag{6.7}$$

be the set of all release times of the jobs and

$$\mathcal{R}(\mathbf{t}) = \{r^i_\ell \mid i \in \mathcal{P}(\mathbf{t}), 1 \leq \ell \leq t_i\} \tag{6.8}$$

Denote now by

$$Q(\mathbf{t}, x, y, z) \tag{6.9}$$

where $\mathbf{t} \neq \mathbf{0}$ and $x \leq y < z$, the set of all jobs among $\bigcup_{i \in \mathcal{P}(\mathbf{t})} \bigcup_{\ell=1}^{t_i} J^i_\ell$ that have release times

$$r^i_\ell \in \begin{cases} [x, z), & \text{if } i = \mathbf{t}_{\max} \text{ and } \ell = t_i \\ [y, z), & \text{otherwise} \end{cases} \tag{6.10}$$

We define for $\mathbf{t} = \mathbf{0}$

$$Q(\mathbf{0}, x, y, z) = \emptyset \tag{6.11}$$

for all values $x \leq y < z$. Moreover, we define for every vector $\mathbf{t}$ and every triple $\{x, y, z\}$, such that $x \leq y$ and $y \geq z$

$$Q(\mathbf{t}, x, y, z) = \emptyset \tag{6.12}$$

Definition 6.1. *The set $Q(\mathbf{t}, x, y, z) \neq \emptyset$ of jobs is called* feasible, *if there exists a feasible schedule of these jobs in the interval $[y, z)$.*

For the case of a feasible set $Q(\mathbf{t}, x, y, z) \neq \emptyset$, denote now by

$$F(\mathbf{t}, x, y, z) \tag{6.13}$$

the value of an optimal schedule of all jobs of the set $Q(\mathbf{t}, x, y, z)$ in the interval $[y, z)$. Due to Lemma 6.3, we allow the variables y, z in (6.9) and (6.13) to take values only from the set T. Also, due to (6.10), since every job is released not earlier than x, it suffices to consider that $x \in \mathcal{R}$. For an arbitrary $y \in T$, let

$$r(y) = \min\{r \in \mathcal{R} \mid r \geq y\} \qquad (6.14)$$

be the smallest release time that equals at least y. For simplicity reasons, we define $r(y) = \max T$ in the case where there exists no release time $r \in \mathcal{R}$ with $r \geq y$, where $\max T$ is the greatest value of the set T, cf. (6.1). In the case where $Q(\mathbf{t}, x, y, z) \neq \emptyset$ is *not* feasible, we define $F(\mathbf{t}, x, y, z) = \infty$. In the case where $Q(\mathbf{t}, x, y, z) = \emptyset$, we define $F(\mathbf{t}, x, y, z) = 0$.

The following lemma uses the release times of the jobs of a set $Q(\mathbf{t}, x, y, z) \neq \emptyset$ in order to decide whether it is feasible, i.e. whether there exists a feasible schedule of these jobs in the interval $[y, z)$.

Lemma 6.4 (feasibility test). *Let $\widetilde{r}_1 \leq \widetilde{r}_2 \leq \ldots \leq \widetilde{r}_q$ be the release times of the jobs of $Q(\mathbf{t}, x, y, z) \neq \emptyset$ and let*

$$\begin{aligned} C_1 &= \max\{\widetilde{r}_1, y\} + p \\ C_\ell &= \max\{\widetilde{r}_\ell, C_{\ell-1}\} + p \end{aligned} \qquad (6.15)$$

for every $\ell \in \{2, 3, \ldots, q\}$. Then, $Q(\mathbf{t}, x, y, z)$ is feasible if and only if $C_q \leq z$.

Proof. The proof is straightforward. The set $Q(\mathbf{t}, x, y, z)$ of jobs is feasible if and only if there exists a schedule of these jobs with makespan $C_{\max}$ not greater than z. Without loss of generality, in a schedule that minimizes $C_{\max}$, every job is scheduled without preemption at the earliest possible point. In particular, the job with the earliest release time $\widetilde{r}_1$ starts at $\max\{\widetilde{r}_1, y\}$. Suppose that the $\ell - 1$ first jobs complete at point $C_{\ell-1}$, for some $\ell \in \{2, 3, \ldots, q\}$. If the ℓth job has release time $\widetilde{r}_\ell > C_{\ell-1}$, then this job starts obviously at $\widetilde{r}_\ell$. In the opposite case $\widetilde{r}_\ell \leq C_{\ell-1}$, it starts at $C_{\ell-1}$. Since every job has processing time p, we obtain (6.15) for the completion times of the scheduled jobs and thus the minimum makespan is C_q. It follows that $Q(\mathbf{t}, x, y, z)$ is feasible, i.e. $F(\mathbf{t}, x, y, z) \neq \infty$, if and only if $C_q \leq z$. □

6.2.2 The recursive computation

Consider a vector $\mathbf{t} \neq \mathbf{0}$ and a set $Q(\mathbf{t}, x, y, z) \neq \emptyset$ of jobs. Then, $y < z$ by the definition of $Q(\mathbf{t}, x, y, z)$. Furthermore, for every index $i \in \mathcal{P}(\mathbf{t}) \setminus \{\mathbf{t}_{\max}\}$, if $r_{t_i}^i \notin [y, z)$, it follows that

$$F(\mathbf{t}, x, y, z) = F(\mathbf{t}'_i, x, y, z) \qquad (6.16)$$

Indeed, in this case $J_{t_i}^i \notin Q(\mathbf{t}, x, y, z)$ by (6.10), and thus we can ignore job $J_{t_i}^i$, i.e. we can replace t_i by $t_i - 1$. Then, all jobs of $Q(\mathbf{t}, x, y, z)$ have release times according to (6.10) and they are scheduled in the interval $[y, z)$. Therefore, (6.16) follows.

On the other hand, for $i = \mathbf{t}_{\max}$, if $r_{t_i}^i \notin [x, z)$, then

$$F(\mathbf{t}, x, y, z) = F(\mathbf{t}'_i, r(y), r(y), z) \qquad (6.17)$$

Indeed, in this case again $J_{t_i}^i \notin Q(\mathbf{t}, x, y, z)$ by (6.10), and thus we can ignore job $J_{t_i}^i$, i.e. we can replace again t_i by $t_i - 1$. Then, all jobs of $Q(\mathbf{t}, x, y, z)$ are released not earlier than y, i.e. not earlier than $r(y)$, and thus they are all scheduled in the interval $[r(y), z)$. Therefore, (6.17) follows. Note here that in the extreme case where $r(y) \geq z$, no job of $Q(\mathbf{t}, x, y, z) \setminus \{J_{t_i}^i\}$ is released in $[y, z)$, and thus $Q(\mathbf{t}, x, y, z) = \emptyset$ by (6.10), which is a contradiction to the assumption that $Q(\mathbf{t}, x, y, z) \neq \emptyset$.

Suppose in the following without loss of generality that $J_{t_i}^i \in Q(\mathbf{t}, x, y, z)$ for every $i \in \mathcal{P}(\mathbf{t})$.

Let C_ℓ^i denote the completion time of job J_ℓ^i, where $i \in \{1, \ldots, k\}$ and $\ell \in \{1, \ldots, n_i\}$. Consider now the vector of the completion times $(C_1^1, C_2^1, \ldots, C_{n_k}^k)$ and the feasible set $Q(\mathbf{t}, x, y, z) \neq \emptyset$. Let $\mathcal{C}(\mathbf{t}, x, y, z)$ be the restriction of the vector $(C_1^1, C_2^1, \ldots, C_{n_k}^k)$ on those values j and ℓ, for which $J_\ell^j \in Q(\mathbf{t}, x, y, z)$. Denote now by $\mathcal{S}(\mathbf{t}, x, y, z)$ the optimal schedule of the jobs of $Q(\mathbf{t}, x, y, z)$ that lexicographically minimizes the vector $\mathcal{C}(\mathbf{t}, x, y, z)$ among all other optimal schedules. In the sequel, we denote $\mathcal{S}(\mathbf{t}, x, y, z)$ by $\mathcal{S}$, whenever the values $\mathbf{t}, x, y, z$ are clear from the context.

Next, we compute in Theorems 6.1 and 6.2 the values $F(\mathbf{t}, x, y, z)$. To this end, we provide first Lemma 6.5 and Corollary 6.1. These results will enable us to partition in the proof of Theorems 6.1 and 6.2 the set $Q(\mathbf{t}, x, y, z)$ into two subsets of jobs according to their release times, such that the jobs of the first set are completely scheduled in the first part $[y, s)$ of the interval $[y, z)$, while the jobs of the second set are completely scheduled

Chapter 6. *Preemptive scheduling of equal-length jobs* 119

in the second part $[s, z)$ of $[y, z)$, for an appropriately chosen time point $s \in (y, z)$. Denote by s_i and e_i the start and completion time of job $J^i_{t_i}$ in $\mathcal{S} = \mathcal{S}(\mathbf{t}, x, y, z)$, respectively. Also, for $i = \mathbf{t}_{\max}$, denote for simplicity $J^i_{t_i}$ and $r^i_{t_i}$ by $J_{\mathbf{t}_{\max}}$ and $r_{\mathbf{t}_{\max}}$, respectively.

Lemma 6.5. *Suppose that $Q(\mathbf{t}, x, y, z) \neq \emptyset$ is feasible and that $J^i_{t_i} \in Q(\mathbf{t}, x, y, z)$ for some $i \in \mathcal{P}(\mathbf{t})$. For every other job $J^j_\ell \in Q(\mathbf{t}, x, y, z) \setminus \{J^i_{t_i}\}$ with $j \leq i$, if J^j_ℓ is completed in $\mathcal{S}$ at a point $C^j_\ell > s_i$, then its release time is $r^j_\ell > s_i$.*

Proof. The proof will be done by contradiction. Consider a job $J^j_\ell \in Q(\mathbf{t}, x, y, z) \setminus \{J^i_{t_i}\}$ with $j \leq i$ and suppose that J^j_ℓ is completed in $\mathcal{S}$ at a point $C^j_\ell > s_i$. We distinguish the cases $C^j_\ell > C^i_{t_i}$ and $C^j_\ell < C^i_{t_i}$, respectively.

Suppose that $C^j_\ell > C^i_{t_i}$ and that J^j_ℓ is executed in $[C^i_{t_i}, z)$ for a time period of total length $L \leq p$, as it is illustrated in Figure 6.2(a). If $r^j_\ell \leq s_i$, then we can exchange the execution of J^j_ℓ in the interval $[C^i_{t_i}, z)$ with the last part of total length L of the execution of $J^i_{t_i}$ in the interval $[s_i, C^i_{t_i})$. In the resulting schedule $\mathcal{S}'$, the completion times C^j_ℓ and $C^i_{t_i}$ exchange values, while the completion times of all other jobs remain the same. Since $j \leq i$, it holds $\alpha_j \geq \alpha_i$ and therefore the schedule $\mathcal{S}'$ is not worse than $\mathcal{S}$. Thus, since $\mathcal{S}$ is optimal, $\mathcal{S}'$ is also optimal. However, $\mathcal{S}'$ is lexicographically smaller than $\mathcal{S}$, which is a contradiction to the assumption on $\mathcal{S}$. It follows that job J^j_ℓ is released not earlier than s_i, i.e. $r^j_\ell > s_i$.

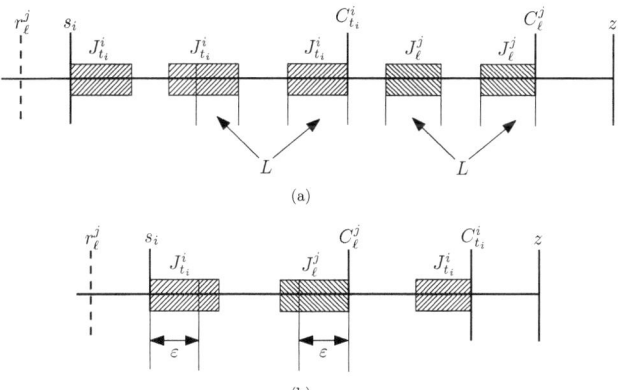

FIGURE 6.2: The impossible case $r^j_\ell \leq s_i$, where $j \leq i$ and $C^j_\ell > s_i$.

Suppose now that $C_\ell^j < C_{t_i}^i$, as it is illustrated in Figure 6.2(b). Then, there exists a sufficiently small time period $\varepsilon > 0$, such that during the time intervals $[s_i, s_i + \varepsilon)$ and $[C_\ell^j - \varepsilon, C_\ell^j)$ the jobs $J_{t_i}^i$ and J_ℓ^j are executed, respectively. If $r_\ell^j \leq s_i$, we can now exchange the execution of the jobs $J_{t_i}^i$ and J_ℓ^j in these intervals, obtaining a completion time of J_ℓ^j at most $C_\ell^j - \varepsilon$, while the completion times of all other jobs remain the same. Since all weights are positive, the resulting schedule is better than $\mathcal{S}$, which is a contradiction to its optimality. This implies again that job J_ℓ^j is released not earlier than s_i, i.e. $r_\ell^j > s_i$. □

Corollary 6.1. *Suppose that $Q(\mathbf{t}, x, y, z) \neq \emptyset$ is feasible and that $J_{t_i}^i \in Q(\mathbf{t}, x, y, z)$ for some $i \in \mathcal{P}(\mathbf{t})$. Then, every other job $J_\ell^i \in Q(\mathbf{t}, x, y, z) \setminus \{J_{t_i}^i\}$ is completed in $\mathcal{S}$ at a point $C_\ell^i \leq s_i$.*

Proof. Consider such a job J_ℓ^i, with $\ell < t_i$ and suppose that J_ℓ^i is completed at a point $C_\ell^i > s_i$. Then, Lemma 6.5 implies that $r_\ell^i > s_i$. On the other hand, it holds due to (6.2) that $r_\ell^i \leq r_{t_i}^i \leq s_i$, which is a contradiction. □

Theorem 6.1. *Let $Q(\mathbf{t}, x, y, z) \neq \emptyset$ be feasible and $J_{t_i}^i \in Q(\mathbf{t}, x, y, z)$ for every $i \in \mathcal{P}(\mathbf{t})$. Suppose that $r_{\mathbf{t}_{\max}} > y$. Then,*

$$F(\mathbf{t}, x, y, z) = F_1 = \min_{\substack{s \in (y,z) \cap T \\ s \notin \mathcal{R}(\mathbf{t}'_{\mathbf{t}_{\max}})}} \left\{ F(\mathbf{t}'_{\mathbf{t}_{\max}}, r(y), r(y), s) + F(\mathbf{t}, x, s, z) \right\} \quad (6.18)$$

Proof. First, recall that s_i and e_i denote the start and completion times of the job $J_{t_i}^i \in Q(\mathbf{t}, x, y, z)$ in $\mathcal{S} = \mathcal{S}(\mathbf{t}, x, y, z)$, for every $i \in \mathcal{P}(\mathbf{t})$. Due to the assumption that $r_{\mathbf{t}_{\max}} > y$, it follows that also $s_{\mathbf{t}_{\max}} > y$.

For every job $J_\ell^j \in Q(\mathbf{t}, x, y, z)$ it holds $j \leq \mathbf{t}_{\max}$, due to (6.6). Thus, Lemma 6.5 implies that all jobs $J_\ell^j \in Q(\mathbf{t}, x, y, z) \setminus \{J_{\mathbf{t}_{\max}}\}$ with release times $r_\ell^j \leq s_{\mathbf{t}_{\max}}$ are scheduled completely in the interval $[y, s_{\mathbf{t}_{\max}})$, while all jobs $J_\ell^j \in Q(\mathbf{t}, x, y, z) \setminus \{J_{\mathbf{t}_{\max}}\}$ with release times $r_\ell^j > s_{\mathbf{t}_{\max}}$ are scheduled in $\mathcal{S}$ completely in the interval $[s_{\mathbf{t}_{\max}}, z)$. Note that the extreme case $r_\ell^j = s_{\mathbf{t}_{\max}}$ is impossible for any job $J_\ell^j \in Q(\mathbf{t}, x, y, z) \setminus \{J_{\mathbf{t}_{\max}}\}$, since otherwise job J_ℓ^j must be scheduled in the empty interval $[s_{\mathbf{t}_{\max}}, s_{\mathbf{t}_{\max}})$, which is a contradiction. That is, $s_{\mathbf{t}_{\max}} \notin \mathcal{R}(\mathbf{t}'_{\mathbf{t}_{\max}})$.

Since $J_{\mathbf{t}_{\max}}$ is scheduled in the second part $[s_{\mathbf{t}_{\max}}, z)$ of $\mathcal{S}$, it follows that every job J_ℓ^j, which is scheduled in the first part $[y, s_{\mathbf{t}_{\max}})$ of $\mathcal{S}$, has release time $r_\ell^j \geq y$, i.e. $r_\ell^j \geq r(y)$.

Thus, the value of this first part of $\mathcal{S}$ equals $F(\mathbf{t}'_{\mathbf{t}_{\max}}, r(y), r(y), s_{\mathbf{t}_{\max}})$. Note here that in the extreme case where $r(y) \geq s_{\mathbf{t}_{\max}}$, no job of $Q(\mathbf{t}, x, y, z) \setminus \{J_{\mathbf{t}_{\max}}\}$ is released in $[y, s_{\mathbf{t}_{\max}})$, and thus no job is scheduled in the first part of $\mathcal{S}$, i.e. the value of this part equals zero. However, in this case, where $r(y) \geq s_{\mathbf{t}_{\max}}$, it holds $Q(\mathbf{t}'_{\mathbf{t}_{\max}}, r(y), r(y), s_{\mathbf{t}_{\max}}) = \emptyset$ by (6.12), and thus $F(\mathbf{t}'_{\mathbf{t}_{\max}}, r(y), r(y), s_{\mathbf{t}_{\max}}) = 0$. Thus, in any case, the value of the first part of $\mathcal{S}$ equals $F(\mathbf{t}'_{\mathbf{t}_{\max}}, r(y), r(y), s_{\mathbf{t}_{\max}})$.

On the other hand, in the second part $[s_{\mathbf{t}_{\max}}, z)$ of $\mathcal{S}$, exactly $J_{\mathbf{t}_{\max}}$ and the jobs $J_\ell^j \in Q(\mathbf{t}, x, y, z) \setminus \{J_{\mathbf{t}_{\max}}\}$ with release times $r_\ell^j > s_{\mathbf{t}_{\max}}$ are scheduled. Thus, since $s_{\mathbf{t}_{\max}} \notin \mathcal{R}(\mathbf{t}'_{\mathbf{t}_{\max}})$, we can state equivalently that in the second part $[s_{\mathbf{t}_{\max}}, z)$ of $\mathcal{S}$, exactly $J_{\mathbf{t}_{\max}}$ and the jobs $J_\ell^j \in Q(\mathbf{t}, x, y, z) \setminus \{J_{\mathbf{t}_{\max}}\}$ with release times $r_\ell^j \geq s_{\mathbf{t}_{\max}}$ are scheduled. Therefore, since $J_{\mathbf{t}_{\max}}$ is released not earlier than x, the value of the second part of $\mathcal{S}$ equals $F(\mathbf{t}, x, s_{\mathbf{t}_{\max}}, z)$. It follows that

$$F(\mathbf{t}, x, y, z) = F(\mathbf{t}'_{\mathbf{t}_{\max}}, r(y), r(y), s_{\mathbf{t}_{\max}}) + F(\mathbf{t}, x, s_{\mathbf{t}_{\max}}, z) \qquad (6.19)$$

Conversely, if the value of (6.19) is finite, then it corresponds to a feasible schedule of the jobs of $Q(\mathbf{t}, x, y, z)$ in the interval $[y, z)$. Thus, since $\mathcal{S}$ is assumed to be optimal, the value $F(\mathbf{t}, x, y, z)$ is the minimum of the expression in (6.19) over all possible values $s = s_{\mathbf{t}_{\max}} \in (y, z) \cap T$, such that $s_{\mathbf{t}_{\max}} \notin \mathcal{R}(\mathbf{t}'_{\mathbf{t}_{\max}})$. $\square$

Theorem 6.2. *Let $Q(\mathbf{t}, x, y, z) \neq \emptyset$ be feasible and $J_{t_i}^i \in Q(\mathbf{t}, x, y, z)$ for every $i \in \mathcal{P}(\mathbf{t})$. Suppose that $r_{\mathbf{t}_{\max}} \leq y$ and let $e = y + p \cdot |Q(\mathbf{t}, x, y, z)|$. If $Q(\mathbf{t}, r(e), r(e), z) \neq \emptyset$, then*

$$F(\mathbf{t}, x, y, z) = \min_{\substack{s \in (y,z) \cap T \\ i \in \mathcal{P}(\mathbf{t}) \setminus \{\mathbf{t}_{\max}\} \\ s \geq r(y),\ s \notin \mathcal{R}(\mathbf{t}'_i)}} \left\{ F_1, F(\mathbf{t}'_i, x, y, s) + F(\mathbf{t}''_i, r(y), s, z) \right\} \qquad (6.20)$$

Otherwise, if $Q(\mathbf{t}, r(e), r(e), z) = \emptyset$, then

$$F(\mathbf{t}, x, y, z) = \min_{\substack{s \in (y,z) \cap T \\ i \in \mathcal{P}(\mathbf{t}) \setminus \{\mathbf{t}_{\max}\} \\ s \geq r(y),\ s \notin \mathcal{R}(\mathbf{t}'_i)}} \left\{ \begin{array}{l} F_1, \\ F(\mathbf{t}'_i, x, y, s) + F(\mathbf{t}''_i, r(y), s, z), \\ F(\mathbf{t}'_{\mathbf{t}_{\max}}, r(y), r(y), e) + e \cdot \alpha_{\mathbf{t}_{\max}} \end{array} \right\} \qquad (6.21)$$

where F_1 is the value computed in (6.18).

Proof. Similarly to the proof of Theorem 6.1, let job $J_{t_i}^i \in Q(\mathbf{t}, x, y, z)$ start at point s_i and complete at point e_i in $\mathcal{S} = \mathcal{S}(\mathbf{t}, x, y, z)$, for every $i \in \mathcal{P}(\mathbf{t})$. In the case where $s_{\mathbf{t}_{\max}} > y$, Theorem 6.1 implies that $F(\mathbf{t}, x, y, z) = F_1$, where F_1 is the value computed in (6.18). Suppose in the sequel of the proof that $s_{\mathbf{t}_{\max}} = y$. We distinguish in the following two cases.

Case 1. Suppose that there exists an index $i \in \mathcal{P}(\mathbf{t})$, such that $s_i \geq e_{\mathbf{t}_{\max}}$, and let i be the greatest among them. Then, $i < \mathbf{t}_{\max}$ and $y < s_i < z$. That is, for every index $j \in \mathcal{P}(\mathbf{t})$ with $j > i$, job $J_{t_j}^j$ starts at a point $s_j \in [s_{\mathbf{t}_{\max}}, e_{\mathbf{t}_{\max}})$ in $\mathcal{S}$, as it is illustrated in Figure 6.3(a). Then, Lemma 6.1 implies that this job completes also in this interval, i.e. $e_j \in [s_{\mathbf{t}_{\max}}, e_{\mathbf{t}_{\max}})$. Furthermore, Corollary 6.1 implies that for every such index $j \in \mathcal{P}(\mathbf{t})$ (where $j > i$), all jobs $J_\ell^j \in Q(\mathbf{t}, x, y, z) \setminus \{J_{t_j}^j\}$ are completed at a point $C_\ell^j \leq s_j$. Then, since $s_j < s_i$, we obtain that $C_\ell^j < s_i$. It follows that for every job J_ℓ^j that is completed at a point $C_\ell^j > s_i$, it holds $j \leq i$. Thus, Lemma 6.5 implies that all jobs $J_\ell^j \in Q(\mathbf{t}, x, y, z) \setminus \{J_{t_i}^i\}$ with release times $r_\ell^j \leq s_i$ are scheduled completely in the interval $[y, s_i)$, while all jobs $J_\ell^j \in Q(\mathbf{t}, x, y, z) \setminus \{J_{t_i}^i\}$ with release times $r_\ell^j > s_i$ are scheduled in $\mathcal{S}$ completely in the interval $[s_i, z)$. Note that the extreme case $r_\ell^j = s_i$ is impossible for any job $J_\ell^j \in Q(\mathbf{t}, x, y, z) \setminus \{J_{t_i}^i\}$, since otherwise job J_ℓ^j must be scheduled in the empty interval $[s_i, s_i)$, which is a contradiction. That is, $s_i \notin \mathcal{R}(\mathbf{t}_i')$. Furthermore, since the release time of $J_{t_i}^i$ is assumed to be $r_{t_i}^i \geq y$, i.e. $r_{t_i}^i \geq r(y)$, and since $s_i \geq r_{t_i}^i$, it follows that $s_i \geq r(y)$.

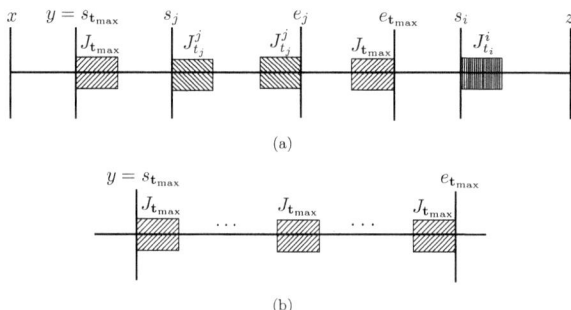

FIGURE 6.3: The case $s_{\mathbf{t}_{\max}} = y$.

Note that $J_{\mathbf{t}_{\max}}$ is scheduled in the first part $[y, s_i)$ of $\mathcal{S}$, since we assumed that $y = s_{\mathbf{t}_{\max}}$, while $J_{t_i}^i$ is scheduled in the second part $[s_i, z)$ of $\mathcal{S}$. Thus, since $J_{\mathbf{t}_{\max}}$ is released not earlier than x, the value of the first part $[y, s_i)$ of $\mathcal{S}$ equals $F(\mathbf{t}_i', x, y, s_i)$.

Chapter 6. *Preemptive scheduling of equal-length jobs* 123

In the second part $[s_i, z)$ of $\mathcal{S}$, exactly $J^i_{t_i}$ and the jobs $J^j_\ell \in Q(\mathbf{t}, x, y, z) \setminus \{J^i_{t_i}\}$ with $j \leq i$ and release times $r^j_\ell > s_i$ are scheduled. Thus, since $s_i \notin \mathcal{R}(\mathbf{t}'_i)$, we can state equivalently that in the second part $[s_i, z)$ of $\mathcal{S}$, exactly $J^i_{t_i}$ and the jobs $J^j_\ell \in Q(\mathbf{t}, x, y, z) \setminus \{J^i_{t_i}\}$ with $j \leq i$ and release times $r^j_\ell \geq s_i$ are scheduled. Since the release time of $J^i_{t_i}$ is assumed to be $r^i_{t_i} \geq y$, i.e. $r^i_{t_i} \geq r(y)$, the value of the second part of $\mathcal{S}$ equals $F(\mathbf{t}''_i, r(y), s_i, z)$. Note here that, since $r(y) \leq s_i < z$, the value $F(\mathbf{t}''_i, r(y), s_i, z)$ is well defined. It follows that

$$F(\mathbf{t}, x, y, z) = F(\mathbf{t}'_i, x, y, s_i) + F(\mathbf{t}''_i, r(y), s_i, z) \qquad (6.22)$$

Conversely, if the value of (6.22) is finite, then it corresponds to a feasible schedule of the jobs of $Q(\mathbf{t}, x, y, z)$ in the interval $[y, z)$. Thus, since $\mathcal{S}$ is assumed to be optimal, the value $F(\mathbf{t}, x, y, z)$ equals (in Case 1) to the minimum of the expression in (6.22) over all possible values of $i \in \mathcal{P}(\mathbf{t}) \setminus \{\mathbf{t}_{\max}\}$ and $s = s_i \in (y, z) \cap T$, such that $s \notin \mathcal{R}(\mathbf{t}'_i)$ and $s \geq r(y)$.

Case 2. Suppose that $s_i < e_{\mathbf{t}_{\max}}$ for every $i \in \mathcal{P}(\mathbf{t})$. Then, Corollary 6.1 implies that for every $i \in \mathcal{P}(\mathbf{t})$, all jobs $J^i_\ell \in Q(\mathbf{t}, x, y, z)$ with $\ell < t_i$ are completed at most at point s_i in $\mathcal{S}$. Thus, in this case all jobs of $Q(\mathbf{t}, x, y, z)$ are scheduled completely in the interval $[y, e_{\mathbf{t}_{\max}})$, as it is illustrated in Figure 6.3(b). Since the processing time of every job equals p, the total processing time of all jobs equals $p \cdot |Q(\mathbf{t}, x, y, z)|$. On the other hand, there is no idle period between y and $e_{\mathbf{t}_{\max}}$, since otherwise $J_{\mathbf{t}_{\max}}$ would be scheduled to complete earlier, resulting thus to a better schedule, which is a contradiction to the optimality of $\mathcal{S}$. Therefore,

$$e_{\mathbf{t}_{\max}} = y + p \cdot |Q(\mathbf{t}, x, y, z)| \qquad (6.23)$$

Note that, since $Q(\mathbf{t}, x, y, z)$ is assumed to be feasible, there exists a feasible schedule of the jobs of $Q(\mathbf{t}, x, y, z)$ in the interval $[y, z)$, and thus, $z \geq e_{\mathbf{t}_{\max}} = y + p \cdot |Q(\mathbf{t}, x, y, z)|$. Furthermore, since all jobs of $Q(\mathbf{t}, x, y, z)$ are scheduled completely in the interval $[y, e_{\mathbf{t}_{\max}})$, it follows in particular that all jobs of $Q(\mathbf{t}, x, y, z)$ are released strictly before $e_{\mathbf{t}_{\max}}$, and thus $Q(\mathbf{t}, r(e_{\mathbf{t}_{\max}}), r(e_{\mathbf{t}_{\max}}), z) = \emptyset$. Note here that, in the extreme case where $r(e_{\mathbf{t}_{\max}}) \geq z$, again $Q(\mathbf{t}, r(e_{\mathbf{t}_{\max}}), r(e_{\mathbf{t}_{\max}}), z) = \emptyset$ by (6.12).

Now, Lemma 6.1 implies that no part of $J_{\mathbf{t}_{\max}}$ is executed in any time interval $[r^i_\ell, C^i_\ell)$, where $J^i_\ell \in Q(\mathbf{t}, x, y, z) \setminus \{J_{\mathbf{t}_{\max}}\}$, since otherwise $J_{\mathbf{t}_{\max}}$ would complete before J^i_ℓ, which is a contradiction. Thus, the completion times of all these jobs remain the same if we remove $J_{t_{\max}}$ from the schedule $\mathcal{S}$. Recall that all jobs $J_\ell^i \in Q(\mathbf{t}, x, y, z) \setminus \{J_{t_{\max}}\}$ have release times $r_\ell^i \geq y$, i.e. $r_\ell^i \geq r(y)$. Thus, since the weight of $J_{t_{\max}}$ is $\alpha_{t_{\max}}$ and its completion time is $e_{t_{\max}}$, it follows in this case that

$$F(\mathbf{t}, x, y, z) = F(\mathbf{t}'_{t_{\max}}, r(y), r(y), e_{t_{\max}}) + e_{t_{\max}} \cdot \alpha_{t_{\max}} \qquad (6.24)$$

Note here that in the extreme case where $r(y) \geq e_{t_{\max}}$, no job of $Q(\mathbf{t}, x, y, z) \setminus \{J_{t_{\max}}\}$ is released in $[y, e_{t_{\max}})$, and thus no job except $J_{t_{\max}}$ is scheduled in $\mathcal{S}$, i.e. $F(\mathbf{t}, x, y, z) = e_{t_{\max}} \cdot \alpha_{t_{\max}}$. In this case, where $r(y) \geq e_{t_{\max}}$, it holds $Q(\mathbf{t}'_{t_{\max}}, r(y), r(y), e_{t_{\max}}) = \emptyset$ by (6.12), and thus $F(\mathbf{t}'_{t_{\max}}, r(y), r(y), e_{t_{\max}}) = 0$. Thus, in any case, the value of $F(\mathbf{t}, x, y, z)$ is given by (6.24).

Conversely, suppose that $Q(\mathbf{t}, r(e_{t_{\max}}), r(e_{t_{\max}}), z) = \emptyset$ and that the value of $F(\mathbf{t}, x, y, z)$ in (6.24) is finite, or equivalently, the value $F(\mathbf{t}'_{t_{\max}}, r(y), r(y), e_{t_{\max}})$ is finite, where $e_{t_{\max}}$ is given by (6.23). Then, since $Q(\mathbf{t}, r(e_{t_{\max}}), r(e_{t_{\max}}), z) = \emptyset$, all jobs $J_\ell^i \in Q(\mathbf{t}, x, y, z) \setminus \{J_{t_{\max}}\}$ have release times r_ℓ^i, such that $r(y) \leq r_\ell^i < e_{t_{\max}}$.

If $F(\mathbf{t}'_{t_{\max}}, r(y), r(y), e_{t_{\max}}) = 0$, then $Q(\mathbf{t}'_{t_{\max}}, r(y), r(y), e_{t_{\max}}) = \emptyset$. Therefore, since also $Q(\mathbf{t}, r(e_{t_{\max}}), r(e_{t_{\max}}), z) = \emptyset$, it follows that $Q(\mathbf{t}, x, y, z) = \{J_{t_{\max}}\}$, and thus $F(\mathbf{t}, x, y, z) = e_{t_{\max}} \cdot \alpha_{t_{\max}}$ corresponds to a feasible schedule of $Q(\mathbf{t}, x, y, z)$ in $[y, z)$.

In the opposite case, where $F(\mathbf{t}'_{t_{\max}}, r(y), r(y), e_{t_{\max}}) \neq 0$, this value corresponds to a feasible schedule $\mathcal{S}_0$ of the jobs of the set $Q(\mathbf{t}, x, y, z) \setminus \{J_{t_{\max}}\}$ in the interval $[y, e_{t_{\max}})$. Since the processing time of each job is p, the total processing time of these jobs in $[y, e_{t_{\max}})$ is $p \cdot (|Q(\mathbf{t}, x, y, z)| - 1)$. Thus, due to (6.23), the machine has idle periods in the interval $[y, e_{t_{\max}})$ of total length p (in the schedule $\mathcal{S}_0$). Therefore, since $r_{t_{\max}} \leq y$ by the assumption, we can schedule the job $J_{t_{\max}}$ in these idle periods, obtaining a feasible schedule of all jobs of $Q(\mathbf{t}, x, y, z)$ in the interval $[y, e_{t_{\max}})$ with value $F(\mathbf{t}, x, y, z)$, as it is expressed in (6.24). That is, if $Q(\mathbf{t}, r(e_{t_{\max}}), r(e_{t_{\max}}), z) = \emptyset$, and if the value of (6.24) is finite, then this value corresponds to a feasible schedule of the jobs of $Q(\mathbf{t}, x, y, z)$ in the interval $[y, z)$. Thus, since $\mathcal{S}$ is assumed to be optimal, the value $F(\mathbf{t}, x, y, z)$ equals (in Case 2) to the expression in (6.24) for $e_{t_{\max}} = y + p \cdot |Q(\mathbf{t}, x, y, z)|$.

Summarizing now Cases 1 and 2, and since $\mathcal{S}$ is optimal, it follows that the optimal value $F(\mathbf{t}, x, y, z)$ is the minimum among the value F_1 (computed in (6.18)) and the values of the expressions in (6.22) and (6.24), over all possible values $s = s_i \in (y, z) \cap T$ and $i \in \mathcal{P}(\mathbf{t}) \setminus \{t_{\max}\}$, such that $s \notin \mathcal{R}(\mathbf{t}'_i)$ and $s \geq r(y)$. This completes the theorem. $\square$

6.2.3 The algorithm

Since the start and completion times of the jobs in an optimal schedule belong to T by Lemma 6.3, the value of such a schedule equals

$$F(\mathbf{t}^*, \min T, \min T, \max T) \qquad (6.25)$$

where

$$\mathbf{t}^* = (n_1, n_2, \ldots, n_k) \qquad (6.26)$$

and $\min T$, $\max T$ denote the smallest and the greatest value of the set T, respectively, cf. (6.1). Note that $\min T$ coincides with the smallest release time. The dynamic programming Algorithm 6.1 follows now by Lemma 6.4 and Theorems 6.1 and 6.2. The correctness and the complexity of this algorithm is proved in the main Theorem 6.3.

Theorem 6.3. *An optimal schedule can be computed in $O((\frac{n}{k}+1)^k n^8)$ time and $O((\frac{n}{k}+1)^k n^6)$ space, while the computation of the value of an optimal schedule needs $O((\frac{n}{k}+1)^k n^5)$ space.*

Proof. We present Algorithm 6.1 that computes the value of an optimal schedule of the given n jobs. A slight modification of this algorithm returns an optimal schedule, instead of its value only. As a preprocessing step, in the first two lines, Algorithm 6.1 partitions the n jobs into the sets $\mathcal{J}^i = \{J_1^i, J_2^i, \ldots, J_{n_i}^i\}$, $i \in \{1, \ldots, k\}$, such that job J_ℓ^i has weight α_i for every $\ell \in \{1, \ldots, n_i\}$, and that, for every i, the jobs $J_\ell^i \in \mathcal{J}^i$ are sorted with respect to ℓ according to (6.2).

In lines 3-6, Algorithm 6.1 initializes $F(\mathbf{0}, x, y, z) = 0$ for all possible values of x, y, z, such that $x \leq y < z$, as well as $F(\mathbf{t}, x, y, z) = 0$ for all possible values of $\mathbf{t}, x, y, z$, such that $x \leq y$ and $y \geq z$, cf. (6.11) and (6.12). It iterates further for every $\mathbf{t}$ between $\mathbf{0}$ and $\mathbf{t}^*$ in lexicographical order and for every possible x, y, z, such that $x \leq y < z$. For every such tuple $(\mathbf{t}, x, y, z)$, the algorithm computes the value $F(\mathbf{t}, x, y, z)$ as follows. At first, it computes the set $Q(\mathbf{t}, x, y, z)$ in line 10. If this set is empty, it defines $F(\mathbf{t}, x, y, z) = 0$. Otherwise, it checks in line 12 its feasibility, using Lemma 6.4 and, if it is not feasible, it defines $F(\mathbf{t}, x, y, z) = \infty$. In the case of feasibility of the set $Q(\mathbf{t}, x, y, z)$, the algorithm checks in lines 15-21 the release times of the jobs $J_{t_i}^i$ for all $i \in \mathcal{P}(\mathbf{t})$. If at least one of these jobs does not belong to $Q(\mathbf{t}, x, y, z)$, it computes $F(\mathbf{t}, x, y, z)$ recursively in lines 18 and 21, due to (6.17) and (6.16), respectively. Finally, if all jobs $J_{t_i}^i$, $i \in \mathcal{P}(\mathbf{t})$ belong to

Algorithm 6.1 Computation of the value of an optimal schedule with n jobs

Input: Jobs $J_1, J_2, \ldots, J_n$ with equal processing time p, release times r_i and positive weights $w_i \in \{\alpha_j\}_{j=1}^k$, $i \in \{1, 2, \ldots, n\}$
Output: The minimum value $\sum_{i=1}^n w_i C_i$ of a feasible preemptive schedule $\mathcal{S}$ of $J_1, J_2, \ldots, J_n$

1: Partition the jobs into the sets $\mathcal{J}^i = \{J_1^i, J_2^i, \ldots, J_{n_i}^i\}$, $i \in \{1, \ldots, k\}$, such that job J_ℓ^i has weight α_i for every $\ell \in \{1, \ldots, n_i\}$
2: For every i, sort the jobs $J_\ell^i \in \mathcal{J}^i$ with respect to ℓ according to (6.2)
3: **for** each $x \in \mathcal{R}$ and $y, z \in T$, with $x \leq y < z$ **do**
4:    $F(\mathbf{0}, x, y, z) \leftarrow 0$ {initialization}
5: **for** each **t** between **0** and $\mathbf{t}^*$, $x \in \mathcal{R}$ and $y, z \in T$, with $x \leq y$ and $y \geq z$ **do**
6:    $F(\mathbf{t}, x, y, z) \leftarrow 0$ {initialization}
7: **for** every **t** between **0** and $\mathbf{t}^*$ in lexicographical order **do**
8:    **for** every $x \in \mathcal{R}$ and $z \in T$ with $x < z$ **do**
9:      **for** $y = z$ downto x (with $y \in T$ and $y \neq z$) **do**
10:        **if** $Q(\mathbf{t}, x, y, z) = \emptyset$ **then**
11:          $F(\mathbf{t}, x, y, z) \leftarrow 0$
12:        **else if** $Q(\mathbf{t}, x, y, z)$ is not feasible **then**
13:          $F(\mathbf{t}, x, y, z) \leftarrow \infty$
14:        **else**
15:          **for** every $i \in \mathcal{P}(\mathbf{t})$ **do**
16:            **if** $i = \mathbf{t}_{\max}$ **then**
17:              **if** $r_{t_i}^i \notin [x, z)$ **then**
18:                $F(\mathbf{t}, x, y, z) \leftarrow F(\mathbf{t}_i', r(y), r(y), z)$
19:            **else** $\{i \neq \mathbf{t}_{\max}\}$
20:              **if** $r_{t_i}^i \notin [y, z)$ **then**
21:                $F(\mathbf{t}, x, y, z) \leftarrow F(\mathbf{t}_i', x, y, z)$
22:          **if** $F(\mathbf{t}, x, y, z)$ has not been computed in lines 18 or 21 **then**
23:            Compute $F(\mathbf{t}, x, y, z)$ by Theorems 6.1 and 6.2
24: **return** $F(\mathbf{t}^*, \min T, \min T, \max T)$

$Q(\mathbf{t}, x, y, z)$, i.e. if the value $F(\mathbf{t}, x, y, z)$ has not been computed in the lines 18 or 21, the algorithm computes $F(\mathbf{t}, x, y, z)$ in line 23 by Theorems 6.1 and 6.2.

Note here that, for every $i \in \mathcal{P}(\mathbf{t})$, the vectors $\mathbf{t}_i'$ and $\mathbf{t}_i''$ are lexicographically smaller than $\mathbf{t}$. Thus, the values $F(\mathbf{t}_i', \cdot, \cdot, \cdot)$ and $F(\mathbf{t}_i'', \cdot, \cdot, \cdot)$, which are used in lines 18 and 21, as well as in equations (6.18), (6.20), and (6.21), have been already computed at a previous iteration of the algorithm. Furthermore, since we iterate for y in line 9 from the value z downwards to the value x, the values $F(\mathbf{t}, x, s, z)$, for every s with $y < s < z$, cf. equation (6.18), have been also computed at a previous iteration of the algorithm. Thus, all recursive values that are used by Theorems 6.1 and 6.2, cf. equations (6.18),

(6.20), and (6.21), have been already computed at a previous iteration of the algorithm. This completes the correctness of Algorithm 6.1.

The running time of the algorithm can be computed as follows. First, the preprocessing step of the first two lines can be done clearly in $O(n \log n)$ time. For each vector $\mathbf{t} = (t_k, t_{k-1}, \ldots, t_1)$, the set $\mathcal{P}(\mathbf{t}) = \{i \mid t_i > 0, 1 \leq i \leq k\}$ and the value $\mathbf{t}_{\max} = \max \mathcal{P}(\mathbf{t})$ can be computed in linear $O(n)$ time, since $k \leq n$. Thus, the computation of the set $Q(\mathbf{t}, x, y, z)$ in line 10 can be done in linear time as well. Indeed, since $y < z$, we can check in linear time whether $\mathbf{t} = \mathbf{0}$, cf. (6.11), while we can check also in linear time in (6.10) the release times of the jobs $\bigcup_{i \in \mathcal{P}(\mathbf{t})} \bigcup_{\ell=1}^{t_i} J_\ell^i$. The feasibility of $Q(\mathbf{t}, x, y, z)$ in line 12 can be checked in $O(n \log n)$ time using Lemma 6.4, by sorting first increasingly the release times $\tilde{r}_1, \tilde{r}_2, \ldots, \tilde{r}_q$ of the jobs in $Q(\mathbf{t}, x, y, z)$ and then, by computing in linear time the value C_q. The execution of lines 15-21 can be simply done in linear time, by checking the release times of the jobs $J_{t_i}^i$, for all $i \in \mathcal{P}(\mathbf{t})$.

For the computation of $F(\mathbf{t}, x, y, z)$ by Theorems 6.1 and 6.2, the algorithm uses for at most every $s \in T$ and every $i \in \mathcal{P}(\mathbf{t}) \setminus \{\mathbf{t}_{\max}\}$ the values of one or two smaller instances that have been already computed at a previous iteration. This takes $O(n^3)$ time, since T has at most n^2 elements and $\mathcal{P}(\mathbf{t})$ has at most n elements. Furthermore, the sets $\mathcal{R}(\mathbf{t}'_{\mathbf{t}_{\max}})$ and $\mathcal{R}(\mathbf{t}'_i)$ in the statements of these theorems can be computed in linear $O(n)$ time by (6.8). Moreover, the set $Q(\mathbf{t}, r(e), r(e), z)$ in the statement of Theorem 6.2 can be computed in linear $O(n)$ time. Indeed, we can check in linear time whether $\mathbf{t} = \mathbf{0}$ or whether $r(e) \geq z$, cf. (6.11) and (6.12), while we can check also in linear time in (6.10) the release times of the jobs $\bigcup_{i \in \mathcal{P}(\mathbf{t})} \bigcup_{\ell=1}^{t_i} J_\ell^i$. Thus, the algorithm needs $O(n^3)$ time for the execution of the lines 10-23.

There are in total $\prod_{i=1}^{k}(n_i + 1)$ possible values of the vector $\mathbf{t}$, where it holds $\sum_{i=1}^{k}(n_i + 1) = n + k$. The product $\prod_{i=1}^{k}(n_i + 1)$ is maximized, when $(n_i + 1) = \frac{n+k}{k}$ for every $i = 1, \ldots, k$. Thus, there are in total at most $O((\frac{n}{k} + 1)^k)$ vectors $\mathbf{t}$ and $O((\frac{n}{k} + 1)^k n^5)$ possible tuples $(\mathbf{t}, x, y, z)$, since $x \in \mathcal{R}$ can take at most $O(n)$ possible values and $y, z \in T$ can take at most $O(n^2)$ possible values each. Since the lines 10-23 are executed for all these tuples, the algorithm needs for the lines 7-23 $O((\frac{n}{k} + 1)^k n^8)$ time. Furthermore, the initialization of the values $F(\mathbf{0}, x, y, z)$ for all possible x, y, z in lines 3-4 takes $O(n^5)$ time. Finally, the initialization of the values $F(\mathbf{t}, x, y, z)$ in lines 5-6 takes $O((\frac{n}{k} + 1)^k n^5)$ time, since it is executed for at most all possible tuples $(\mathbf{t}, x, y, z)$. Summarizing, the running time of Algorithm 6.1 is $O((\frac{n}{k} + 1)^k n^8)$.

The space complexity of Algorithm 6.1 can be computed as follows. For the computation of the optimal value, the algorithm stores for every tuple $(\mathbf{t}, x, y, z)$ the value $F(\mathbf{t}, x, y, z)$ in an array of size $O((\frac{n}{k}+1)^k n^5)$. The storage of the release and completion times in Lemmas 6.4 and Theorem 6.1 can be done in an array of linear size $O(n)$. In order to build the optimal schedule, instead of its value, we need to store at every entry of these arrays the corresponding schedule. For each one of them we store the start and completion times of the jobs in an array of size $O(n)$. Then, the optimal schedule can be easily computed by sorting these start and completion times in non-decreasing order, storing the interrupted jobs in a stack. This implies space complexity $O((\frac{n}{k}+1)^k n^6)$. □

Chapter 7

Concluding remarks

In this thesis we mainly investigated some classes of perfect graphs that have been widely studied due to their interesting structure, as well as due to their numerous applications. In particular, we investigated the classes of interval, proper interval graphs, tolerance, and bounded tolerance graphs. Furthermore, we investigated a scheduling problem from the algorithmic point of view, which is related to the concept of interval and tolerance graphs.

In Chapters 2 and 3 we dealt with interval and proper interval graphs, and especially with representations and path problems on these graph classes. Interval and proper interval graphs find many applications in genetics, molecular biology, scheduling, VLSI circuit design, information storage retrieval, as well as in archaeology, psychology, and social sciences in general. Moreover, several problems that are NP-hard on general graphs, admit polynomial time algorithms on interval graphs. These algorithms exploit the special structure of them. Two such problems are the Hamiltonian path problem and the path cover problem, which are well known to be solvable in linear time by a greedy approach. One of the most natural optimization versions of the Hamiltonian path problem is the longest path problem. However, in contrast to the Hamiltonian path problem, there are only few known polynomial algorithms for the longest path problem, and these restrict to trees and some other small graph classes. In particular, the complexity status of the longest path problem on interval graphs was as an open question. In Chapter 2 we presented the first polynomial algorithm for this problem on interval graphs [P1]. This algorithm is based on a dynamic programming approach and its running time is $O(n^4)$, when applied to an interval graph with n vertices.

Two other graph classes, which have a similar structure to that of interval graphs, are the classes of convex and biconvex graphs. The complexity status of the longest path problem on these classes is open; the only known result is that the longest path problem on interval graphs can be reduced in polynomial time to the one for convex graphs [113, 114]. However, since convex and biconvex graphs have a similar structure with interval graphs, the complexity of the longest path problem on interval graphs and convex graphs is expected to be essentially the same [113, 114]. Therefore, it would be interesting to see whether the techniques presented in Chapter 2 can be applied to derive polynomial algorithms for the longest path problem on convex and on biconvex graphs.

In Chapter 3 we introduced a new matrix characterization of the classes of interval and of proper interval graphs, called the *Normal Interval Representation (NIR)* and the *Stair Normal Interval Representation (SNIR)* matrix, respectively [P2]. Namely, every (proper) interval graph G can be represented by a (S)NIR matrix H_G, which is a special form of its adjacency matrix, according to a specific ordering of the vertices of G. In contrast to the $O(n^2)$ space that is needed in worst case to represent an arbitrary graph G with n vertices by its adjacency matrix, the whole information of the (S)NIR matrix H_G can be captured in $O(n)$ space. Furthermore, given an interval representation of a (proper) interval graph G with sorted intervals, the whole information of the corresponding (S)NIR matrix H_G can be computed in $O(n)$ time.

Apart of being important on its own, we use this succinct representation (SNIR) of proper interval graphs to derive an optimal $O(n)$ algorithm for another optimization variant of the Hamiltonian path problem, which also generalizes the path cover problem, namely the k-fixed-endpoint path cover problem on proper interval graphs [P5]. The *k-fixed-endpoint path cover* problem is, given a graph G and k arbitrary vertices of G, to cover all vertices of G with the smallest possible number of simple paths, such that the given k vertices are only allowed to be endpoints of these paths. An interesting open question would be whether the k-fixed-endpoint path cover problem is polynomially solvable on the class of interval graphs.

In Chapters 4 and 5 we dealt with tolerance and bounded tolerance graphs, and especially with representations and the recognition problems of these classes. Tolerance graphs find many applications in bioinformatics, constrained-based temporal reasoning, resource allocation, and scheduling problems, among others. They have been introduced by Golumbic and Monma in 1982, mainly motivated by the need to to solve scheduling

Chapter 7. *Concluding remarks* 131

problems in which resources that would be normally used exclusively, like rooms or vehicles, can tolerate some sharing among users. Since then, tolerance graphs have been widely studied, as they generalize in a natural way both interval and permutation graphs.

In Chapter 4 we presented the first non-trivial intersection model for tolerance graphs, given by three-dimensional parallelepipeds [P3], which extends the widely known intersection model of parallelograms in the plane that characterizes bounded tolerance graphs [18,83]. This new intersection model can be computed in $O(n)$ time for a tolerance graph with n vertices, when a tolerance representation of it is given. Furthermore, this new model proved to be useful for the design of efficient algorithms on tolerance graphs. Namely, we illustrated its usefulness by presenting in Chapter 4 optimal $O(n \log n)$ time algorithms for the minimum coloring and the maximum clique problems, as well as an improved $O(n^2)$ time algorithm for the maximum weight independent set problem on a tolerance graph G with n vertices [P3].

In spite of the extensive study of tolerance graphs, the recognition problems of both tolerance and bounded tolerance graphs have been the main open problems since their introduction. Therefore, all existing algorithms on these classes of graphs assumed that a (bounded) tolerance representation of the input (bounded) tolerance graph is given. Since very few subclasses of perfect graphs are known to be NP-hard to recognize, it was believed that the recognition of tolerance graphs was polynomial. On the other hand, bounded tolerance graphs –which are equivalent to parallelogram graphs– form a natural subclass of trapezoid graphs and share a very similar structure with them. Thus, it was plausible that bounded tolerance graphs could be recognized in polynomial time, since trapezoid graphs can be recognized in polynomial time as well.

In Chapter 5 we proved that the recognition of both tolerance and bounded tolerance graphs is surprisingly NP-complete, by providing a reduction from the monotone-Not-All-Equal-3-SAT (monotone-NAE-3-SAT) problem [P4]. For our reduction we extend the notion of an acyclic orientation of permutation and trapezoid graphs. Our main tool is a new algorithm that transforms a given trapezoid graph into a permutation graph by splitting some specific vertices, while preserving this new acyclic orientation property. One of the main advantages of this algorithm is that the constructed permutation graph does not depend on any particular trapezoid representation of the input trapezoid graph. The recognition of unit and of proper tolerance graphs, as well as of any other subclass

Chapter 7. *Concluding remarks*

of tolerance graphs, except bounded tolerance and bipartite tolerance graphs, remain interesting open problems [62]. It would be interesting to see whether the approach based on splitting vertices presented in Chapter 5 can be applied to derive a polynomial recognition algorithm or an NP-completeness reduction for the recognition problem of any of these subclasses of tolerance graphs.

Finally, we investigated in Chapter 6 a preemptive scheduling model, in which several jobs $J_1, J_2, \ldots, J_n$ have to be scheduled on a single machine. In the model under consideration, every job J_i has a release time r_i and a positive weight w_i. A schedule of the given jobs is feasible if the execution of every job J_i starts not earlier than its release time r_i. Furthermore, all jobs have equal length, i.e. equal processing time. The objective is to find a feasible preemptive schedule of the given n jobs that minimizes the weighted sum $\sum_{i=1}^{n} w_i C_i$ of the completion times. The complexity status of this problem has been stated as an open question. In Chapter 6, we provided for this problem a polynomial algorithm, assuming that the number of different weights of the jobs is constant [P6]. It would be interesting to see whether the general problem, i.e. when there are arbitrarily many different weights of the jobs, admits a polynomial algorithm. In particular, it would be interesting to investigate whether the techniques presented in Chapter 6 can be extended to the general case.

Publications

[P1] · K. Ioannidou, G. B. Mertzios, and S. D. Nikolopoulos. The longest path problem is polynomial on interval graphs. In *Proceedings of the 34th International Symposium on Mathematical Foundations of Computer Science (MFCS)*, pages 403–414, High Tatras, Slovakia, August 2009.

· Technical Report AIB-2009-11, RWTH Aachen University, April 2009.

[P2] G. B. Mertzios. A matrix characterization of interval and proper interval graphs. *Applied Mathematics Letters*, Elsevier, 21(4):332–337, 2008.

[P3] · G. B. Mertzios, I. Sau, and S. Zaks. A new intersection model and improved algorithms for tolerance graphs. In *Proceedings of the 35th International Workshop on Graph-Theoretic Concepts in Computer Science (WG)*, pages 285–295, Montpelier, France, June 2009.

· *SIAM Journal on Discrete Mathematics*, Society for Industrial and Applied Mathematics, 23(4):1800-1813, 2009.

· Technical Report AIB-2009-05, RWTH Aachen University, March 2009.

[P4] · G. B. Mertzios, I. Sau, and S. Zaks. The recognition of tolerance and bounded tolerance graphs. In *27th International Symposium on Theoretical Aspects of Computer Science (STACS)*, Nancy, France, March 2010, pp. 585-596.

· Technical Report AIB-2009-06, RWTH Aachen University, April 2009.

[P5] · G. B. Mertzios and W. Unger. An optimal algorithm for the k-fixed-endpoint path cover on proper interval graphs. In *Proceedings of the 19th International Workshop on Combinatorial Algorithms (IWOCA)*, pages 197–211, Nagoya, Japan, September 2008.

· *Mathematics in Computer Science Special Issue on "Advances in Combinatorial Algorithms I"*. Birkhäuser/Springer, 3(1), pp. 85-96, 2010.

· Technical Report AIB-2008-09, RWTH Aachen University, May 2008.

[P6] · G. B. Mertzios and W. Unger. Preemptive scheduling of equal-length jobs in polynomial time. Poster presentation in the *19th International Workshop on Combinatorial Algorithms (IWOCA)*, Nagoya, Japan, September 2008.

· *Mathematics in Computer Science Special Issue on "Advances in Combinatorial Algorithms I"*. Birkhäuser/Springer, 3(1), pp. 73-84, 2010.

· Technical Report AIB-2008-10, RWTH Aachen University, May 2008.

References

[1] G. S. Adhar and S. Peng. Parallel algorithms for path covering, hamiltonian path and hamiltonian cycle in cographs. In *International Conference on Parallel Processing*, volume 3, pages 364–365, 1990.

[2] S. F. Altschul, W. Gish, W. Miller, E. W. Myers, and D. J. Lipman. Basic local alignment search tool. *Journal of Molecular Biology*, 215(3):403–410, 1990.

[3] S. R. Arikati and C. P. Rangan. Linear algorithm for optimal path cover problem on interval graphs. *Information Processing Letters*, 35(3):149–153, 1990.

[4] K. Asdre, K. Ioannidou, and S. D. Nikolopoulos. The harmonious coloring problem is NP-complete for interval and permutation graphs. *Discrete Applied Mathematics*, 155:2377–2382, 2007.

[5] K. Asdre and S. D. Nikolopoulos. A linear-time algorithm for the k-fixed-endpoint path cover problem on cographs. *Networks*, 50:231–240, 2007.

[6] K. Asdre and S. D. Nikolopoulos. A polynomial solution to the k-fixed-endpoint path cover problem on proper interval graphs. In *18th International Conference on Combinatorial Algorithms (IWOCA)*, Newcastle, Australia, 2007.

[7] K. Asdre and S. D. Nikolopoulos. The 1-fixed-endpoint path cover problem is polynomial on interval graphs. *Algorithmica*, 2009.

[8] K. R. Baker. *Introduction to Sequencing and Scheduling*. John Wiley & Sons, Inc., New York, 1974.

[9] P. Baptiste. An $O(n^4)$ algorithm for preemptive scheduling of a single machine to minimize the number of late jobs. *Operations Research Letters*, 24:175–180, 1999.

[10] P. Baptiste. Polynomial time algorithms for minimizing the weighted number of late jobs on a single machine when processing times are equal. *Journal of Scheduling*, 2:245–252, 1999.

[11] P. Baptiste. Scheduling equal-length jobs on identical parallel machines. *Discrete Applied Mathematics*, 103:21–32, 2000.

[12] P. Baptiste, P. Brucker, M. Chrobak, C. Durr, S. A. Kravchenko, and F. Sourd. The complexity of mean flow time scheduling problems with release times. *Journal of Scheduling*, 10(2):139–146, 2007.

[13] P. Baptiste, M. Chrobak, C. Dürr, W. Jawor, and N. Vakhania. Preemptive scheduling of equal-length jobs to maximize weighted throughput. *Operation Research Letters*, 32(3):258–264, 2004.

[14] P. Baptiste and C. Dürr. http://www.lix.polytechnique.fr/~durr/OpenProblems/1_rj_pmtn_pjp_sumWjCj/.

[15] A. A. Bertossi. Finding hamiltonian circuits in proper interval graphs. *Information Processing Letters*, 17(2):97–101, 1983.

[16] A. A. Bertossi and M. A. Bonucelli. Finding hamiltonian circuits in interval graph generalizations. *Information Processing Letters*, 23:195–200, 1986.

[17] H. L. Bodlaender. Achromatic number is NP-complete for cographs and interval graphs. *Information Processing Letters*, 31:135–138, 1989.

[18] K. P. Bogart, P. C. Fishburnb, G. Isaak, and L. Langley. Proper and unit tolerance graphs. *Discrete Applied Mathematics*, 60(1-3):99–117, 1995.

[19] K. P. Bogart and D. B. West. A short proof that "proper = unit". *Discrete Mathematics*, 201:21–23, 1999.

[20] K. S. Booth and G. S. Lueker. Testing for the consecutive ones property, interval graphs, and graph planarity using PQ-tree algorithms. *Journal of Computer and System Sciences*, 13:335–379, 1976.

[21] A. Brandstädt, V. B. Le, and J. P. Spinrad. *Graph classes: a survey*. Society for Industrial and Applied Mathematics (SIAM), 1999.

[22] P. Brucker. *Scheduling algorithms*. Springer Verlag, Heidelberg, 5 edition, 2007.

[23] P. Brucker and S. Knust. Complexity results for scheduling problems. http://www.mathematik.uni-osnabrueck.de/research/OR/class/.

[24] R. W. Bulterman, F. W. van der Sommen, G. Zwaan, T. Verhoeff, A. J. M. van Gasteren, and W. H. J. Feijen. On computing a longest path in a tree. *Information Processing Letters*, 81(2):93–96, 2002.

[25] P. Buneman. A characterisation of rigid circuit graphs. *Discrete Mathematics*, 9:205–212, 1974.

[26] A. H. Busch. A characterization of triangle-free tolerance graphs. *Discrete Applied Mathematics*, 154(3):471–477, 2006.

[27] A. H. Busch and G. Isaak. Recognizing bipartite tolerance graphs in linear time. In *Proceedings of the 33rd International Workshop on Graph-Theoretic Concepts in Computer Science (WG)*, pages 12–20, 2007.

[28] A. V. Carrano. Establishing the order to human chromosome-specific DNA fragments. *Biotechnology and the Human Genome*, pages 37–50, 1988.

[29] M. S. Chang, S. L. Peng, and J. L. Liaw. Deferred-query - an efficient approach for problems on interval and circular-arc graphs (extended abstract). In *Proceedings of the third Workshop on Algorithms and Data Structures (WADS)*, pages 222–233, 1993.

[30] F. Cheah and D. G. Corneil. On the structure of trapezoid graphs. *Discrete Applied Mathematics*, 66(2):109–133, 1996.

[31] F. Cheah and D. G. Corneil, 2009. Personal communication.

[32] M. Chudnovsky, G. Cornuéjols, X. Liu, P. Seymour, and K. Vušković. Recognizing berge graphs. *Combinatorica*, 25(2):143–186, 2005.

[33] M. Chudnovsky, N. Robertson, P. Seymour, and R. Thomas. The strong perfect graph theorem. *Annals of Mathematics*, 164:51–229, 2006.

[34] J. Cohen, F. Fomin, P. Heggernes, D. Kratsch, and G. Kucherov. Optimal linear arrangement of interval graphs. In *Proceedings of the 31st International Symposium on Mathematical Foundations of Computer Science (MFCS)*, pages 267–279, 2006.

[35] D. G. Corneil. A simple 3-sweep LBFS algorithm for the recognition of unit interval graphs. *Discrete Applied Mathematics*, 138(3):371–379, 2004.

[36] D. G. Corneil, H. Kim, S. Natarajan, S. Olariu, and A. P. Sprague. Simple linear time recognition of unit interval graphs. *Information Processing Letters*, 55(2):99–104, 1995.

[37] D. G. Corneil, S. Olariu, and L. Stewart. The ultimate interval graph recognition algorithm? In *Proceedings of the 9th annual ACM-SIAM symposium on Discrete algorithms (SODA)*, pages 175–180, 1998.

[38] D. G. Corneil, S. Olariu, and L. Stewart. The LBFS structure and recognition of interval graphs. *SIAM Journal of Discrete Mathematics*, 2009. To appear.

[39] P. Damaschke. The hamiltonian circuit problem for circle graphs in NP-complete. *Information Processing Letters*, 32(1):1–2, 1989.

[40] P. Damaschke. Paths in interval graphs and circular arc graphs. *Discrete Mathematics*, 112(1-3):49–64, 1993.

[41] P. Damaschke, J. S. Deogun, D. Kratsch, and G. Steiner. Finding hamiltonian paths in cocomparability graphs using the bump number algorithm. *Order*, 8:383–391, 1992.

[42] C. M. H. de Figueiredo, J. Meidanis, and C. P. de Mello. A linear-time algorithm for proper interval graph recognition. *Information Processing Letters*, 56:179–184, 1995.

[43] X. Deng, P. Hell, and J. Huang. Linear-time representation algorithms for proper circular-arc graphs and proper interval graphs. *SIAM Journal on Computing*, 25(2):390–403, 1996.

[44] M. I. Dessouky, B. J. Lageweg, J. K. Lenstra, and S. L. van de Velde. Scheduling identical jobs on uniform parallel machines. *Statistica Neerlandica*, 44:115–123, 1990.

[45] R. Diestel. *Graph Theory*. Springer, Berlin, 3rd edition, 2005.

[46] S. Felsner. Tolerance graphs and orders. *Journal of Graph Theory*, 28:129–140, 1998.

[47] S. Felsner, R. Müller, and L. Wernisch. Trapezoid graphs and generalizations, geometry and algorithms. *Discrete Applied Mathematics*, 74:13–32, 1997.

[48] P. C. Fishburn and W. T. Trotter. Split semiorders. *Discrete Mathematics*, 195:111–126, 1999.

[49] M. L. Fredman. On computing the length of longest increasing subsequences. *Discrete Mathematics*, 11:29–35, 1975.

[50] D. R. Fulkerson and O. A. Gross. Incidence matrices and interval graphs. *Pacific Journal of Mathematics*, 15:835–855, 1965.

[51] R. Gandhi, B. G. Jr, S. Pemmaraju, and R. Raman. Sub-coloring and hypo-coloring interval graphs. In *Proceedings of the 35rd International Workshop on Graph-Theoretic Concepts in Computer Science (WG)*, 2009. To appear.

[52] M. R. Garey, D. R. Johnson, B. B. Simons, and R. E. Tarjan. Scheduling unit-time tasks with arbitrary release times and deadlines. *SIAM Journal on Computing*, 10:256–269, 1981.

[53] M. R. Garey and D. S. Johnson. *Computers and intractability: A guide to the theory of NP-completeness*. W. H. Freeman & Co., New York, NY, USA, 1979.

[54] M. R. Garey, D. S. Johnson, and R. E. Tarjan. The planar hamiltonian circuit problem is NP-complete. *SIAM Journal on Computing*, 5:704–714, 1976.

[55] F. Gavril. The intersection graphs of subtrees in trees are exactly the chordal graphs. *Journal of Combinatorial Theory*, 16:47–56, 1974.

[56] P. W. Goldberg, M. C. Golumbic, H. Kaplan, and R. Shamir. Four strikes against physical mapping of DNA. *Journal of Computational Biology*, 2(1):139–152, 1995.

[57] M. C. Golumbic. *Algorithmic graph theory and perfect graphs (Annals of Discrete Mathematics, Vol. 57)*. North-Holland Publishing Co., 2004.

[58] M. C. Golumbic and R. E. Jamison. Edge and vertex intersection of paths in a tree. *Discrete Mathematics*, 55(2):151–159, 1985.

[59] M. C. Golumbic and C. L. Monma. A generalization of interval graphs with tolerances. In *Proceedings of the 13th Southeastern Conference on Combinatorics, Graph Theory and Computing, Congressus Numerantium 35*, pages 321–331, 1982.

[60] M. C. Golumbic, C. L. Monma, and W. T. Trotter. Tolerance graphs. *Discrete Applied Mathematics*, 9(2):157–170, 1984.

[61] M. C. Golumbic and A. Siani. Coloring algorithms for tolerance graphs: reasoning and scheduling with interval constraints. In *Proceedings of the Joint International*

Conferences on Artificial Intelligence, Automated Reasoning, and Symbolic Computation (AISC/Calculemus), pages 196–207, 2002.

[62] M. C. Golumbic and A. N. Trenk. *Tolerance Graphs*. Cambridge studies in advanced mathematics, 2004.

[63] M. Grötschel, L. Lovász, and A. Schrijver. *Geometric algorithms and combinatorial optimization*. Springer, 1988.

[64] U. I. Gupta, D. T. Lee, and J. Y. T. Leung. Efficient algorithms for interval graphs and circular-arc graphs. *Networks*, pages 459–467, 1982.

[65] M. Habib, R. M. McConnell, C. Paul, and L. Viennot. Lex-BFS and partition refinement, with applications to transitive orientation, interval graph recognition and consecutive ones testing. *Theoretical Computer Science*, 234(1-2):59–84, 2000.

[66] R. B. Hayward and R. Shamir. A note on tolerance graph recognition. *Discrete Applied Mathematics*, 143(1-3):307–311, 2004.

[67] P. Heggernes, D. Meister, and C. Papadopoulos. A new representation of proper interval graphs with an application to clique-width. *Electronic Notes in Discrete Mathematics*, 32:27–34, 2009.

[68] L. A. Herrbach and J. Y.-T. Leung. Preemptive scheduling of equal length jobs on two machines to minimize mean flow time. *Operations Research*, 38:487–494, 1990.

[69] J. Y. Hsiao and C. Y. Tang. An efficient algorithm for finding a maximum weight 2-independent set on interval graphs. *Information Processing Letters*, 43(5):229–235, 1992.

[70] R. W. Hung and M. S. Chang. Solving the path cover problem on circular-arc graphs by using an approximation algorithm. *Discrete Applied Mathematics*, 154(1):76–105, 2006.

[71] G. Isaak, K. L. Nyman, and A. N. Trenk. A hierarchy of classes of bounded bitolerance orders. *Ars Combinatoria*, 69, 2003.

[72] A. Itai, C. H. Papadimitriou, and J. L. Szwarcfiter. Hamiltonian paths in grid graphs. *SIAM Journal on Computing*, 11:676–686, 1982.

[73] Z. Jackowski. A new characterization of proper interval graphs. *Discrete Mathematics*, 105(1-3):103–109, 1992.

[74] D. R. Karger, R. Motwani, and G. D. S. Ramkumar. On approximating the longest path in a graph. *Algorithmica*, 18:82–98, 1997.

[75] M. Kaufmann, J. Kratochvil, K. A. Lehmann, and A. R. Subramanian. Max-tolerance graphs as intersection graphs: cliques, cycles, and recognition. In *Proceedings of the 17th annual ACM-SIAM symposium on Discrete Algorithms (SODA)*, pages 832–841, 2006.

[76] J. M. Keil. Finding hamiltonian circuits in interval graphs. *Information Processing Letters*, 20:201–206, 1985.

[77] J. M. Keil and P. Belleville. Dominating the complements of bounded tolerance graphs and the complements of trapezoid graphs. *Discrete Applied Mathematics*, 140(1-3):73–89, 2004.

[78] N. Korte and R. H. Möhring. A simple linear-time algorithm to recognize interval graphs. In *Proceedings of the 35rd International Workshop on Graph-Theoretic Concepts in Computer Science (WG)*, pages 1–16, 1986.

[79] N. Korte and R. H. Möhring. An incremental linear-time algorithm for recognizing interval graphs. *SIAM Journal on Computing*, 18(1):68–81, 1989.

[80] D. Kratsch, R. M. McConnell, K. Mehlhorn, and J. P. Spinrad. Certifying algorithms for recognizing interval graphs and permutation graphs. *SIAM Journal on Computing*, 36(2):326–353, 2006.

[81] M. S. Krishnamoorthy. An NP-hard problem in bipartite graphs. *SIGACT News*, 7(1):26–26, 1975.

[82] J. Labetoulle, E. L. Lawler, J. K. Lenstra, and A. H. G. R. Kan. Preemptive scheduling of uniform machines subject to release dates. In *Progress in Combinatorial Optimization*, pages 245–261. Academic Press, Toronto, 1984.

[83] L. Langley. *Interval tolerance orders and dimension*. PhD thesis, Dartmouth College, 1993.

[84] E. L. Lawler. A dynamic programming algorithm for preemptive scheduling of a single machine to minimize the number of late jobs. *Annals of Discrete Mathematics*, 26(1–4):125–133, 1990.

[85] J. K. Lenstra, A. H. G. R. Kan, and P. Brucker. Complexity of machine scheduling problems. *Annals of Discrete Mathematics*, 1:343–362, 1977.

[86] G. S. Leuker. Structured breadth first search and chordal graphs. Technical Report TR-158, Princeton University, 1974.

[87] J. Y.-T. Leung and G. H. Young. Preemptive scheduling to minimize mean weighted flow time. *Information Processing Letters*, 34:47–50, 1990.

[88] R. Lin, S. Olariu, and G. Pruesse. An optimal path cover algorithm for cographs. *Computers and Mathematics with Applications*, 30:75–83, 1995.

[89] L. Lovász. Normal hypergraphs and the perfect graph conjecture. *Discrete Mathematics*, 2:253–267, 1972.

[90] T.-H. Ma and J. P. Spinrad. On the 2-chain subgraph cover and related problems. *Journal of Algorithms*, 17(2):251–268, 1994.

[91] D. Marx. A short proof of the NP-completeness of minimum sum interval coloring. *Operations Research Letters*, 33(4):382–384, 2005.

[92] T. A. McKee and F. R. McMorris. *Topics in intersection graph theory*. SIAM Monographs on Discrete Mathematics and Applications, Philadelphia, 1999.

[93] M. Middendorf and F. Pfeiffer. On the complexity of recognizing perfectly orderable graphs. *Discrete Mathematics*, 80(3):327–333, 1990.

[94] H. Müller. Hamiltonian circuits in chordal bipartite graphs. *Discrete Mathematics*, 156(1-3):291–298, 1996.

[95] G. Narasimhan and R. Manber. Stability and chromatic number of tolerance graphs. *Discrete Applied Mathematics*, 36:47–56, 1992.

[96] S. Olariu. An optimal greedy heuristic to color interval graphs. *Information Processing Letters*, 37(1):21–25, 1991.

[97] B. S. Panda and S. K. Das. A linear time recognition algorithm for proper interval graphs. *Information Processing Letters*, 87(3):153–161, 2003.

[98] A. Pnueli, A. Lempel, and S. Even. Transitive orientation of graphs and identification of permutation graphs. *Canadian Journal of Mathematics*, 23(1):160–175, 1971.

[99] G. Ramalingam and C. P. Rangan. A unified approach to domination problems on interval graphs. *Information Processing Letters*, 27(5):271–274, 1988.

[100] J. L. Ramírez-Alfonsín and B. A. Reed, editors. *Perfect graphs*. Wiley-Interscience Series in Discrete Mathematics and Optimization. John Wiley & Sons, Inc., 2001.

[101] F. S. Roberts. Indifference graphs. In F. Harary, editor, *Proof Techniques in Graph Theory*, pages 139–146. Academic Press, New York, 1969.

[102] D. J. Rose and R. E. Tarjan. Algorithmic aspects of vertex elimination. In *Proceedings of seventh annual ACM symposium on theory of computing (STOC)*, pages 245–254, 1975.

[103] S. P. Ryan. Trapezoid order classification. *Order*, 15:341–354, 1998.

[104] T. J. Schaefer. The complexity of satisfiability problems. In *Proceedings of the 10th annual ACM symposium on Theory of computing (STOC)*, pages 216–226, 1978.

[105] K. Simon. A new simple linear algorithm to recognize interval graphs. In *Proceedings of the International Workshop on Computational Geometry - Methods, Algorithms and Applications (CG)*, pages 289–308. Springer, 1991.

[106] B. Simons. Multiprocessor scheduling of unit-time jobs with arbitrary release times and deadlines. *SIAM Journal on Computing*, 12:294–299, 1983.

[107] J. P. Spinrad. *Efficient graph representations*, volume 19 of *Fields Institute Monographs*. American Mathematical Society, 2003.

[108] A. P. Sprague. An $O(n \log n)$ algorithm for bandwidth of interval graphs. *SIAM Journal on Discrete Mathematics*, 7(2):213–220, 1994.

[109] R. Srikant, R. Sundaram, K. S. Singh, and C. P. Rangan. Optimal path cover problem on block graphs and bipartite permutation graphs. *Theoretical Computer Science*, 115:351–357, 1993.

[110] T. Szkaliczki. Routing with minimum wire length in the dogleg-free manhattan model is NP-complete. *SIAM Journal on Computing*, 29(1):274–287, 2000.

[111] Y. Takahara, S. Teramoto, and R. Uehara. Longest path problems on ptolemaic graphs. *IEICE Transactions on Information and Systems*, E91-D(2):170–177, 2008.

[112] Z. Tian, C. T. Ng, and T. C. E. Cheng. An $O(n^2)$ algorithm for scheduling equal-length preemptive jobs on a single machine to minimize total tardiness. *SIAM Journal on Computing*, 9(4):343–364, 2006.

[113] R. Uehara and Y. Uno. Efficient algorithms for the longest path problem. In *15th Annual International Symposium on Algorithms and Computation (ISAAC)*, pages 871–883, 2004.

[114] R. Uehara and Y. Uno. On computing longest paths in small graph classes. *International Journal of Foundations of Computer Science*, 18(5):911–930, 2007.

[115] R. Uehara and G. Valiente. Linear structure of bipartite permutation graphs and the longest path problem. *Information Processing Letters*, 103(2):71–77, 2007.

[116] J. R. Walter. *Representations of rigid cycle graphs*. PhD thesis, Wayne State University, 1972.

[117] P. Zhang, E. A. Schon, S. G. Fischer, E. Cayanis, J. Weiss, S. Kistler, and P. E. Bourne. An algorithm based on graph theory for the assembly of contigs in physical mapping of DNA. *Computer Applications in the Biosciences*, 10:309–317, 1994.

Die VDM Verlagsservicegesellschaft sucht für wissenschaftliche Verlage abgeschlossene und herausragende

Dissertationen, Habilitationen, Diplomarbeiten, Master Theses, Magisterarbeiten usw.

für die kostenlose Publikation als Fachbuch.

Sie verfügen über eine Arbeit, die hohen inhaltlichen und formalen Ansprüchen genügt, und haben Interesse an einer honorarvergüteten Publikation?

Dann senden Sie bitte erste Informationen über sich und Ihre Arbeit per Email an *info@vdm-vsg.de*.

Sie erhalten kurzfristig unser Feedback!

VDM Verlagsservicegesellschaft mbH
Dudweiler Landstr. 99   Telefon +49 681 3720 174
D - 66123 Saarbrücken   Fax   +49 681 3720 1749
www.vdm-vsg.de

Die VDM Verlagsservicegesellschaft mbH vertritt

Printed by Books on Demand GmbH, Norderstedt / Germany